FRANCIS BACON

Texts in English Literature

FRANCIS
BACON

Selected and edited by
ARTHUR JOHNSTON
Professor of English at the
University College of Wales
Aberystwyth

SCHOCKEN BOOKS   NEW YORK

First published in the U.S.A. 1965

Library of Congress Catalog Card Number: 65–18635

Printed in Great Britain

Contents

CONTENTS

Preface

Bacon is read because he is a great writer in English, and because he is an interesting, and occasionally great, thinker. I have therefore tried to represent his many interests by selecting passages from his English works, including passages translated from the Latin only where their omission would leave an obvious gap. Bacon disapproved of epitomes, but I am confident that any passages selected from his works can only whet the reader's appetite for the complete works edited by Ellis, Spedding and Heath, and for the letters and speeches in Spedding's *Life* of Bacon. It is from these volumes that the translations have been taken. In all texts except the *Essays*, spelling and punctuation have been modernized; the *Essays* have been left in their antique garb, since this can give some readers an added pleasure. I have not entered into the biography of Bacon; the best short account is still that by R. W. Church in the 'English Men of Letters' series.

I have had great pleasure in choosing the passages and in writing the introductions and notes to them. For making that pleasure possible, I dedicate my share in this volume to my mother and father.

Chronology of Bacon's Life and Writings

1561, 22 Jan.	Born at York House in the Strand, son of Sir Nicholas Bacon, Lord Keeper of the Seal, and Anne Cooke, daughter of the tutor to Edward VI
1573, April	Entered Trinity College, Cambridge
1576, June	Admitted to Gray's Inn
Sept.	Went to Paris with Sir Amyas Paulet
1579, Feb./March	Death of his father and return to England
1582, June	Admitted Utter Barrister at Gray's Inn
1584, Nov.	Member of Parliament for Melcombe in Dorsetshire (he was a Member for various constituencies until he went to the Lords in 1618)
1591	Acquaintance with Essex begins
1592	*A Conference of Pleasure* written (published 1870)
1595–6	*Formularies and Elegancies* written (published 1883)
1597	*Essays, Colours of Good and Evil, Meditationes Sacrae*
1601, Feb.	Trial of Essex
1601	*Declaration of the Practises and Treasons attempted and committed by Robert late Earl of Essex*
1603, 24 March	Death of Elizabeth, Accession of James I
23 July	Bacon knighted
1604	*Apology in certain imputations concerning the late Earl of Essex*
1605	*Advancement of Learning*
1606, 10 May	Marriage to Alice Barnham

1607, 25 June	Appointed Solicitor General
1609	*De Sapientia Veterum*
1610	Death of his mother
1612	*Essays*, enlarged
1613, 26 Oct.	Appointed Attorney General
1616, 9 June	Made a Privy Councillor
1617, 7 March	Made Lord Keeper
1618, 4 Jan.	Made Lord Chancellor
12 July	Created Baron Verulam
1620, Oct.	*Novum Organum*
1621, 27 Jan.	Created Viscount St Albans
30 Jan.	Meeting of Parliament
3 May	Sentenced by House of Lords for accepting bribes
Nov.	Limited pardon sealed by James I
1622, March	*History of Henry VII*
1622–3	Published monthly instalments of his Natural History—*Historia Ventorum* and *Historia Vitae et Mortis*
1623, Oct.	*De Augmentis Scientiarum*
1625, 27 March	Death of James I
	Essays, much enlarged
1626, 9 April	Bacon died at Highgate

Bacon used the time when he was out of office, and the vacations, for his writing. To the bare outline above should be added all the speeches, legal and parliamentary, the volumes of legal arguments, and the drafts of parts of the Instauration, at which he was constantly working. These were published in various collections during the century after his death.

INTRODUCTION

'*What is Truth?* said jesting Pilate, and would not stay for an answer.' Everyone knows this sentence of Bacon's, and everyone responds to its combination of strangeness and familiarity. It uses a Gospel episode with which everyone is familiar, but presents it in a manner and a context so unusual that it is puzzling. Bacon has obviously read the episode in a way that has not occurred to any other reader, and the realization of this produces excitement. This combination of strangeness, familiarity and excitement characterizes our response to Bacon both as a man and as a writer.

As we read the life of Bacon we must accustom ourselves to the intermingling of two figures. One is that of Bacon involved in the highest affairs of state: familiar with Elizabeth and James; prosecuting his one-time patron, the Earl of Essex; an active member of the House of Commons in the Parliaments called between 1584 and 1618; Solicitor-General; Attorney-General; and Lord Chancellor of England for three years. The other is that of Bacon the learned lawyer, the historian, the essayist, the logician, the philosophical speculator, the careful student of natural history. More than once we hear him say that he was 'a man naturally fitted for literature rather than for anything else, and borne by some destiny against the inclination of his genius into the business of active life'. In his speech on taking his place in Chancery in 1618 he said as he accepted the burden: 'Only the depth of the three long vacations I would reserve in some measure free from business of estate, and for studies, arts and sciences, to which in my own nature I am most inclined.'

This basic contradiction between his nature and activities is partly responsible for our feeling of the strangeness of the man, but other reasons contribute to it. Reading his works we become aware of the intense idealism of which he was capable, coupled with an understanding of 'serpentine wisdom' which has shocked many a commentator.

I

The man who wrote the noble essay 'Of Judicature' was the man who was condemned for accepting gifts while holding the highest judicial post in the country. His greatest anxiety was for the furtherance of scientific knowledge, yet he was unappreciative of the actual scientific work being done in his own time, and of his many investigations in natural history none was useful. He often speaks of the collection of experiments in natural history as a work that *he* should not be expected to do, yet in the absence of helpers he abandoned the completion of his New Method of scientific investigation in order to compile experiments himself. The experiments, he saw, were in the long run more important than the expounding of method.

He was a master of writing and speaking in English, and clearly took pains with all his compositions. Ben Jonson said of him what he had said also of Shakespeare (adapting some words of Seneca), that he had 'performed that in our tongue which may be compared or preferred either to insolent Greece or haughty Rome'. But Bacon himself thought that only works in Latin had a chance of survival, and had all his English works translated into Latin.

As we read his works we become aware of a contradiction that is also characteristic of him as a man. At an early age he declares, 'I have taken all knowledge to be my province.' This confidence in his own powers is borne out by all he did, his mastery of so many branches of learning, his map of the whole world of learning and declaration of what areas were yet uncultivated, his plan for the Great Instauration or Regeneration of learning, with its new method of inductive investigation into Nature, his project of collecting Natural History, his plans for a digest of English law. But with this confident undertaking goes a modesty that delights. Though immersed in the affairs of state and not strong in health he feels that he has 'advanced these matters some little way' (*Novum Organum*, I.113), saying it not boastingly but to encourage others. He declares: 'My purpose is to try whether I cannot in very fact lay more firmly the foundations, and extend more widely the limits, of the power and greatness of man . . . sowing for future ages the seeds of purer truth' (I.116). But he attributes his own part in all this 'rather to good luck than to ability', and accounts it 'a birth of time rather than of wit' (I.122). The *Advancement* seems to him 'not much better than that noise or sound which musicians make while they are tuning their instruments'; of his own rôle he says, 'I am but a trumpeter.' The judgment he expected posterity to pronounce on him is equally modest, 'that I did no great things, but simply made less account of things that were accounted great' (*Novum Organum*, I.97).

Some of the strangeness that strikes the modern reader of Bacon's works is attributable to the unfamiliarity of the contents of Bacon's mind. When we read, 'There were under the law, excellent King, both daily sacrifices and freewill offerings', few readers will know of the Jewish law of sacrifice as laid down in the books of *Exodus*, *Leviticus* and *Numbers*, and practised by the Jews until the destruction of the Temple. But Bacon constantly refers to Biblical passages in the Vulgate with an ease that indicates how much of his mental equipment was derived from a source which is no longer familiar. Contributing even more to the sense of strangeness is the way in which Bacon writes with ease of reference to the works of Aristotle, Plato, the early Greek philosophers from Pythagoras to Protagoras, and the Latin historians, especially Tacitus and Livy, to the works of Cicero, Seneca, Pliny, Plutarch and the Latin poets. The gap left in one's understanding at such points can normally be filled by a note. But lying below the surface is the whole body of formative reading not only in these works, but in writers whose works Bacon rarely mentions—men of the previous century such as Cardan, Telesius, Porta, Scaliger, Paracelsus, Patrizzi, Severinus, Agrippa, Ramus and Robert Fludd. When we read Bacon's account of the Methods and Illustration of Tradition (see p. 69) we are conscious that Bacon is moving confidently in a discussion of a topic which had its roots in Aristotle and Cicero and the Ramist controversy of the day. But the whole concept has vanished. To understand Bacon here, we must be prepared to learn about Logic and Rhetoric and have the agility to translate the concepts into modern terms. These things were important not merely for Bacon, but for any educated man until the eighteenth century.

The unfamiliar content of Bacon's mind produced habits of thought which are equally arresting. It was not only the encyclopaedic tradition which encouraged Bacon's love of categorizing knowledge. He was by patient training a lawyer, and the training is seen in his marshalling and weighing of evidence, in his love of organising a discourse into clear divisions, in his careful selection and placing of the most telling points in an argument, and of the most telling phrases. He was trained as a persuader, and perfected his art with the greatest attention to detail. Thus he collected and compiled what he called *Antitheta*, lists of arguments for and against any topic, for example:

KNOWLEDGE AND CONTEMPLATION

For	*Against*
That pleasure only is according to nature which never cloys.	A contemplative life is but a specious laziness.
The sweetest prospect is that below, into the errors of others.	To think well is little better than to dream well.
It is best to have the orbits of the mind concentric with those of the universe.	Divine Providence regards the world, but man regards only his country.
All depraved affections are false valuations, but goodness and truth are ever the same.	A political man sows even his thoughts.

As he pointed out when collecting these for the *De Augmentis*, they are topics suitable more for expansion in discourses of praise and dispraise, than of proving and disproving, or of persuading or dissuading.

He compiled also a series of refutations of rhetorical sophisms, in which he lists arguments against popular sayings, such as 'What men praise and celebrate is good; what they dispraise and censure, evil.' His aim is to show in what ways such sayings, often used as easy persuaders in discourse, are fallacious. The habits of mind indicated by such exercises are foreign to a modern reader.

A writer whose field of reference is unfamiliar will often draw his images from sources that no longer illuminate what is said for the modern reader. When Donne writes

> *Let Man's soul be a sphere, and then, in this,*
> *The intelligence that moves, devotion is,*

the image now puzzles. With Bacon it is usually true to say, as Shelley does, that his 'words unveil the permanent analogy of things by images which participate in the life of truth'. His delight in imagery normally results in clear and simple illumination: 'The knowledge of man is as the waters, some descending from above, and some springing from beneath; the one informed by the light of nature, the other inspired by divine revelation.' But while this does not puzzle, it is in the same form as the following: 'By all means it is to be procured that the Trunk of Nebuchadnezzar's Tree of Monarchy be great enough to bear the branches and the boughs.' If Bacon did not go on, 'That is, that the natural subjects of the crown or state bear a sufficient proportion to the stranger subjects that they govern', we should be at a loss for the meaning. Sometimes it seems that Bacon carried ideas in his head not as abstract statements but as vivid images or emblems, such as this of Nebuchadnezzar's tree. It was a common recommendation of those who wrote of Memory; Bacon states it thus: 'Emblem reduceth conceits intellectual to images sensible, which strike the memory more.' Where the emblem was a private one, the ensuing image in prose will not be readily understood unless the 'conceit intellectual' is attached to it.

Any difficulty the reader may have in understanding Bacon is not to be attributed to any deliberate obscurity on Bacon's part, but to lack of acquaintance with his references and to unfamiliarity with accepted topics of discussion in his day. But he is usually writing not about subjects which have ceased to interest men—indeed it is true of almost all his works that they 'come home to men's business and bosoms'. There is little in the *Advancement of Learning* that is without its relevance to the modern world. The defence of learning and the proof of its dignity is an appeal to men to set learning as the highest ideal of a civilized state. When Bacon discusses Universities (see p. 63) everything he says—that university salaries should be such as to attract the best teachers, that adequate provision be made for the tools of scholarship, books and equipment, that the syllabuses be kept under constant review—is still being said. Bacon always thinks clearly and thinks about ordinary things. He is not ashamed to be interested in how to prepare a hot-bed with manure for the early germination of seeds, just as he is willing to explain how to manipulate a committee-meeting or how to produce a masque. He knows his way about in the world of particulars as well as in the world of speculation. He wanted to understand the world, and had the optimism which springs from believing it easier to understand than it is. One can adapt Bertrand Russell's description of the Greek philosophers before Socrates as a just picture of Bacon—in spite of the prejudices of his day, his attitude was scientific, 'but it was not *only* scientific; it was imaginative and vigorous and filled with the delight of adventure. He was interested in everything—meteors and eclipses, fishes and whirlwinds, religion and morality. With a penetrating intellect he combined the zest of a child.'

This breadth of interest ensures that much of Bacon's writing strikes us as familiar. We know where we are with a man who writes 'Riches are for spending', 'The ways to enrich are many, and most of them foul', 'Money is like muck, not good except it be spread', or 'A man that hath no virtue in himself ever envieth virtue in others.' We are on familiar ground when Bacon picks up proverbs as though they were of his own manufacture—'There is commonly less money, less wisdom, and less good faith than men do account upon.' Neither the expression nor the idea presents any difficulty. What we derive from them is excitement—the excitement we feel when an idea has achieved memorable expression.

This excitement Bacon constantly arouses. In small areas of discourse it is often associated with the habit of conveying an abstract idea in terms of an image or emblem. Thus he uses the story that Pan 'by a happy accident when he was hunting' was the god who succeeded in finding Proserpine, to coin the phrase 'the hunt of Pan' (*venatio Panis*, *De Augmentis*, V.2) to mean proceeding with order and direction in experiments, not haphazardly. The phrase is exciting; its meaning springs from his interpretation of the episode in the fable of Pan. Similarly he creates other phrases—the Idols of the Tribe, the Cave, the Market-Place, the Theatre and, to describe his investigation into 'the appetite and will of man', the wonderful phrase 'The Georgics of the Mind' (*Advancement*, II.xx.3).

Sometimes it is the whole sentence which excites. We are struck simultaneously by the truth of what is said and by the memorable wording and rhythm of how it is said. Some of the quotations already made illustrate this; others spring to mind—'Doctrine should be such as should make one in love with the lesson, and not with the teacher'; 'Indeed the strength of all sciences is as the strength of the old man's faggot, in the bond'; 'His mother he reverenced much, heard little.'

The Essays, especially the opening sentences, provide many examples. Thought packed close and rendered portable was Macaulay's description of this quality. It is a quality which Bacon shares with Dr Johnson, whose knowledge was equally wide-ranging, and who was anxious also that men should live in the clear daylight of Truth. Both have minds that turn to aphoristic statement; Johnson's aphorisms in *Rasselas* are equally characteristic of him—'Human life is everywhere a state in which much is to be endured and little to be enjoyed', 'There may be community of material possessions, but there can never be community of love or of esteem', 'Marriage has many pains, but celibacy has no pleasures.' For Bacon the aphorism was a form of presenting knowledge that was still in growth, it invited thought and comment; in fact the effect is often the reverse—his aphorisms less often invite thought than command assent.

The excitement of Bacon as a writer is not confined to pointed sentences. He is equally concerned for the movement of a paragraph and the rhythms of larger units. The penultimate paragraph of Book I of the *Advancement of Learning* (see p. 61) is famous. Here, wrote F. P. Wilson, 'Bacon is using eloquence, as Cicero and St Augustine had used it, to sway the mind to truth and stir the will to right action.' But the paragraph in Book II. xviii.2 (see p. 73) shows Bacon delighting in the three-fold balance of his argument and matching his phrases, clauses and rhythms to the same movement. Again it is in accordance with his own doctrine that 'it is a thing not hastily to be condemned, to clothe and adorn the obscurity even of philosophy itself with sensible and plausible elocution' (I.iv.4). Bacon respects matter more than words, but he never, even when dictating the *Sylva Sylvarum* to Rawley, showed any sign that he despised words and rhythm.

A writer who is no more than an assembly of purple passages, whether sentences or paragraphs, is in the end dull. The pleasure in reading Bacon extends over large areas, where the controlled arrangement of the material is exciting. The arrangement of the *Advancement of Learning*, with its masterly divisions of the subject, is constantly before the reader, as he moves through the varied forms of distinction, 'This knowledge hath two parts', 'First therefore in this', 'Another article of knowledge' and so on, to the climax, 'Thus have I concluded this portion of learning touching civil knowledge; and with civil knowledge have concluded human philosophy; and with human philosophy, philosophy in general.' But even in simpler works the arrangement gives pleasure, whether it is the interest of watching the skilful lawyer build up the evidence against Somerset, or the strange delight in observing the allegorical interpretation, element by element, of the fables in *The Wisdom of the Ancients*.

The brilliance of Bacon's thinking mind grips the reader as he is led through the inevitable progression of the argument. In reading the *Novum Organum* now, we are aware that we no longer need to be persuaded that a new scientific method is required. The effect of this is to make the second book not much more than an historical oddity, since the method there propounded corresponds to no method that has ever been used by scientists. But the first book is busy clearing the ground before the method is expounded, and so is an examination of the hindrances to learning in the human mind generally. Here anyone who is interested in the processes of learning and teaching will find in the doctrine of Idols observations relevant to every age.

Bacon's own excitement as he delights in his power and command over words, over organization, over argument, over illustration, over rhythm, communicates itself to the reader. Excitement, too, is engendered by Bacon's hopes and by his vision. As a philosopher of science, what he has to offer is in the region of generalities, not particulars. 'Nature to be commanded must be obeyed; and that which in contemplation is as the cause is in operation as the rule', is the sort of statement which embodies truth. The College of the Six Days' Works is a vision of an organization of good men who are working for 'an improvement of man's estates and an enlargement of his power over nature'. The plan of the Great Instauration was a plan for the future, a plan which Bacon could do no more than bequeath to men in hope: 'The fortune of the human race will give the issue, such an issue, it may be, as in the present condition of things, and men's minds cannot easily be conceived or imagined. For the matter in hand is no mere felicity of speculation, but the real business and fortunes of the human race.'

The century following his death provides testimony of the high regard paid to Bacon's scientific and philosophical work by such men as Boyle and the founders of the Royal Society. Because he had pointed out the way to increase of scientific knowledge, and eloquently argued that this was the only fruitful way, with all the force of his power of argument and language, and all the dignity of his position as Lord Chancellor, Dryden's exaggerated praise of him was not uncommon:

> The world to Bacon does not only owe
> Its present knowledge, but its future too.

Bacon was not alone in opposing experiment and observation to authority, but no other writer made his attacks and his recommendations so forcefully. He persuaded men who read his *Novum Organum* that the world lay open for exciting discoveries, though the methods they used were not exactly those he described. By the nineteenth century the investigations he advocated were gathering momentum when, between 1825 and 1834, Basil Montagu published his edition of Bacon's works in 16 volumes. This edition and the review of it by Macaulay in the *Edinburgh Review* (1837) began a period of intense study of Bacon to which we owe the great edition by Ellis and Spedding. But out of the study came also the only careful discussions of Bacon's Inductive philosophy—in William Whewell's *Philosophy of the Inductive Sciences* (1840) and Fowler's edition of the *Novum Organum* (1889), but also reflected in Richard Whately's *Logic* (1826, expanded in later editions) and in Mill's *System of Logic* (1843). Montagu's edition, and the growing interest in the method whereby scientific discoveries were made, gave Bacon new importance in the eyes of scholars. Macaulay's essay, and the numerous essays by lesser men in the periodicals of the time, made Bacon a widely read author. The late seventeenth century had been called 'this Bacon-faced generation'. The mid-nineteenth century merited the same name. For science now attracted the best brains and made its most startling discoveries. Looking back over the century, estimating what had been achieved, Alfred Russell Wallace wrote, echoing Bacon's words:

> In order to estimate its full importance and grandeur—more especially as regards man's increased power over nature, and the application of that power to the needs of his life today, with unlimited possibilities in the future —we must compare it, not with any preceding century, or even with the last millennium, but with the whole historical period—perhaps even with the whole period that has elapsed since the stone age.
>
> (*This Wonderful Century*, 1898, p. 2)

But coincident with the increase in scientific knowledge, and to some extent occasioned by it, was the loosening of men's belief in Christianity. Darwinism versus Christianity was the great discussion of the 1860s. Even without Darwin's particular discoveries and theories the result would have been the same; before Darwin, Charles Kingsley was dramatizing in his novels the clash between his Baconian heroes and the old beliefs, and recommending that Baconian induction be applied to Christianity. He had no doubts that Christianity would survive the application. The conflict was one which Bacon had foreseen and which he had prayed might not happen. In his Preface to the Great Instauration he wrote:

> At the outset of this work I most humbly and fervently pray to God the Father, God the Son, and God the Holy Ghost, that remembering the sorrows of mankind and the pilgrimage of this our life wherein we wear out days few and evil, they will vouchsafe through my hands to endow the human family with new mercies. This likewise I humbly pray, that things human may not interfere with things divine, and that from the opening of the ways of sense and the increase of natural light there may arise in our minds no incredulity or darkness with regard to the divine mysteries, but rather that the understanding being thereby purified and purged of fancies and vanity, and yet not the less subject and entirely submissive to the divine oracles, may give to faith that which is faith's. Lastly, that knowledge being now discharged of that venom which the serpent infused into it, and which makes the mind of man to swell, we may not be wise above measure and sobriety, but cultivate truth in charity.

Reading this we know we are on the threshold of the modern world. Bacon expresses here a hope which is not yet fulfilled.

A Conference of Pleasure
In Praise of Knowledge

For the anniversary of the coronation of Queen Elizabeth, on 17 November 1592, Bacon wrote a 'device' or entertainment which was presented by the Earl of Essex for the Queen's amusement. In this, four characters spoke in praise of that which they held most worthy—Fortitude, Love, Knowledge, and lastly, of the Queen herself. The only complete text to have survived, a manuscript, badly burned, belonging to the Duke of Northumberland, was printed by Spedding in 1870. The last two speeches are also found in Harley MS. 6797, and were first printed in the supplement to the edition of Bacon's *Letters* published by Stephens in 1734. The following text combines readings from both manuscripts (though spelling and punctuation are modernized).

The speech in praise of knowledge is doubly interesting, as showing that Bacon's ideas were fixed at an early age, and as an example of a formal exercise in rhetorical praise. In the first book of the *Advancement of Learning* (especially Sections vi–vii) and in the first book of the *Novum Organum*, we find Bacon's final elaboration of the ideas he expressed here. And between this brief discourse and those finished works stand the many English and Latin fragments in which, with many false starts, he began his elaboration. At the first entry into Bacon's works it is important to grasp the basic elements of this speech. First, that the highest of all pleasures are those of the intellect, in particular, the delight in observing and understanding the order which is in Nature. But this is not delight only; it is also, if properly pursued, likely to lead to inventions for the relief of man's estate. Second, that the concept of knowledge commonly held is incapable of showing the way to inventions. The logic in use may be valuable for decorating what is known, but is incapable of pointing the way to the unknown. The only philosophies available are the Greek, which is merely verbal, and the alchemical, which is full of impostures. Third, that the Universities are seats of uncritical learning which is always at a stand. Fourth, that we have a vision of what could lie in the future for man when we consider the effect on men's lives of three inventions—printing, gunpowder and the magnetic compass. But these we owe to chance and to 'rude mechanicals', not to an ordered process of investigation of Nature based on scientific method. Last, that we must subject ourselves to the discipline of investigating Nature's laws if we would be able to control and direct the powerful forces we should thus discover.

Bacon's style in this piece is already aphoristic. His great gift is, in Macaulay's phrase, his 'wonderful talent for packing thought close and rendering it portable'. The form he uses here is his favourite one, the Demonstrative, that is, the form of Praise (or Dispraise). It is the form he used in many of the *Essays*. He is not Judicial, i.e. proving or disproving a case, nor Deliberative, i.e. persuading or dissuading, but is engaged in praising knowledge as it could be and dispraising knowledge as it is and has been. Like the *Essays*, this speech grew out of his collection of *Antitheta* (those on 'Knowledge and Contemplation' and 'Learning'), which he compiled in his youth and published in the *De Augmentis Scientiarum* (VI.3) at the end of his life.

In Praise of Knowledge

Silence were the best celebration of that, which I mean to commend; for who would not use silence, there where silence is not made? and what crier can make silence in such a noise and tumult of vain and popular opinions? My praise shall be dedicate to the mind itself. The mind is the man,[1] and knowledge mind. A man is but what he knoweth. The mind itself is but an accident[2] to knowledge; for knowledge is a double of that which is.[3] The truth of being, and the truth of knowing, is all one. Are the pleasures of the affections greater than the pleasures of the senses? And are not the pleasures of the intellect greater than the pleasures of the affections? Is not that only a true and natural pleasure, whereof there is no satiety?[4] Is not that knowledge alone that doth clear the mind of all perturbations? How many things be there which we imagine are not? How many things do we esteem and value otherwise than they are? These vain imaginations, these ill-proportioned estimations, these be the clouds of error that turn into the storms of perturbations. Is there then any such happiness as for a man's mind to be raised above the confusion of things; where he may have a prospect of the order of nature, and the error of men?[5] Is this but a view only of delight, and not of discovery? of contentment, and not of benefit? Shall we not discern as well the riches of nature's warehouse, as the beauty of her shop? Is truth barren? Shall we not thereby be able to produce worthy effects, and to endow the life of man with infinite commodities?

But shall I make this garland to be put upon a wrong head? Would any man believe me, if I should verify this, upon the knowledge that is now in use? Are we the richer by one poor invention, by reason of all the learning that hath been this many hundred years? The industry of artificers maketh some small improvements of things invented; and chance sometimes in experimenting, makes us to stumble upon somewhat that is new: but all the disputations of the learned never brought to light one effect of nature before unknown.[6] When things are known and found out, then they can descant upon them, they can knit them into certain causes, they can reduce them to their principles. If any instance of experience stand against them, they can range it in order by some distinctions. But all this is but a web of the wit, it can work nothing. I do not doubt but that common notions which we call reason, and the knitting of them together, which we call logic or the art of reason, may have use in popular studies. But they rather cast obscurity, than give light to the contemplation of nature. All the philosophy of nature which is now received, is either the philosophy of the Grecians, or that other of the alchemists.[7] That of the Grecians hath the foundation in words, in ostentation, in confutation, in sects, in Auditories, in schools, in disputations. The Grecians are, as one of themselves saith, 'you Grecians, ever children.' They knew little antiquity; they knew, except fables, not much above five hundred years before themselves. They knew but a small portion of the world. That of the alchemists hath the foundation in imposture, in auricular traditions and obscurity. It was catching hold of religion, but the principle of it is, 'Populus vult decipi.'[8] So that I know no great difference between these great philosophies, but that the one is a loud crying folly, the other a whispering folly. The one is gathered out of a few vulgar observations, and the other out of a few experiments of the furnace. The one never faileth to multiply words, and the other ever faileth to multiply gold.

Who would not smile at Aristotle, when he admireth the eternity and invariableness of the heavens, as if there were not the like in the bowels of the earth? They be the confines and borders of these two kingdoms, where the continual alterations and incursions are. The superficies and upper parts of the earth is full of variety. The superficies and lower part of the heavens, which we call the middle region of the air, is full of varieties. There is much spirit in the one place, that cannot be brought into mass. There is much massy body in the other place, that cannot be refined into spirit.[9] The common air is as the waste ground between the borders. Who would not smile at the astronomers, I mean not these new carmen which drive the earth about, but the ancient astronomers,[10] which feign the moon to be the swiftest of the planets in motion, and the rest in order, the higher the slower; and so are compelled to imagine a double motion: whereas how evident is it, that that which they call a contrary motion, is but an abatement of motion. The fixed stars overgo Saturn and Saturn leaveth behind him Jupiter, and so in them and the rest, all is but one motion, and the nearer the earth the slower. A motion also whereof the air and the water do participate, though much interrupted.

But why do I in a conference of pleasure enter into these great matters, in sort that pretending to know much, I should know not season? Pardon me, it was because all [other] things may be endowed and adorned with speeches, but knowledge itself is more beautiful than any apparel of words that can be put upon it. And let me not seem arrogant without respect to these great reputed authors. Let me so give every man his due, as I give time his due, which is to discover truth. Many of these men had greater wits, far above mine own, and so are many in the Universities of Europe at this day. But alas, they learn nothing there but to believe: first, to believe that others know that which they know not; and after [that] themselves know that which they know not.[11] But indeed facility to believe, impatience to doubt, temerity to asseter,[12] glory to know, doubt to contradict, end to gain, sloth to search, seeking things in words, resting in a part of nature; these and the like, have been the things which have forbidden the happy match between the mind of man and the nature of things; and in place thereof have married it to vain notions and blind experiments: and what the posterity and issue of so honourable a match may be, it is not hard to consider. Printing, a gross invention; artillery, a thing that lay not far out of the way; the needle, a thing partly known before: what a change have these three made in the world in these times;[13] the one in state of learning, the other in the state of war, the third in the state of treasure, commodities, and navigation? And these were, as I say, but stumbled upon and lighted on by chance. Therefore, no doubt, the sovereignty of man lieth hid in knowledge; wherein many things are reserved, which kings with their treasure cannot buy, nor with their force command; their spials[14] and intelligencers can give no news of them, their seamen and discoverers cannot sail where they grow; now we govern nature in opinions, but are thrall to her in necessities; but if we would be led by her in invention, we should command her in action.

The Advancement of Learning

The publication of the *Advancement of Learning* coincided with the discovery of the Gunpowder Plot on 5 November 1605. Bacon composed quickly, and probably wrote the book during the long adjournment of Parliament from January to October. He enjoyed writing it, he told Sir Thomas Bodley, and he dedicated it to the King because James was 'the learnedest king that hath reigned'. His aim in writing it was to demonstrate the dignity of learning and defend it against its detractors and then to survey all branches of learning and to estimate which were inadequately developed and indicate how they could usefully be more thoroughly investigated. It is usually said that Bacon wrote the book in order to attract the attention of James to his ideas about the ways to increase human knowledge. Certainly the King seemed no more prepared than Elizabeth had been to advance him in his civil capacity. But Bacon was eager to be heard by anyone. 'I have been content to tune the instruments of the Muses, that they may play that have better hands', he wrote at the end of his survey of the state of human learning. '*Verbera, sed audi.*' No matter what you may think of my works, listen to what I have to say.

The *Advancement of Learning* is Bacon's greatest English work, his only considerable discussion of philosophy in English, his most carefully written and arranged piece of prose, his most exciting and most varied account of all his basic ideas, his most noble and sustained work in thought and expression. In the first Book, which is printed here with the omission of only three paragraphs, he expands the 'Praise of Knowledge' of 1592. He defends learning and learned men, that is, men learned in secular knowledge, against various charges—those brought by divines who see in secular learning a threat to religion, those brought by men engaged in government who see learning as inimical to the State, and those brought against defects thought to be inherent in learning itself. For Bacon it was not scientific knowledge that was evil, but the sort of knowledge pursued by the Schoolmen. A learned man was not a danger to the State, nor useless to it, but its greatest ornament. Learning suffered not because scholars were poor, or were employed to teach the young, but because they had so far studied the wrong things—words instead of things, useless knowledge; and in the wrong spirit —contentiously, or for the sake of ornament; and by the wrong methods—using only the syllogism, abandoning universality, over-valuing human reason, hastening to reduce everything to rational systems, and neglecting to doubt and verify. But true knowledge is to be seen in the wisdom of God in the Creation, in the learning of Moses, Job and Solomon, and of such leaders as Caesar, Alexander and Elizabeth I, in the use of learning to relieve man's estate, to civilize mankind, to encourage our progress in virtue, to provide the purest and deepest of pleasures, and to ensure the only immortality that man can win by his own efforts.

Bacon knew that he was living on the verge of a revival of learning which could be compared only with the periods of Greek and Roman learning. This 'third visitation' had been a long time in coming, well over a thousand years, and since its first dawning had shown signs of dissipating its energies in religious controversies and mere imitation of the ancients. But there were other signs that promised a glorious future, such as the invention of printing and the improvement in navigation, the increase of leisure, the hopes of European peace, and the exhaustion of the religious quarrels. These Bacon was anxious to encourage by showing that learning is the ideal to which civilization should devote its energies and that in order to pursue the ideal men must know their own strength and weakness, learn to co-operate in research instead of quarrel, and investigate in the spirit of a quest for Truth (II.xxiv).

The second Book of the *Advancement* is a survey of the state of learning. Bacon is in the tradition of the medieval and Renaissance encyclopaedists who organized all knowledge according to some scheme—the six days of Creation, or the seven liberal arts (grammar, rhetoric, logic, arithmetic, geometry, astronomy and music) and the three philosophies (natural, moral and rational). The resulting works— Bartholomew's *Liber de Proprietatibus Rerum*, Vincent of Beauvais'

Specula, La Primaudaye's *The French Academy*, Agrippa's *De Incertitudine et Vanitate Omnium Scientiarum et Artium*, and so on—expounded all that was known on each topic, arranged according to the chosen scheme. What Bacon does in Book II is to arrange all knowledge according to his own scheme, but instead of outlining what is known of each subject, he assesses its importance and reports where it is not adequately investigated. The scheme might be described thus—the seat of learning is the Understanding, which has three faculties, Memory, Imagination and Reason. To each of these faculties particular branches of knowledge belong. To the Memory belong types of History—(1) Natural (subdivided into Histories of Creatures, Marvels and Arts), (2) Civil, (3) Ecclesiastical, (4) Literary. To the Imagination belongs Poetry, Narrative, Dramatic and Allegorical (see pp. 126 ff.). To the Reason belongs Philosophy, divided into—(1) Natural Theology, (2) Natural Philosophy, which is either Speculative (Physical and Metaphysical, including mathematics) or Operative (Experimental, Philosophical, and Magical), (3) Human Philosophy. This last division occupies the bulk of the work and is subdivided to include, among other things, the studies of Mind and its faculties (logic, invention, judgment and rhetoric), of the nature of Good, both private and in communities, of the 'culture of the mind', and of the 'architecture of fortune', a long essay on how to succeed in politics. Divinity has a short section to itself.

Bacon's delight is in the beautiful symmetry of his arrangement—it is characteristic that he does not question this, partly because the book is offered as a 'just Treatise', or work in which part of the persuasive skill lies in its arrangement, and partly because Bacon himself was one of those disposed to find more pattern in things than is actually there. But Bacon also enjoys explaining what parts of this great map of knowledge have not yet been properly explored. He hoped that the map would encourage both government and individuals to set to work to occupy the territory he had plotted.

Three sections from the second Book are printed: the account of Poetry (taken from the expanded Latin version of the *De Augmentis Scientiarum* of 1623, see pp. 126-45); the introductory paragraphs on education and the defects of the universities (pp. 63-68); and the paragraphs on the transferring of knowledge to others (pp. 69-75).

As a preparation for his 'perambulation of learning, with an inquiry what parts thereof lie fresh and waste', which is all that the private individual can do, Bacon explains to the King what aspects of learning kings can assist. These are all related to the universities—to the provision of books and apparatus for experiments, to the proper remuneration of university teachers in order to attract the best men, to the encouraging of intercourse between English and Continental universities, and to the need to keep the syllabuses of study under constant review. Bacon, rightly, had no hope that either of the universities would reform itself, according to his principles, from within; hence the appeal to the King to impose reform. Here the proposals are three—(1) that to the present subjects of study, which are all professional (divinity, law and medicine) be added such subjects as history, modern languages and politics ,and also such general philosophical subjects as have no immediate practical value but are 'pure' (he is thinking of scientific investigations), (2) that logic and rhetoric, the subjects normally studied for the first two years, be left for maturer study, (3) that men be appointed to investigate those parts of learning so far but thinly explored.

The *New Atlantis* incorporates Bacon's plan for an ideal university; but the early paragraphs of the second book of the *Advancement* are equally eloquent in describing the places, the books and the persons of the learned. The irritating actuality of a university he described in Book I when dealing with the indignity that learning receives from the studies pursued by learned men. By his will he endowed two lectureships at the universities, one to be devoted to natural philosophy or science. They were not limited to Englishmen, but no holder was to be a professional man—in law, medicine or divinity. The stipend was generous, £200 a year. Unfortunately Bacon's debts swallowed up his endowment.

The third extract printed here presents Bacon's thoughts on the theory of communication—on methods of arranging and presenting knowledge, and on the illumination of knowledge when offered to an audience, whether learned or popular. It is an important part of Bacon's ideas, partly because it shows him criticizing and making advances on the theories of Ramus, who had reformed Aristotelian logic and rhetoric, and partly because it describes various aspects of his own practice in presenting his own material. The whole discussion is about what we should now call 'style' and must form the basis for any assessment of Bacon's own differing styles. The notes to this section are fuller than usual and could usefully be read before the passage itself.

First Book of Francis Bacon
Of the Proficience and
Advancement of Learning
Divine and Human

To the King

1. There were under the law,[1] excellent King, both daily sacrifices and free-will offerings; the one proceeding upon ordinary observance, the other upon a devout cheerfulness: in like manner there belongeth to kings from their servants both tribute of duty and presents of affection. In the former of these I hope I shall not live to be wanting, according to my most humble duty, and the good pleasure of your Majesty's employments: for the latter, I thought it more respective to make choice of some oblation, which might rather refer to the propriety and excellency of your individual person, than to the business of your crown and state. . . .

3. Therefore I did conclude with myself, that I could not make unto your Majesty a better oblation than of some treatise tending to that end, whereof the sum will consist of these two parts; the former concerning the excellency of learning and knowledge, and the excellency of the merit and true glory in the augmentation and propagation thereof: the latter, what the particular acts and works are, which have been embraced and undertaken for the advancement of learning; and again, what defects and undervalues I find in such particular acts: to the end that though I cannot positively or affirmatively advise your Majesty, or propound unto you framed particulars, yet I may excite your princely cogitations to visit the excellent treasure of your own mind, and thence to extract particulars for this purpose, agreeable to your magnanimity and wisdom.

I. 1. In the entrance to the former of these, to clear the way, and as it were to make silence, to have the true testimonies concerning the dignity of learning to be better heard, without the interruption of tacit objections; I think it good to deliver it from the discredits and disgraces which it hath received, all from ignorance; but ignorance severally disguised; appearing sometimes in the zeal and jealousy of divines; sometimes in the severity and arrogancy of politiques;[2] and sometimes in the errors and imperfections of learned men themselves.

2. I hear the former sort say, that knowledge is of those things which are to be accepted of with great limitation and caution: that the aspiring to overmuch knowledge was the original temptation and sin whereupon ensued the fall of

man: that knowledge hath in it somewhat of the serpent, and therefore where it entereth into a man it makes him swell; *Scientia inflat*: that Salomon gives a censure, *That there is no end of making books, and that much reading is weariness of the flesh*; and again in another place, *That in spacious knowledge there is much contristation,*[3] *and that he that increaseth knowledge increaseth anxiety*: that Saint Paul gives a caveat, *That we be not spoiled through vain philosophy*: that experience demonstrates how learned men have been arch-heretics, how learned times have been inclined to atheism, and how the contemplation of second causes[4] doth derogate from our dependence upon God, who is the first cause.

3. To discover then the ignorance and error of this opinion, and the mis-understanding in the grounds thereof, it may well appear these men do not observe or consider that it was not the pure knowledge of nature and univer-sality,[5] a knowledge by the light whereof man did give names unto other creatures in Paradise, as they were brought before him, according unto their proprieties, which gave the occasion to the fall: but it was the proud knowledge of good and evil, with an intent in man to give law unto himself, and to depend no more upon God's commandments, which was the form of the temptation. Neither is it any quantity of knowledge, how great soever, that can make the mind of man to swell; for nothing can fill, much less extend the soul of man, but God and the contemplation of God; and therefore Salomon, speaking of the two principal senses of inquisition, the eye and the ear, affirmeth that *the eye is never satisfied with seeing, nor the ear with hearing*; and if there be no fulness, then is the continent greater than the content: so of knowledge itself, and the mind of man, whereto the senses are but reporters, he defineth likewise in these words, placed after that Kalendar or Ephemerides[6] which he maketh of the diversities of times and seasons for all actions and purposes; and concludeth thus: *God hath made all things beautiful, or decent, in the true return of their seasons: Also he hath placed the world in man's heart, yet cannot man find out the work which God worketh from the beginning to the end*: declaring not obscurely, that God hath framed the mind of man as a mirror or glass, capable of the image of the universal world, and joyful to receive the impression thereof, as the eye joyeth to receive light; and not only delighted in beholding the variety of things and vicissitude of times, but raised also to find out and discern the ordinances and decrees, which throughout all those changes are infallibly observed. And al-though he doth insinuate that the supreme or summary law of nature, which he calleth *The work which God worketh from the beginning to the end*, is not possible to be found out by man; yet that doth not derogate from the capacity of the mind, but may be referred to the impediments, as of shortness of life, ill conjunction of labours, ill tradition[7] of knowledge over from hand to hand, and many other inconveniences, whereunto the condition of man is subject.

For that nothing parcel of the world is denied to man's inquiry and invention, he doth in another place rule over, when he saith, *The spirit of man is as the lamp of God, wherewith he searcheth the inwardness of all secrets*. If then such be the capacity and receipt of the mind of man, it is manifest that there is no danger at all in the proportion or quantity of knowledge, how large soever, lest it should make it swell or out-compass itself; no, but it is merely the quality of knowledge, which, be it in quantity more or less, if it be taken without the true corrective thereof, hath in it some nature of venom or malignity, and some effects of that venom, which is ventosity or swelling. This corrective spice, the mixture whereof maketh knowledge so sovereign, is charity, which the Apostle immediately addeth to the former clause: for so he saith, *Knowledge bloweth up, but charity buildeth up*; not unlike unto that which he delivereth in another place: *If I spake*, saith he, *with the tongues of men and angels, and had not charity, it were but as a tinkling cymbal*; not but that it is an excellent thing to speak with the tongues of men and angels, but because, if it be severed from charity, and not referred to the good of men and mankind, it hath rather a sounding and unworthy glory, than a meriting and substantial virtue. And as for that censure of Salomon, concerning the excess of writing and reading books, and the anxiety of spirit which redoundeth from knowledge; and that admonition of Saint Paul, *That we be not seduced by vain philosophy* let those places be rightly understood, and they do indeed excellently set forth the true bounds and limitations, whereby human knowledge is confined and circumscribed; and yet without any such contracting or coarctation,[8] but that it may comprehend all the universal nature of things; for these limitations are three: the first, That we do not so place our felicity in knowledge, as we forget our mortality: the second, That we make application of our knowledge, to give ourselves repose and contentment, and not distaste or repining: the third, That we do not presume by the contemplation of nature to attain to the mysteries of God. For as touching the first of these, Salomon doth excellently expound himself in another place of the same book, where he saith: *I saw well that knowledge recedeth as far from ignorance as light doth from darkness; and that the wise man's eyes keep watch in his head, whereas the fool roundeth about in darkness: but withal I learned, that the same mortality involveth them both*. And for the second, certain it is, there is no vexation or anxiety of mind which resulteth from knowledge otherwise than merely by accident; for all knowledge and wonder (which is the seed of knowledge) is an impression of pleasure in itself: but when men fall to framing conclusions out of their knowledge, applying it to their particular,[9] and ministering to themselves thereby weak fears or vast desires, there groweth that carefulness and trouble of mind which is spoken of: for then knowledge is no more *Lumen siccum*,[10] whereof Heraclitus the profound said, *Lumen siccum optima anima*; but it becometh *Lumen madidum* or *maceratum*, being steeped and infused in the humours of the affections. And as for the third point, it deserveth to be a little stood upon, and not to be lightly passed over: for if any man shall think by view and inquiry into these sensible and material things to attain that light, whereby he may reveal unto himself the nature or will of God, then indeed is he spoiled by vain philosophy: for the contemplation of God's creatures and works produceth (having regard to the works and creatures themselves) knowledge, but having regard to God, no perfect knowledge, but wonder which is broken[11] knowledge. And therefore it was most aptly said by one of Plato's school, *That the sense of man carrieth a resemblance with the sun, which (as we see) openeth and revealeth all the terrestrial globe; but then again it obscureth and concealeth the stars and celestial globe: so doth the sense discover natural things, but it darkeneth and shutteth up divine.* And hence it is true that it hath proceeded, that divers great learned men have been heretical, whilst they have sought to fly up to the secrets of the Deity by the waxen wings of the senses. And as for the conceit that too much knowledge should incline a man to atheism, and that the ignorance of second causes should make a more devout dependence upon God, which is the first cause; first, it is good to ask the question which Job asked of his friends: *Will you lie for God, as one man will do for another, to gratify him?* For certain it is that God worketh nothing in nature but by second causes: and if they would have it otherwise believed, it is mere imposture, as it were in favour towards God; and nothing else but to offer to the author of truth the unclean sacrifice of a lie. But further, it is an assured truth, and a conclusion of experience, that a little or superficial knowledge of philosophy may incline the mind of man to atheism, but a further proceeding therein doth bring the mind back again to religion. For in the entrance of philosophy, when the second causes, which are next unto the senses, do offer themselves to the mind of man, if it dwell and stay there it may induce some oblivion of the highest cause; but when a man passeth on further, and seeth the dependence of causes, and the works of Providence, then, according to the allegory of the poets, he will easily believe that the highest link of nature's chain[12] must needs be tied to the foot of Jupiter's chair. To conclude, therefore, let no man upon a weak conceit of sobriety or an ill-applied moderation think or maintain, that a man can search too far, or be too well studied in the book of God's word, or in the book of God's works, divinity or philosophy; but rather let men endeavour an endless progress or proficience in both; only let men beware that they apply both to charity, and not to swelling; to use, and not to ostentation; and again, that they do not unwisely mingle or confound these learnings together.

II. 1. And as for the disgraces which learning receiveth from politiques, they be of this nature; that learning doth soften men's minds, and makes them more unapt for the honour and exercise of arms; that it doth mar and pervert men's dispositions for matter of government and policy, in making them too curious and irresolute by variety of reading, or too peremptory or positive by strictness of rules and axioms, or too immoderate and overweening by reason of the greatness of examples, or too incompatible and differing from the times by reason of the dissimilitude of examples; or at least, that it doth divert men's travails from action and business, and bringeth them to a love of leisure and privateness; and that it doth bring into states a relaxation of discipline, whilst every man is more ready to argue than to obey and execute. Out of this conceit, Cato, surnamed the Censor, one of the wisest men indeed that ever lived, when Carneades the philosopher came in embassage to Rome, and that the young men of Rome began to flock about him, being allured with the sweetness and majesty of his eloquence and learning, gave counsel in open senate that they should give him his dispatch with all speed, lest he should infect and enchant the minds and affections of the youth, and at unawares bring in an alteration of the manners and customs of the state. Out of the same conceit or humour did Virgil, turning his pen to the advantage of his country, and the disadvantage of his own profession, make a kind of separation between policy and government, and between arts and sciences, in the verses so much renowned, attributing and challenging the one to the Romans, and leaving and yielding the other to the Grecians: *Tu regere imperio populos, Romane, memento, Hae tibi erunt artes,* &c.[13] So likewise we see that Anytus the accuser of Socrates,[14] laid it as an article of charge and accusation against him, that he did, with the variety and power of his discourses and disputations, withdraw young men from due reverence to the laws and customs of their country, and that he did profess a dangerous and pernicious science, which was, to make the worse matter seem the better, and to suppress truth by force of eloquence and speech.

2. But these and the like imputations have rather a countenance of gravity than any ground of justice: for experience doth warrant, that both in persons and in times there hath been a meeting and concurrence in learning and arms, flourishing and excelling in the same men and the same ages. For as for men, there cannot be a better nor the like instance, as of that pair, Alexander the Great and Julius Caesar the Dictator; whereof the one was Aristotle's scholar in philosophy, and the other was Cicero's rival in eloquence: or if any man had rather call for scholars that were great generals, than generals that were great scholars, let him take Epaminondas the Theban, or Xenophon the Athenian; whereof the one was the first that abated the power of Sparta, and the other was the first that made way to the overthrow of the monarchy of Persia. And this concurrence is yet more visible in times than in persons, by how much an

age is [a] greater object than a man. For both in Egypt, Assyria, Persia, Grecia, and Rome, the same times that are most renowned for arms, are likewise most admired for learning; so that the greatest authors and philosophers and the greatest captains and governors have lived in the same ages. Neither can it otherwise be: for as in man the ripeness of strength of the body and mind cometh much about an age, save that the strength of the body cometh somewhat the more early, so in states, arms and learning, whereof the one correspondeth to the body, the other to the soul of man, have a concurrence or near sequence in times.[15]

3. And for matter of policy and government, that learning should rather hurt, than enable thereunto, is a thing very improbable: we see it is accounted an error to commit a natural body to empiric physicians,[16] which commonly have a few pleasing receipts whereupon they are confident and adventurous, but know neither the causes of diseases, nor the complexions of patients, nor peril of accidents, nor the true method of cures: we see it is a like error to rely upon advocates or lawyers, which are only men of practice and not grounded in their books, who are many times easily surprised when matter falleth out besides their experience, to the prejudice of the causes they handle: so by like reason it cannot be but a matter of doubtful consequence if states be managed by empiric statesmen, not well mingled with men grounded in learning. But contrariwise, it is almost without instance contradictory that ever any government was disastrous that was in the hands of learned governors. For howsoever it hath been ordinary with politique men to extenuate and disable learned men by the names of *pedantes*; yet in the records of time it appeareth in many particulars that the governments of princes in minority (notwithstanding the infinite disadvantage of that kind of state) have nevertheless excelled the government of princes of mature age, even for that reason which they seek to traduce, which is, that by that occasion the state hath been in the hands of *pedantes*:[17] for so was the state of Rome for the first five years, which are so much magnified, during the minority of Nero, in the hands of Seneca a *pedanti*: so it was again, for ten years' space or more, during the minority of Gordianus the younger, with great applause and contentation in the hands of Misitheus a *pedanti*: so was it before that, in the minority of Alexander Severus, in like happiness, in hands not much unlike, by reason of the rule of the women, who were aided by the teachers and preceptors. Nay, let a man look into the government of the bishops of Rome, as by name, into the government of Pius Quintus and Sextus Quintus in our times, who were both at their entrance esteemed but as pedantical friars, and he shall find that such popes do greater things, and proceed upon truer principles of estate, than those which have ascended to the papacy from an education and breeding in affairs of

estate and courts of princes; for although men bred in learning are perhaps to seek[18] in points of convenience and accommodating for the present, which the Italians call *ragioni di stato*, whereof the same Pius Quintus could not hear spoken with patience, terming them inventions against religion and the moral virtues; yet on the other side, to recompense that, they are perfect in those same plain grounds of religion, justice, honour and moral virtue, which if they be well and watchfully pursued, there will be seldom use of those other, no more than of physic in a sound or well-dieted body. Neither can the experience of one man's life furnish examples and precedents for the events of one man's life. For as it happeneth sometimes that the grand-child, or other descendant, resembleth the ancestor more than the son; so many times occurrences of present times may sort better with ancient examples than with those of the later or immediate times: and lastly, the wit of one man can no more countervail learning than one man's means can hold way with[19] a common purse.

4. And as for those particular seducements or indispositions of the mind for policy and government, which learning is pretended to insinuate; if it be granted that any such thing be, it must be remembered withal, that learning ministereth in every of them greater strength of medicine or remedy than it offereth cause of indisposition or infirmity. For if by a secret operation it make men perplexed and irresolute, on the other side by plain precept it teacheth them when and upon what ground to resolve; yea, and how to carry things in suspense without prejudice, till they resolve. If it make men positive and regular,[20] it teacheth them what things are in their nature demonstrative, and what are conjectural, and as well the use of distinctions and exceptions, as the latitude of principles and rules. If it mislead by disproportion or dissimilitude of examples, it teacheth men the force of circumstances, the errors of comparisons, and all the cautions of application; so that in all these it doth rectify more effectually than it can pervert. And these medicines it conveyeth into men's minds much more forcibly by the quickness and penetration of examples. For let a man look into the errors[21] of Clement the seventh, so lively described by Guicciardine, who served under him, or into the errors of Cicero, painted out by his own pencil in his Epistles to Atticus, and he will fly apace from being irresolute. Let him look into the errors of Phocion, and he will beware how he be obstinate or inflexible. Let him but read the fable of Ixion, and it will hold him from being vaporous or imaginative. Let him look into the errors of Cato the second, and he will never be one of the Antipodes, to tread opposite to the present world.

5. And for the conceit that learning should dispose men to leisure and privateness, and make men slothful; it were a strange thing if that which accustometh the mind to a perpetual motion and agitation should induce slothfulness:

whereas contrariwise it may be truly affirmed, that no kind of men love business for itself but those that are learned; for other persons love it for profit, as an hireling, that loves the work for the wages; or for honour, as because it beareth them up in the eyes of men, and refresheth their reputation, which otherwise would wear; or because it putteth them in mind of their fortune, and giveth them occasion to pleasure and displeasure; or because it exerciseth some faculty wherein they take pride, and so entertaineth them in good humour and pleasing conceits toward themselves; or because it advanceth any other their ends. So that as it is said of untrue valours, that some men's valours are in the eyes of them that look on; so such men's industries are in the eyes of others, or at least in regard of their own designments: only learned men love business as an action according to nature, as agreeable to health of mind as exercise is to health of body, taking pleasure in the action itself, and not in the purchase: so that of all men they are the most indefatigable, if it be towards any business which can hold or detain their mind.

6. And if any man be laborious in reading and study and yet idle in business and action, it groweth from some weakness of body or softness of spirit; such as Seneca[22] speaketh of: *Quidam tam sunt umbratiles, ut putent in turbido esse quicquid in luce est*; and not of learning: well may it be that such a point of a man's nature may make him give himself to learning, but it is not learning that breedeth any such point in his nature.

7. And that learning should take up too much time or leisure; I answer, the most active or busy man that hath been or can be, hath (no question) many vacant times of leisure, while he expecteth the tides and returns of business (except he be either tedious and of no dispatch, or lightly and unworthily ambitious to meddle in things that may be better done by others), and then the question is but how those spaces and times of leisure shall be filled and spent; whether in pleasures or in studies; as was well answered by Demosthenes[23] to his adversary Aeschines, that was a man given to pleasure and told him *That his orations did smell of the lamp: Indeed* (said Demosthenes) *there is a great difference between the things that you and I do by lamp-light.* So as no man need doubt[24] that learning will expulse business, but rather it will keep and defend the possession of the mind against idleness and pleasure, which otherwise at unawares may enter to the prejudice of both.

8. Again, for that other conceit that learning should undermine the reverence of laws and government, it is assuredly a mere depravation and calumny, without all shadow of truth. For to say that a blind custom of obedience should be a surer obligation than duty taught and understood, it is to affirm, that a blind man may tread surer by a guide than a seeing man can by a light. And it is without all controversy, that learning doth make the minds of men

gentle, generous, maniable,[25] and pliant to government; whereas ignorance makes them churlish, thwart, and mutinous: and the evidence of time doth clear this assertion, considering that the most barbarous, rude, and unlearned times have been most subject to tumults, seditions, and changes.

9. And as to the judgment of Cato the Censor,[26] he was well punished for his blasphemy against learning, in the same kind wherein he offended; for when he was past threescore years old, he was taken with an extreme desire to go to school again, and to learn the Greek tongue, to the end to peruse the Greek authors; which doth well demonstrate that his former censure of the Grecian learning was rather an affected gravity, than according to the inward sense of his own opinion. And as for Virgil's verses, though it pleased him to brave the world in taking to the Romans the art of empire, and leaving to others the arts of subjects; yet so much is manifest that the Romans never ascended to that height of empire, till the time they had ascended to the height of other arts. For in the time of the two first Caesars, which had the art of government in greatest perfection, there lived the best poet, Virgilius Maro; the best historiographer, Titus Livius; the best antiquary, Marcus Varro; and the best, or second orator, Marcus Cicero, that to the memory of man are known. As for the accusation of Socrates,[27] the time must be remembered when it was prosecuted; which was under the Thirty Tyrants, the most base, bloody, and envious persons that have governed; which revolution of state was no sooner over, but Socrates, whom they had made a person criminal, was made a person heroical, and his memory accumulate with honours divine and human; and those discourses of his which were then termed corrupting of manners, were after acknowledged for sovereign medicines of the mind and manners, and so have been received ever since till this day. Let this therefore serve for answer to politiques, which in their humorous severity, or in their feigned gravity, have presumed to throw imputations upon learning; which redargution[28] nevertheless (save that we know not whether our labours may extend to other ages) were not needful for the present, in regard of the love and reverence towards learning, which the example and countenance of two so learned princes, Queen Elizabeth and your Majesty, being as Castor and Pollux, *lucida sidera*;[29] stars of excellent light and most benign influence, hath wrought in all men of place and authority in our nation.

III. 1. Now therefore we come to that third sort of discredit or diminution of credit that groweth unto learning from learned men themselves, which commonly cleaveth fastest: it is either from their fortune, or from their manners, or from the nature of their studies. For the first, it is not in their power; and the second is accidental; the third only is proper to be handled: but because we are not in hand with true measure, but with popular estimation and conceit, it is not amiss to speak somewhat of the two former. The derogations therefore which grow to learning from the fortune or condition of learned men, are either in respect of scarcity of means, or in respect of privateness of life and meanness of employments.

2. Concerning want, and that it is the case of learned men usually to begin with little, and not to grow rich so fast as other men, by reason they convert not their labours chiefly to lucre and increase, it were good to leave the common-place in commendation of poverty to some friar to handle, to whom much was attributed by Machiavel in this point; when he said, *That the kingdom of the clergy had been long before at an end, if the reputation and reverence towards the poverty of friars had not borne out the scandal of the superfluities and excesses of bishops and prelates.* So a man might say that the felicity and delicacy of princes and great persons had long since turned to rudeness and barbarism, if the poverty of learning had not kept up civility and honour of life: but without any such advantages, it is worthy the observation what a reverent and honoured thing poverty of fortune was for some ages in the Roman state, which never-theless was a state without paradoxes. For we see what Titus Livius[30] saith in his introduction: *Caeterum aut me amor negotii suscepti fallit, aut nulla unquam respublica nec major, nec sanctior, nec bonis exemplis ditior fuit; nec in quam tam serae avaritia luxuriaque immigraverint: nec ubi tantus ac tam diu paupertati ac parsimoniae honos fuerit.* We see likewise, after that the state of Rome was not itself, but did degenerate, how that person that took upon him to be counsellor to Julius Caesar after his victory where to begin his restoration of the state, maketh it of all points the most summary to take away the estimation of wealth: *Verum haec et omnia mala pariter cum honore pecuniae desinent; si neque magistratus, neque alia vulgo cupienda, venalia erunt.*[31] To conclude this point, as it was truly said, that *Rubor est virtutis color*, though sometime it come from vice; so it may be fitly said that *Paupertas est virtutis fortuna*,[32] though some-times it may proceed from misgovernment and accident. Surely Salomon[33] hath pronounced it both in censure, *Qui festinat ad divitias non erit insons*; and in precept, *Buy the truth and sell it not; and so of wisdom and knowledge;* judging that means were to be spent upon learning, and not learning to be applied to means. And as for the privateness or obscureness (as it may be in vulgar estima-tion accounted) of life of contemplative men; it is a theme so common to extol a private life, not taxed with sensuality and sloth, in comparison and to the disadvantage of a civil life, for safety, liberty, pleasure, and dignity, or at least freedom from indignity, as no man handleth it but handleth it well; such a consonancy it hath to men's conceits in the expressing, and to men's consents in the allowing. This only I will add, that learned men forgotten in states and not living in the eyes of men, are like the images of Cassius and Brutus in the

funeral of Junia; of which not being represented, as many others were, Tacitus[34] saith, *Eo ipso praefulgebant, quod non visebantur.*

3. And for meanness of employment, that which is most traduced to contempt[35] is that the government of youth is commonly allotted to them; which age, because it is the age of least authority, it is transferred to the disesteeming of those employments wherein youth is conversant, and which are conversant about youth. But how unjust this traducement is (if you will reduce things from popularity of opinion to measure of reason) may appear in that we see men are more curious what they put into a new vessel than into a vessel seasoned; and what mould they lay about a young plant than about a plant corroborate;[36] so as the weakest terms and times of all things use to have the best applications and helps. And will you hearken to the Hebrew rabbins? *Your young men shall see visions, and your old men shall dream dreams*; say they youth is the worthier age, for that visions are nearer apparitions of God than dreams? And let it be noted, that howsoever the condition of life of *pedantes* hath been scorned upon theatres,[37] as the ape of tyranny; and that the modern looseness or negligence hath taken no due regard to the choice of schoolmasters and tutors; yet the ancient wisdom of the best times did always make a just complaint, that states were too busy with their laws and too negligent in point of education: which excellent part of ancient discipline hath been in some sort revived of late times by the colleges of the Jesuits;[38] of whom, although in regard of their superstition I may say, *Quo meliores, eo deteriores*; yet in regard to this, and some other points concerning human learning and moral matters, I may say, as Agesilaus said to his enemy Pharnabazus, *Talis quum sis, utinam noster esses.* And thus much touching the discredits drawn from the fortunes of learned men.

4. As touching the manners of learned men, it is a thing personal and individual: and no doubt there be amongst them, as in other professions, of all temperatures: but yet so as it is not without truth which is said, that *Abeunt studia in mores*,[39] studies have an influence and operation upon the manners of those that are conversant in them.

5. But upon an attentive and indifferent[40] review, I for my part cannot find any disgrace to learning can proceed from the manners of learned men; not inherent to them as they are learned; except it be a fault (which was the supposed fault of Demosthenes, Cicero, Cato the second, Seneca, and many more) that because the times they read of are commonly better than the times they live in, and the duties taught better than the duties practised, they contend sometimes too far to bring things to perfection, and to reduce the corruption of manners to honesty of precepts or examples of too great height. And yet hereof they have caveats enough in their own walks. For Solon, when he was asked whether

he had given his citizens the best laws, answered wisely, *Yea of such as they would receive*: and Plato, finding that his own heart could not agree with the corrupt manners of his country, refused to bear place or office; saying, *That a man's country was to be used as his parents were, that is, with humble persuasions, and not with contestations*. And Caesar's counsellor put in the same caveat, *Non ad vetera instituta revocans quae jampridem corruptis moribus ludibrio sunt*:[41] and Cicero noteth this error directly in Cato the second, when he writes to his friend Atticus, *Cato optime sentit, sed nocet interdum reipublicae; loquitur enim tanquam in republica Platonis, non tanquam in faece Romuli*.[42] And the same Cicero doth excuse and expound[43] the philosophers for going too far and being too exact in their prescripts, when he saith, *Isti ipsi praeceptores virtutis et magistri videntur fines officiorum paulo longius quam natura vellet protulisse, ut cum ad ultimum animo contendissemus, ibi tamen, ubi oportet, consisteremus*:[44] and yet himself might have said, *Monitis sum minor ipse meis*;[45] for it was his own fault though not in so extreme a degree.

6. Another fault likewise much of this kind hath been incident to learned men; which is, that they have esteemed the preservation, good and honour of their countries or masters before their own fortunes or safeties. For so saith Demosthenes unto the Athenians, *If it please you to note it, my counsels unto you are not such whereby I should grow great amongst you, and you become little amongst the Grecians; but they be of that nature, as they are sometimes not good for me to give, but are always good for you to follow*. And so Seneca, after he had consecrated that *Quinquennium Neronis*[46] to the eternal glory of learned governors, held on his honest and loyal course of good and free counsel, after his master grew extremely corrupt in his government. Neither can this point otherwise be; for learning endueth men's minds with a true sense of the frailty of their persons, the casualty of their fortunes, and the dignity of their soul and vocation; so that it is impossible for them to esteem that any greatness of their own fortune can be a true or worthy end of their being and ordainment; and therefore are desirous to give their account to God, and so likewise to their masters under God (as kings and the states that they serve) in these words; *Ecce tibi lucrefeci*,[47] and not *Ecce mihi lucrefeci*: whereas the corrupter sort of mere politiques that have not their thoughts established by learning in the love and apprehension of duty, nor never look abroad into universality, do refer all things to themselves, and thrust themselves into the centre of the world, as if all lines should meet in them and their fortunes; never caring in all tempests what becomes of the ship of estates, so they may save themselves in the cockboat of their own fortune: whereas men that feel the weight of duty and know the limits of self-love, use to make good their places and duties, though with peril; and if they stand[48] in seditious and violent alterations, it is rather the reverence which many times

both adverse parts do give to honesty, than any versatile advantage of their own carriage. But for this point of tender sense and fast obligation of duty which learning doth endue the mind withal, howsoever fortune may tax it, and many in the depth of their corrupt principles may despise it, yet it will receive an open allowance, and therefore needs the less disproof or excusation.

7. Another fault incident commonly to learned men, which may be more probably defended than truly denied, is, that they fail sometimes in applying themselves to particular persons: which want of exact application ariseth from two causes; the one, because the largeness of their mind can hardly confine itself to dwell in the exquisite observation or examination of the nature and customs of one person: for it is a speech for a lover, and not for a wise man, *Satis magnum alter alteri theatrum sumus.*[49] Nevertheless I shall yield, that he that cannot contract the sight of his mind as well as disperse and dilate it, wanteth a great faculty. But there is a second cause, which is no inability, but a rejection upon choice and judgement. For the honest and just bounds of observation by one person upon another, extend no further but to understand him sufficiently, whereby not to give him offence, or whereby to be able to give him faithful counsel or whereby to stand upon reasonable guard and caution in respect of a man's self. But to be speculative into another man to the end to know how to work him, or wind him, or govern him, proceedeth from a heart that is double and cloven and not entire and ingenuous; which as in friendship it is want of integrity, so towards princes or superiors is want of duty. For the custom of the Levant, which is that subjects do forbear to gaze or fix their eyes upon princes, is in the outward ceremony barbarous, but the moral is good: for men ought not by cunning and bent observations to pierce and penetrate into the hearts of kings, which the scripture hath declared to be inscrutable.

8. There is yet another fault (with which I will conclude this part) which is often noted in learned men, that they do many times fail to observe decency and discretion in their behaviour and carriage, and commit errors in small and ordinary points of action, so as the vulgar sort of capacities do make a judgement of them in greater matters by that which they find wanting in them in smaller. But this consequence doth oft deceive men, for which I do refer them over to that which was said by Themistocles, arrogantly and uncivilly being applied to himself out of his own mouth, but, being applied to the general state of this question, pertinently and justly; when being invited to touch a lute he said *He could not fiddle, but he could make a small town a great state.* So no doubt many may be well seen in the passages of government and policy, which are to seek in little and punctual occasions. I refer them also to that which Plato said of his master Socrates,[50] whom he compared to the gallipots of apothecaries, which

on the outside had apes and owls and antiques but contained within sovereign and precious liquors and confections; acknowledging that to an external report he was not without superficial levities and deformities, but was inwardly replenished with excellent virtues and powers. And so much touching the point of manners of learned men.

9. But in the mean time I have no purpose to give allowance to some conditions and courses base and unworthy, wherein divers professors of learning have wronged themselves and gone too far; such as were those trencher philosophers which in the later age of the Roman state were usually in the houses of great persons, being little better than solemn parasites; of which kind, Lucian[51] maketh a merry description of the philosopher that the great lady took to ride with her in her coach, and would needs have him carry her little dog, which he doing officiously and yet uncomely, the page scoffed and said, *That he doubted the philosopher of a Stoic would turn to be a Cynic.* But above all the rest, the gross and palpable flattery, whereunto many not unlearned have abased and abused their wits and pens, turning (as Du Bartas[52] saith) Hecuba into Helena, and Faustina into Lucretia, hath most diminished the price and estimation of learning. Neither is the modern dedication of books and writings, as to patrons, to be commended: for that books (such as are worthy the name of books) ought to have no patrons but truth and reason. And the ancient custom was to dedicate them only to private and equal friends, or to entitle the books with their names: or if to kings and great persons, it was to some such as the argument of the book was fit and proper for: but these and the like courses may deserve rather reprehension than defence.

10. Not that I can tax or condemn the morigeration[53] or application of learned men to men in fortune. For the answer was good that Diogenes made to one that asked him in mockery, *How it came to pass that philosophers were the followers of rich men, and not rich men of philosophers?* He answered soberly, and yet sharply, *Because the one sort knew what they had need of, and the other did not.* And of the like nature was the answer which Aristippus made, when having a petition to Dionysius, and no ear given to him, he fell down at his feet; whereupon Dionysius stayed and gave him the hearing, and granted it: and afterward some person, tender on the behalf of philosophy, reproved Aristippus that he would offer the profession of philosophy such an indignity as for a private suit to fall at a tyrant's feet: but he answered, *It was not his fault, but it was the fault of Dionysius, that had his ears in his feet.* Neither was it accounted weakness but discretion in him that would not dispute his best with Adrianus Caesar; excusing himself, *That it was reason to yield to him that commanded thirty legions.* These and the like applications and stooping to points of necessity and convenience cannot be disallowed; for though they may have some out-

ward baseness, yet in a judgement truly made they are to be accounted submissions to the occasion and not to the person.

IV. 1. Now I proceed to those errors and vanities which have intervened amongst the studies themselves of the learned, which is that which is principal and proper to the present argument; wherein my purpose is not to make a justification of the errors, but by a censure and separation of the errors to make a justification of that which is good and sound, and to deliver that from the aspersion of the other. For we see that it is the manner of men to scandalize and deprave that which retaineth the state[54] and virtue, by taking advantage upon that which is corrupt and degenerate as the heathens in the primitive church used to blemish and taint[55] the Christians with the faults and corruptions of heretics. But nevertheless I have no meaning at this time to make any exact animadversion of the errors and impediments in matters of learning, which are more secret and remote from vulgar opinion, but only to speak unto such as do fall under or near unto a popular observation.

2. There be therefore chiefly three vanities in studies, whereby learning hath been most traduced. For those things we do esteem vain, which are either false or frivolous, those which either have no truth or no use: and those persons we esteem vain, which are either credulous or curious;[56] and curiosity is either in matter or words: so that in reason as well as in experience there fall out to be these three distempers (as I may term them) of learning: the first, fantastical *l*earning; the second, contentious learning; and the last, delicate learning; vain imaginations, vain altercations, and vain affectations; and with the last I will begin. Martin Luther, conducted (no doubt) by an higher providence, but in discourse of reason,[57] finding what a province he had undertaken against the bishop of Rome and the degenerate traditions of the church, and finding his own solitude, being no ways aided by the opinions of his own time, was enforced to awake all antiquity, and to call former times to his succours to make a party against the present time: so that the ancient authors, both in divinity and in humanity, which had long time slept in libraries, began generally to be read and revolved. This by consequence did draw on a necessity of a more exquisite travail in the languages original, wherein those authors did write, for the better understanding of those authors, and the better advantage of pressing[58] and applying their words. And thereof grew again a delight in their manner of style and phrase, and an admiration of that kind of writing; which was much furthered and precipitated by the enmity and opposition that the propounders of those primitive but seeming new opinions had against the Schoolmen; who were generally of the contrary part, and whose writings were altogether in a different style and form; taking liberty to coin and frame new terms of art to express their own sense, and to avoid circuit of speech, without regard to the

pureness, pleasantness, and (as I may call it) lawfulness of the phrase or word. And again, because the great labour then was with the people (of whom the Pharisees were wont to say, *Execrabilis ista turba, quae non novit legem*),[59] for the winning and persuading of them, there grew of necessity in chief price and request eloquence and variety of discourse, as the fittest and forciblest access into the capacity of the vulgar sort: so that these four causes concurring, the admiration of ancient authors, the hate of the Schoolmen, the exact study of languages, and the efficacy of preaching, did bring in an affectionate study of eloquence and copie[60] of speech, which then began to flourish. This grew speedily to an excess; for men began to hunt more after words than matter;[61] more after the choiceness of the phrase, and the round and clean composition of the sentence, and the sweet falling of the clauses, and the varying and illustration of their works with tropes and figures, than after the weight of matter, worth of subject, soundness of argument, life of invention, or depth of judgement. Then grew the flowing and watery vein of Osorius,[62] the Portugal bishop, to be in price. Then did Sturmius spend such infinite and curious pains upon Cicero the Orator, and Hermogenes the Rhetorician, besides his own books of Periods and Imitation, and the like. Then did Car of Cambridge and Ascham with their lectures and writings almost deify Cicero and Demosthenes, and allure all young men that were studious unto that delicate and polished kind of learning. Then did Erasmus take occasion to make the scoffing echo, *Decem annos consumpsi in legendo Cicerone*; and the echo answered in Greek, *One, Asine*. Then grew the learning of the Schoolmen to be utterly despised as barbarous. In sum, the whole inclination and bent of those times was rather towards copie than weight.[63]

3. Here therefore is the first distemper of learning, when men study words and not matter; whereof, though I have represented an example of late times, yet it hath been and will be *secundum majus et minus*[64] in all time. And how is it possible but this should have an operation to discredit learning, even with vulgar capacities, when they see learned men's works like the first letter of a patent, or limned book;[65] which though it hath large flourishes, yet it is but a letter? It seems to me that Pygmalion's frenzy is a good emblem or portraiture of this vanity: for words are but the images of matter; and except they have life of reason and invention, to fall in love with them is all one as to fall in love with a picture.

4. But yet notwithstanding it is a thing not hastily to be condemned, to clothe and adorn the obscurity even of philosophy itself with sensible and plausible elocution.[66] For hereof we have great examples in Xenophon, Cicero, Seneca, Plutarch, and of Plato also in some degree; and hereof likewise there is great use: for surely, to the severe inquisition of truth and the deep progress

into philosophy, it is some hindrance; because it is too early satisfactory to the mind of man, and quencheth the desire of further search, before we come to a just period.[67] But then if a man be to have any use of such knowledge in civil occasions, of conference, counsel, persuasion, discourse, or the like, then shall he find it prepared to his hands in those authors which write in that manner. But the excess of this is so justly contemptible, that as Hercules, when he saw the image of Adonis, Venus' minion, in a temple, said in disdain, *Nil sacri es*;[68] so there is none of Hercules' followers in learning, that is, the more severe and laborious sort of inquirer into truth, but will despise those delicacies and affectations, as indeed capable of no divineness. And thus much of the first disease or distemper of learning.[69]

5. The second which followeth is in nature worse than the former: for as substance of matter is better than beauty of words, so contrariwise vain matter is worse than vain words: wherein it seemeth the reprehension of Saint Paul was not only proper for those times, but prophetical for the times following; and not only respective to divinity, but extensive to all knowledge: *Devita profanas vocum novitates, et oppositiones falsi nominis scientiae*.[70] For he assigneth two marks and badges of suspected and falsified science: the one, the novelty and strangeness of terms; the other, the strictness of positions,[71] which of necessity doth induce oppositions, and so questions and altercations. Surely, like as many substances in nature which are solid do putrify and corrupt into worms; so it is the property of good and sound knowledge to putrify and dissolve into a number of subtle, idle, unwholesome, and (as I may term them) vermiculate[72] questions, which have indeed a kind of quickness and life of spirit, but no soundness of matter or goodness of quality. This kind of degenerate learning did chiefly reign amongst the Schoolmen: who having sharp and strong wits, and abundance of leisure, and small variety of reading, but their wits being shut up in the cells of a few authors (chiefly Aristotle[73] their dictator) as their persons were shut up in the cells of monasteries and colleges, and knowing little history, either of nature or time, did out of no great quantity of matter and infinite agitation of wit spin out unto us those laborious webs of learning which are extant in their books. For the wit and mind of man, if it work upon matter, which is the contemplation of the creatures of God, worketh according to the stuff and is limited thereby; but if it work upon itself, as the spider worketh his web, then it is endless, and brings forth indeed cobwebs of learning, admirable for the fineness of thread and work, but of no substance or profit.

6. This same unprofitable subtility or curiosity is of two sorts; either in the subject itself that they handle, when it is a fruitless speculation or controversy (whereof there are no small number both in divinity and philosophy), or in

the manner or method of handling of a knowledge, which amongst them was this; upon every particular position or assertion to frame objections, and to those objections, solutions; which solutions were for the most part not confutations, but distinctions: whereas indeed the strength of all sciences, is as the strength of the old man's faggot, in the bond. For the harmony of a science, supporting each part the other, is and ought to be the true and brief confutation and suppression of all the smaller sort of objections. But, on the other side, if you take out every axiom, as the sticks of the faggot, one by one, you may quarrel with them and bend them and break them at your pleasure: so that as was said of Seneca, *Verborum minutiis rerum frangit pondera*[74] so a man may truly say of the Schoolmen, *Quaestionum minutiis scientiarum frangunt soliditatem.* For were it not better for a man in a fair room to set up one great light, or branching candlestick of lights, than to go about with a small watch candle into every corner? And such is their method, that rests not so much upon evidence of truth proved by arguments, authorities, similitudes, examples, as upon particular confutations and solutions of every scruple, cavillation, and objection; breeding for the most part one question as fast as it solveth another; even as in the former resemblance, when you carry the light into one corner, you darken the rest; so that the fable and fiction of Scylla seemeth to be a lively image of this kind of philosophy or knowledge; which was transformed into a comely virgin for the upper parts; but then *Candida succinctam latrantibus inguina monstris:*[75] so the generalities of the Schoolmen are for a while good and proportionable; but then when you descend into their distinctions and decisions, instead of a fruitful womb for the use and benefit of man's life, they end in monstrous altercations and barking questions. So as it is not possible but this quality of knowledge must fall under popular contempt, the people being apt to contemn truth upon occasion of controversies and altercations, and to think they are all out of their way which never meet; and when they see such digladiation[76] about subtilties, and matter of no use or moment, they easily fall upon that judgement of Dionysius of Syracusa, *Verba ista sunt senum otiosorum.*[77]

7. Notwithstanding, certain it is that if those Schoolmen to their great thirst of truth and unwearied travail of wit had joined variety and universality of reading and contemplation, they had proved excellent lights, to the great advancement of all learning and knowledge; but as they are, they are great undertakers indeed, and fierce with dark keeping.[78] But as in the inquiry of the divine truth, their pride inclined to leave the oracle of God's word, and to vanish in the mixture of their own inventions; so in the inquisition of nature, they ever left the oracle of God's works,[79] and adored the deceiving and deformed images which the unequal mirror of their own minds, or a few received

authors or principles, did represent unto them. And thus much for the second disease of learning.

8. For the third vice or disease of learning, which concerneth deceit or untruth, it is of all the rest the foulest; as that which doth destroy the essential form of knowledge, which is nothing but a representation of truth: for the truth of being and the truth of knowing are one, differing no more than the direct beam and the beam reflected. This vice therefore brancheth itself into two sorts; delight in deceiving and aptness to be deceived; imposture and credulity; which, although they appear to be of a diverse nature, the one seeming to proceed of cunning and the other of simplicity, yet certainly they do for the most part concur: for, as the verse noteth,

> Percontatorem fugito, nam garrulus idem est,[80]

an inquisitive man is a prattler; so upon the like reason a credulous man is a deceiver: as we see it in fame, that he that will easily believe rumours, will as easily augment rumours and add somewhat to them of his own; which Tacitus wisely noteth, when he saith, *Fingunt simul creduntque*:[81] so great an affinity hath fiction and belief.

9. This facility of credit and accepting or admitting things weakly authorized or warranted, is of two kinds according to the subject; for it is either a belief of history, or, as the lawyers speak, matter of fact; or else of matter of art and opinion. As to the former, we see the experience and inconvenience of this error in ecclesiastical history; which hath too easily received and registered reports and narrations of miracles wrought by martyrs, hermits, or monks of the desert, and other holy men, and their relics, shrines, chapels, and images: which though they had a passage for a time by the ignorance of the people, the superstitious simplicity of some, and the politic toleration of others, holding them but as divine poesies; yet after a period of time, when the mist began to clear up, they grew to be esteemed but as old wives' fables, impostures of the clergy, illusions of spirits, and badges of Antichrist, to the great scandal and detriment of religion.

10. So in natural history, we see there hath not been that choice and judgement used as ought to have been; as may appear in the writings of Plinius, Cardanus, Albertus, and divers of the Arabians,[82] being fraught with much fabulous matter, a great part not only untried, but notoriously untrue, to the great derogation of the credit of natural philosophy with the grave and sober kind of wits: wherein the wisdom and integrity of Aristotle is worthy to be observed; that, having made so diligent and exquisite a history of living creatures, hath mingled it sparingly with any vain or feigned matter: and yet on the other side hath cast all prodigious narrations, which he thought worthy the recording, into one book:[83] excellently discerning that matter of manifest

truth, such whereupon observation and rule was to be built, was not to be mingled or weakened with matter of doubtful credit; and yet again, that rarities and reports that seem uncredible are not to be suppressed or denied to the memory of men.

11. And as for the facility of credit which is yielded to arts and opinions, it is likewise of two kinds; either when too much belief is attributed to the arts themselves, or to certain authors in any art. The sciences themselves, which have had better intelligence and confederacy with the imagination of man than with his reason, are three in number; astrology, natural magic, and alchemy; of which sciences, nevertheless, the ends or pretences are noble. For astrology pretendeth to discover that correspondence or concatenation which is between the superior globe and the inferior: natural magic pretendeth to call and reduce natural philosophy from variety of speculations to the magnitude of works: and alchemy pretendeth to make separation of all the unlike parts of bodies which in mixtures of nature are incorporate. But the derivations and prosecutions[84] to these ends, both in the theories and in the practices, are full of error and vanity; which the great professors themselves have sought to veil over and conceal by enigmatical writings, and referring themselves to auricular traditions and such other devices, to save the credit of impostures. And yet surely to alchemy this right is due, that it may be compared to the husbandman whereof Aesop makes the fable; that, when he died, told his sons that he had left unto them gold buried under ground in his vineyard; and they digged over all the ground, and gold they found none; but by reason of their stirring and digging the mould about the roots of their vines, they had a great vintage the year following; so assuredly the search and stir to make gold hath brought to light a great number of good and fruitful inventions and experiments, as well for the disclosing of nature as for the use of man's life.[85]

12. And as for the overmuch credit that hath been given unto authors in sciences, in making them dictators, that their words should stand, and not consuls to give advice; the damage is infinite that sciences have received thereby, as the principal cause that hath kept them low at a stay without growth or advancement. For hence it hath comen, that in arts mechanical the first deviser comes shortest, and time addeth and perfecteth; but in sciences the first author goeth furthest, and time leeseth and corrupteth.[86] So we see, artillery, sailing, printing, and the like, were grossly managed at the first, and by time accommodated and refined: but contrariwise, the philosophies and sciences of Aristotle, Plato, Democritus, Hippocrates, Euclides, Archimedes, of most vigour at the first and by time degenerate and imbased; whereof the reason is no other, but that in the former many wits and industries have contributed in one; and in the latter many wits and industries have been spent about the wit of some

one, whom many times they have rather depraved than illustrated. For as water will not ascend higher than the level of the first springhead from whence it descendeth, so knowledge derived from Aristotle and exempted from liberty of examination, will not rise again higher than the knowledge of Aristotle. And therefore although the position be good, *Oportet discentem credere*, yet it must be coupled with this, *Oportet edoctum judicare*[87]; for disciples do owe unto masters only a temporary belief and a suspension of their own judgement till they be fully instructed, and not an absolute resignation or perpetual captivity: and therefore, to conclude this point, I will say no more, but so let great authors have their due, as time, which is the author of authors, be not deprived of his due, which is, further and further to discover truth. Thus have I gone over these three diseases of learning; besides the which there are some other rather peccant[88] humours than formed diseases, which nevertheless are not so secret and intrinsic but that they fall under a popular observation and traducement, and therefore are not to be passed over.

V. 1. The first of these is the extreme affecting of two extremities: the one antiquity, the other novelty; wherein it seemeth the children of time do take after the nature and malice of the father. For as he devoureth[89] his children, so one of them seeketh to devour and suppress the other; while antiquity envieth there should be new additions, and novelty cannot be content to add but it must deface: surely the advice of the prophet is the true direction in this matter, *State super vias antiquas, et videte quaenam sit via recta et bona et ambulate in ea.*[90] Antiquity deserveth that reverence, that men should make a stand thereupon and discover what is the best way; but when the discovery is well taken, then to make progression. And to speak truly, *Antiquitas saeculi juventus mundi.*[91] These times are the ancient times, when the world is ancient, and not those which we account ancient *ordine retrogrado*, by a computation backward from ourselves.

2. Another error induced by the former is a distrust that anything should be now to be found out, which the world should have missed and passed over so long time; as if the same objection were to be made to time, that Lucian[92] maketh to Jupiter and other the heathen gods; of which he wondereth that they begot so many children in old time, and begot none in his time; and asketh whether they were become septuagenary, or whether the law *Papia*, made against old men's marriages, had restrained them. So it seemeth men doubt lest time is become past children and generation;[93] wherein contrariwise we see commonly the levity and unconstancy of men's judgements, which till a matter be done, wonder that it can be done; and as soon as it is done, wonder again that it was no sooner done: as we see in the expedition of Alexander into Asia, which at first was prejudged as a vast and impossible enterprise; and yet afterwards it pleaseth Livy[94] to make no more of it than this, *Nil aliud quam*

bene ausus vana contemnere. And the same happened to Columbus in the western navigation. But in intellectual matters it is much more common; as may be seen in most of the propositions of Euclid; which till they be demonstrate, they seem strange to our assent; but being demonstrate, our mind accepteth of them by a kind of relation (as the lawyers speak) as if we had known them before.

3. Another error, that hath also some affinity with the former, is a conceit that of former opinions or sects after variety and examination the best hath still prevailed and suppressed the rest; so as if a man should begin the labour of a new search, he were but like to light upon somewhat formerly rejected, and by rejection brought into oblivion; as if the multitude, or the wisest for the multitude's sake, were not ready to give passage rather to that which is popular and superficial, than to that which is substantial and profound; for the truth is, that time[95] seemeth to be of the nature of a river or stream, which carrieth down to us that which is light and blown up, and sinketh and drowneth that which is weighty and solid.

4. Another error, of a diverse nature from all the former, is the over-early and peremptory reduction of knowledge into arts and methods;[96] from which time commonly sciences receive small or no augmentation. But as young men, when they knit and shape perfectly, do seldom grow to a further stature; so knowledge, while it is in aphorisms and observations, it is in growth: but when it once is comprehended in exact methods, it may perchance be further polished and illustrate and accommodated for use and practice; but it increaseth no more in bulk and substance.

5. Another error which doth succeed that which we last mentioned, is, that after the distribution of particular arts and sciences, men have abandoned universality, or *philosophia prima*:[97] which cannot but cease and stop all progression. For no perfect discovery can be made upon a flat or a level: neither is it possible to discover the more remote and deeper parts of any science, if you stand but upon the level of the same science, and ascend not to a higher science.

6. Another error hath proceeded from too great a reverence, and a kind of adoration of the mind and understanding of man; by means whereof, men have withdrawn themselves too much from the contemplation of nature, and the observations of experience, and have tumbled up and down in their own reason and conceits. Upon these intellectualists, which are notwithstanding commonly taken for the most sublime and divine philosophers, Heraclitus gave a just censure, saying, *Men sought truth in their own little worlds, and not in the great and common world*; for they disdain to spell, and so by degrees to read in the volume of God's works: and contrariwise by continual meditation and agitation of wit do urge and as it were invocate their own spirits to divine and give oracles unto them, whereby they are deservedly deluded.

7. Another error that hath some connexion with this latter is, that men have used to infect their meditations, opinions, and doctrines, with some conceits which they have most admired, or some sciences which they have most applied; and given all things else a tincture according to them, utterly untrue and unproper. So hath Plato intermingled his philosophy with theology, and Aristotle with logic; and the second school of Plato, Proclus and the rest, with the mathematics.[98] For these were the arts which had a kind of primogeniture with them severally. So have the alchemists made a philosophy out of a few experiments of the furnace; and Gilbertus our countryman hath made a philosophy out of the observations of a loadstone. So Cicero,[99] when, reciting the several opinions of the nature of the soul, he found a musician that held the soul was but a harmony, saith pleasantly, *Hic ab arte sua non recessit, &c.* But of these conceits Aristotle speaketh seriously and wisely when he saith, *Qui respiciunt ad pauca de facili pronunciant.*

8. Another error is an impatience of doubt, and haste to assertion without due and mature suspension of judgement. For the two ways of contemplation are not unlike the two ways of action commonly spoken of by the ancients: the one plain and smooth in the beginning, and in the end impassable; the other rough and troublesome in the entrance, but after a while fair and even: so it is in contemplation; if a man will begin with certainties, he shall end in doubts; but if he will be content to begin with doubts, he shall end in certainties.

9. Another error is in the manner of the tradition and delivery of knowledge, which is for the most part magistral[100] and peremptory, and not ingenuous and faithful; in a sort as may be soonest believed, and not easiliest examined. It is true that in compendious treatises for practice that form is not to be disallowed: but in the true handling of knowledge, men ought not to fall either on the one side into the vein of Velleius the Epicurean, *Nil tam metuens, quam ne dubitare aliqua de re videretur*;[101] nor on the other side into Socrates his ironical doubting of all things; but to propound things sincerely with more or less asseveration, as they stand in a man's own judgement proved more or less.

10. Other errors there are in the scope that men propound to themselves, whereunto they bend their endeavours; for whereas the more constant and devote kind of professors of any science ought to propound to themselves to make some additions to their science, they convert their labours to aspire to certain second prizes: as to be a profound interpreter or commenter, to be a sharp champion or defender, to be a methodical compounder or abridger, and so the patrimony of knowledge cometh to be sometimes improved, but seldom augmented.

11. But the greatest error of all the rest is the mistaking or misplacing of the last or furthest end of knowledge. For men have entered into a desire of

learning and knowledge, sometimes upon a natural curiosity and inquisitive appetite; sometimes to entertain their minds with variety and delight; sometimes for ornament and reputation; and sometimes to enable them to victory of wit and contradiction; and most times for lucre and profession; and seldom sincerely to give a true account of their gift of reason, to the benefit and use of men: as if there were sought in knowledge a couch whereupon to rest a searching and restless spirit; or a terrace for a wandering and variable mind to walk up and down with a fair prospect; or a tower of state for a proud mind to raise itself upon; or a fort or commanding ground for strife and contention; or a shop for profit or sale; and not a rich storehouse for the glory of the Creator and the relief of man's estate. But this is that which will indeed dignify and exalt knowledge, if contemplation and action may be more nearly and straitly conjoined and united together than they have been; a conjunction like unto that of the two highest planets, Saturn, the planet of rest and contemplation, and Jupiter, the planet of civil society and action. Howbeit, I do not mean, when I speak of use and action, that end before-mentioned of the applying of knowledge to lucre and profession; for I am not ignorant how much that diverteth and interrupteth the prosecution and advancement of knowledge, like unto the golden ball thrown before Atalanta, which while she goeth aside and stoopeth to take up, the race is hindered,

> Declinat cursus, aurumque volubile tollit.[102]

Neither is my meaning, as was spoken of Socrates, to call philosophy down from heaven to converse upon the earth; that is, to leave natural philosophy aside, and to apply knowledge only to manners and policy. But as both heaven and earth do conspire and contribute to the use and benefit of man; so the end ought to be, from both philosophies to separate and reject vain speculations, and whatsoever is empty and void, and to preserve and augment whatsoever is solid and fruitful: that knowledge may not be as a courtesan, for pleasure and vanity only, or as a bond-woman, to acquire and gain to her master's use; but as a spouse, for generation, fruit and comfort.

12. Thus have I described and opened, as by a kind of dissection, those peccant humours (the principal of them) which have not only given impediment to the proficience of learning, but have given also occasion to the traducement thereof: wherein if I have been too plain, it must be remembered, *fidelia vulnera amantis, sed dolosa oscula malignantis.*[103] This I think I have gained, that I ought to be the better believed in that which I shall say pertaining to commendation; because I have proceeded so freely in that which concerneth censure. And yet I have no purpose to enter into a laudative of learning, or to make a hymn to the Muses, (though I am of opinion that it is long since their

rites were duly celebrated), but my intent is, without varnish or amplification justly to weigh the dignity of knowledge in the balance with other things, and to take the true value thereof by testimonies and arguments divine and human.

VI. 1. First therefore let us seek the dignity of knowledge in the arch-type or first platform,[104] which is in the attributes and acts of God, as far as they are revealed to man and may be observed with sobriety; wherein we may not seek it by the name of learning; for all learning is knowledge acquired, and all knowledge in God is original: and therefore we must look for it by another name, that of wisdom or sapience, as the scriptures call it.

2. It is so then, that in the work of the creation we see a double emanation of virtue from God; the one referring more properly to power, the other to wisdom; the one expressed in making the subsistence of the matter, and the other in disposing the beauty of the form. This being supposed, it is to be observed that for anything which appeareth in the history of the creation, the confused mass and matter of heaven and earth was made in a moment; and the order and disposition of that chaos or mass was the work of six days; such a note of difference it pleased God to put upon the works of power, and the works of wisdom: wherewith concurreth, that in the former, it is not set down that God said, *Let there be heaven and earth*, as it is set down of the works following; but actually, that God made heaven and earth: the one carrying the style of a manufacture, and the other of a law, decree, or counsel.

3. To proceed to that which is next in order from God to spirits; we find, as far as credit is to be given to the celestial hierarchy of that supposed Dionysius[105] the senator of Athens, the first place or degree is given to the angels of love, which are termed seraphim; the second to the angels of light, which are termed cherubim; and the third, and so following places, to thrones, principalities, and the rest, which are all angels of power and ministry; so as the angels of knowledge and illumination are placed before the angels of office and domination.

4. To descend from spirits and intellectual forms to sensible and material forms, we read the first form that was created was light, which hath a relation and correspondence in nature and corporal things to knowledge in spirits and incorporal things.

5. So in the distribution of days we see the day wherein God did rest and contemplate his own works, was blessed above all the days wherein he did effect and accomplish them.

6. After the creation was finished, it is set down unto us that man was placed in the garden to work therein; which work, so appointed to him, could be no other than work of contemplation; that is, when the end of work is but for exercise and experiment, not for necessity; for there being then no

reluctation of the creature, nor sweat of the brow, man's employment must of consequence have been matter of delight in the experiment, and not matter of labour for the use. Again, the first acts which man performed in Paradise consisted of the two summary parts of knowledge; the view of creatures, and the imposition of names. As for the knowledge which induced the fall, it was, as was touched before, not the natural knowledge of creatures, but the moral knowledge of good and evil; wherein the supposition was, that God's commandments or prohibitions were not the originals of good and evil, but that they had other beginnings, which man aspired to know; to the end to make a total defection from God and to depend wholly upon himself.

7. To pass on: in the first event or occurrence after the fall of man, we see (as the scriptures have infinite mysteries, not violating at all the truth of the story or letter) an image of the two estates,[106] the contemplative state and the active state, figured in the two persons of Abel and Cain, and in the two simplest and most primitive trades of life; that of the shepherd (who, by reason of his leisure, rest in a place, and living in view of heaven, is a lively image of a contemplative life), and that of the husbandman: where we see again the favour and election of God went to the shepherd, and not to the tiller of the ground.

8. So in the age before the flood, the holy records within those few memorials which are there entered and registered, have vouchsafed to mention and honour the name of the inventors and authors of music and works in metal. In the age after the flood, the first great judgement of God upon the ambition of man was the confusion of tongues: whereby the open trade and intercourse of learning and knowledge was chiefly imbarred.

9. To descend to Moyses the lawgiver, and God's first pen: he is adorned by the scriptures with this addition and commendation, *That he was seen in all the learning of the Egyptians*; which nation we know was one of the most ancient schools of the world: for so Plato brings in the Egyptian priest saying unto Solon, *You Grecians are ever children; you have no knowledge of antiquity, nor antiquity of knowledge*.[107] Take a view of the ceremonial law of Moyses; you shall find, besides the prefiguration of Christ, the badge or difference of the people of God, the exercise and impression of obedience, and other divine uses and fruits thereof, that some of the most learned Rabbins have travailed profitably and profoundly to observe, some of them a natural, some of them a moral, sense or reduction of many of the ceremonies and ordinances. As in the law of the leprosy, where it is said, *If the whiteness have overspread the flesh, the patient may pass abroad for clean; but if there be any whole flesh remaining, he is to be shut up for unclean*; one of them noteth a principle of nature, that putrefaction is more contagious before maturity than after: and another noteth a position of moral philosophy, that men abandoned to vice do not so much corrupt manners,

as those that are half good and half evil. So in this and very many other places in that law, there is to be found, besides the theological sense, much aspersion of philosophy.

10. So likewise in that excellent book of Job, if it be revolved with diligence, it will be found pregnant and swelling with natural philosophy; ...

11. So likewise in the person of Salomon[108] the king, we see the gift or endowment of wisdom and learning, both in Salomon's petition and in God's assent thereunto, preferred before all other terrene and temporal felicity. By virtue of which grant or donative of God Salomon became enabled not only to write those excellent parables or aphorisms concerning divine and moral philosophy; but also to compile a natural history of all verdure, from the cedar upon the mountain to the moss upon the wall (which is but a rudiment between putrefaction and an herb), and also of all things that breathe or move. Nay, the same Salomon the king, although he excelled in the glory of treasure and magnificent buildings, of shipping and navigation, of service and attendance, of fame and renown, and the like, yet he maketh no claim to any of those glories, but only to the glory of inquisition of truth; for so he saith expressly, *The Glory of God is to conceal a thing, but the glory of the king is to find it out*; as if, according to the innocent play of children, the Divine Majesty took delight to hide his works, to the end to have them found out; and as if kings could not obtain a greater honour than to be God's play-fellows in that game; considering the great commandment of wits and means, whereby nothing needeth to be hidden from them.

12. Neither did the dispensation of God vary in the times after our Saviour came into the world; for our Saviour himself did first show his power to subdue ignorance, by his conference with the priests and doctors of the law, before he showed his power to subdue nature by his miracles. And the coming of the Holy Spirit was chiefly figured and expressed in the similitude and gift of tongues, which are but *vehicula scientiae*.

13. So in the election of those instruments, which it pleased God to use for the plantation of the faith, notwithstanding that at the first he did employ persons altogether unlearned, otherwise than by inspiration, more evidently to declare his immediate working, and to abase all human wisdom or knowledge; yet nevertheless that counsel of his was no sooner performed, but in the next vicissitude and succession he did send his divine truth into the world, waited on with other learnings, as with servants or handmaids: for so we see Saint Paul, who was only[109] learned amongst the Apostles, had his pen most used in the scriptures of the New Testament.

14. So again we find that many of the ancient bishops and fathers of the Church were excellently read and studied in all the learning of the heathen;

insomuch that the edict of the Emperor Julianus[110] (whereby it was interdicted unto Christians to be admitted into schools, lectures, or exercises of learning) was esteemed and accounted a more pernicious engine and machination against the Christian Faith, than were all the sanguinary prosecutions of his predecessors; neither could the emulation and jealousy of Gregory the first[111] of that name, bishop of Rome, ever obtain the opinion of piety or devotion; but contrariwise received the censure of humour, malignity and pusillanimity, even amongst holy men; in that he designed to obliterate and extinguish the memory of heathen antiquity and authors. But contrariwise it was the Christian Church, which, amidst the inundations of the Scythians on the one side from the north-west, and the Saracens from the east, did preserve in the sacred lap and bosom thereof the precious relics even of heathen learning, which otherwise had been extinguished as if no such thing had ever been.

15. And we see before our eyes, that in the age of ourselves and our fathers, when it pleased God to call the Church of Rome to account for their degenerate manners and ceremonies, and sundry doctrines obnoxious and framed to uphold the same abuses; at one and the same time it was ordained by the Divine Providence, that there should attend withal a renovation and new spring of all other knowledges. And, on the other side we see the Jesuits, who partly in themselves and partly by the emulation and provocation of their example, have much quickened and strengthened the state of learning, we see (I say) what notable service and reparation they have done to the Roman see.

16. Wherefore to conclude this part, let it be observed, that there be two principal duties and services, besides ornament and illustration, which philosophy and human learning do perform to faith and religion. The one, because they are an effectual inducement to the exaltation of the glory of God. For as the Psalms and other scriptures do often invite us to consider and magnify the great and wonderful works of God, so if we should rest only in the contemplation of the exterior of them as they first offer themselves to our senses, we should do a like injury unto the majesty of God, as if we should judge or construe of the store of some excellent jeweller, by that only which is set out toward the street in his shop. The other, because they minister a singular help and preservative against unbelief and error. For our Saviour saith, *You err, not knowing the scriptures, nor the power of God*; laying before us two books or volumes to study, if we will be secured from error; first the scriptures, revealing the will of God, and then the creatures expressing his power; whereof the latter is a key unto the former: not only opening our understanding to conceive the true sense of the scriptures, by the general notions of reason and rules of speech; but chiefly opening our belief, in drawing us into a due meditation of the omnipotency of God, which is chiefly signed and engraven upon his

works. Thus much therefore for divine testimony and evidence concerning the true dignity and value of learning.

VII. 1. As for human proofs, it is so large a field, as in a discourse of this nature and brevity it is fit rather to use choice of those things which we shall produce, than to embrace the variety of them. First therefore, in the degrees of human honour amongst the heathen, it was the highest to obtain to a veneration and adoration as a God. This unto the Christians is as the forbidden fruit. But we speak now separately of human testimony: according to which, that which the Grecians call *apotheosis*, and the Latins *relatio inter divos*, was the supreme honour which man could attribute unto man: specially when it was given, not by a formal decree or act of state, as it was used among the Roman Emperors, but by an inward assent and belief. Which honour, being so high, had also a degree or middle term: for there were reckoned above human honours, honours heroical and divine: in the attribution and distribution of which honours we see antiquity made this difference: that whereas founders and uniters of states and cities, lawgivers, extirpers of tyrants, fathers of the people, and other eminent persons in civil merit, were honoured but with the titles of worthies or demi-gods; such as were Hercules, Theseus, Minos, Romulus and the like: on the other side, such as were inventors and authors of new arts, endowments, and commodities towards man's life, were ever consecrated amongst the gods themselves; as was Ceres, Bacchus, Mercurius, Apollo, and others; and justly; for the merit of the former is confined within the circle of an age or a nation; and is like fruitful showers, which though they be profitable and good, yet serve but for that season, and for a latitude of ground where they fall; but the other is indeed like the benefits of heaven, which are permanent and universal. The former again is mixed with strife and perturbation; but the latter hath the true character of Divine Presence, coming in *aura leni*,[112] without noise or agitation.

2. Neither is certainly that other merit of learning, in repressing the inconveniences which grow from man to man, much inferior to the former, of relieving the necessities which arise from nature; which merit was lively set forth by the ancients in that feigned relation of Orpheus' theatre, where all beasts and birds assembled; and forgetting their several appetites, some of prey, some of game, some of quarrel, stood all sociably together listening unto the airs and accords of the harp; the sound whereof so sooner ceased, or was drowned by some louder noise, but every beast returned to his own nature: wherein is aptly described the nature and condition of men, who are full of savage and unreclaimed desires, of profit, of lust, of revenge; which as long as they give ear to precepts, to laws, to religion, sweetly touched with eloquence and persuasion of books, of sermons, of harangues, so long is society

and peace maintained; but if these instruments be silent, or that sedition and tumult make them not audible, all things dissolve into anarchy and confusion.

3. But this appeareth more manifestly, when kings themselves, or persons of authority under them, or other governors in commonwealths and popular estates, are endued with learning. For although he might be thought partial to his own profession, that said, *Then should people and estates be happy, when either kings were philosophers, or philosophers kings*;[113] yet so much is verified by experience, that under learned princes and governors there have been ever the best times; for howsoever kings may have their imperfections in their passions and customs; yet if they be illuminate by learning, they have those notions of religion, policy, and morality, which do preserve them and refrain them from all ruinous and peremptory errors and excesses; whispering evermore in their ears, when counsellors and servants stand mute and silent. And senators or counsellors likewise, which be learned, do proceed upon more safe and substantial principles, than counsellors which are only men of experience: the one sort keeping dangers afar off, whereas the other discover them not till they come near hand, and then trust to the agility of their wit to ward or avoid them.

4. Which felicity of times under learned princes (to keep still the law of brevity, by using the most eminent and selected examples) doth best appear in the age which passed from the death of Domitianus the emperor until the reign of Commodus; comprehending a succession of six princes,[114] all learned, or singular favourers and advancers of learning, which age for temporal respects was the most happy and flourishing that ever the Roman empire (which then was a model of the world) enjoyed; a matter revealed and prefigured unto Domitian in a dream the night before he was slain; for he thought there was grown behind upon his shoulders a neck and a head of gold: which came accordingly to pass in those golden times which succeeded: of which princes we will make some commemoration; wherein although the matter will be vulgar, and may be thought fitter for a declamation than agreeable to a treatise infolded[115] as this is, yet because it is pertinent to the point in hand, *Neque semper arcum tendit Apollo*,[116] and to name them only were too naked and cursory, I will not omit it altogether. The first was Nerva; the excellent temper of whose government is by a glance in Cornelius Tacitus touched to the life: *Postquam divus Nerva res olim insociabiles miscuisset, imperium et libertatem*.[117] And in token of his learning, the last act of his short reign left to memory was a missive to his adopted son Trajan, proceeding upon some inward discontent at the ingratitude of the times, comprehended in a verse of Homer's

Telis, Phoebe, tuis lacrymas ulciscere nostras.[118]

5. Trajan, who succeeded, was for his person not learned: but if we will

hearken to the speech of our Saviour, that saith, *He that receiveth a prophet in the name of a prophet shall have a prophet's reward*, he deserveth to be placed amongst the most learned princes: for there was not a greater admirer of learning or benefactor of learning; a founder of famous libraries, a perpetual advancer of learned men to office, and a familiar converser with learned professors and preceptors, who were noted to have then most credit in court. On the other side, how much Trajan's virtue and government was admired and renowned, surely no testimony of grave and faithful history doth more lively set forth, than that legend tale of Gregorius Magnus, bishop of Rome, who was noted for the extreme envy he bare towards all heathen excellency: and yet he is reported, out of the love and estimation of Trajan's moral virtues,[119] to have made unto God passionate and fervent prayers for the delivery of his soul out of hell: and to have obtained it, with a caveat that he should make no more such petitions. In this prince's time also the persecutions against the Christians received intermission, upon the certificate of Plinius Secundus, a man of excellent learning and by Trajan advanced.

6. Adrian, his successor, was the most curious[120] man that lived, and the most universal inquirer; insomuch as it was noted for an error in his mind, that he desired to comprehend all things, and not to reserve himself for the worthiest things: falling into the like humour that was long before noted in Philip of Macedon; who, when he would needs over-rule and put down an excellent musician in an argument touching music, was well answered by him again, *God forbid, sir* (saith he), *that your fortune should be so bad, as to know these things better than I.* It pleased God likewise to use the curiosity of this emperor as an inducement to the peace of his Church in those days. For having Christ in veneration, not as a God or Saviour but as a wonder or novelty, and having his picture in his gallery, matched with Apollonius[121] (with whom in his vain imagination he thought he had some conformity), yet it served the turn to allay the bitter hatred of those times against the Christian name, so as the Church had peace during his time. And for his government civil, although he did not attain to that of Trajan's in glory of arms or perfection of justice, yet in deserving of the weal of the subject he did exceed him. For Trajan erected many famous monuments and buildings; insomuch as Constantine the Great in emulation was wont to call him *Parietaria*, wallflower, because his name was upon so many walls: but his buildings and works were more of glory and triumph than use and necessity. But Adrian spent his whole reign, which was peaceable, in a perambulation or survey of the Roman empire; giving order and making assignation where he went, for re-edifying of cities, towns and forts decayed; and for cutting of rivers and streams, and for making bridges and passages, and for policing of cities and commonalties with new

ordinances and constitutions, and granting new franchises and incorporations; so that his whole time was a very restoration of all the lapses and decays of former times.

7. Antoninus Pius, who succeeded him, was a prince excellently learned, and had the patient and subtle wit of a Schoolman; insomuch as in common speech (which leaves no virtue untaxed) he was called *Cymini Sector*, a carver or a divider of cummin seed, which is one of the least seeds; such a patience he had and settled spirit, to enter into the least and most exact differences of causes; a fruit no doubt of the exceeding tranquillity and serenity of his mind; which being no ways charged or incumbered, either with fears, remorses, or scruples, but having been noted for a man of the purest goodness, without all fiction or affectation, that hath reigned or lived, made his mind continually present and entire. He likewise approached a degree nearer unto Christianity, and became, as Agrippa said unto Saint Paul, *half a Christian*; holding their religion and law in good opinion, and not only ceasing persecution, but giving way to the advancement of Christians.

8. There succeeded him the first *Divi fratres*, the two adoptive brethren, Lucius Commodus Verus, son to Aelius Verus, who delighted much in the softer kind of learning, and was wont to call the poet Martial his Virgil; and Marcus Aurelius Antoninus; whereof the latter, who obscured his colleague and survived him long, was named the Philosopher; who, as he excelled all the rest in learning, so he excelled them likewise in perfection of all royal virtues; insomuch as Julianus the emperor, in his book intituled *Caesares*, being as a pasquil or satire to deride all his predecessors, feigned that they were all invited to a banquet of the gods, and Silenus the jester sat at the nether end of the table, and bestowed a scoff on every one as they came in; but when Marcus Philosophus came in, Silenus was gravelled and out of countenance, not knowing where to carp at him; save at the last he gave a glance at his patience towards his wife. And the virtue of this prince, continued with that of his predecessor, made the name of Antoninus so sacred in the world, that though it were extremely dishonoured in Commodus, Caracalla, and Heliogabalus, who all bare the name, yet when Alexander Severus refused the name because he was a stranger to the family, the senate with one acclamation said, *Quomodo Augustus, sic et Antoninus*.[122] In such renown and veneration was the name of these two princes in those days, that they would have had it as a perpetual addition in all the emperors' style. In this emperor's time also the Church for the most part was in peace; so as in this sequence of six princes we do see the blessed effects of learning in sovereignty, painted forth in the greatest table of the world.

9. But for a tablet or picture of smaller volume (not presuming to speak of your Majesty that liveth), in my judgement the most excellent is that of Queen

Elizabeth,[123] your immediate predecessor in this part of Britain; a prince that, if Plutarch were now alive to write lives by parallels, would trouble him I think to find for her a parallel amongst women. This lady was endued with learning in her sex singular, and rare even amongst masculine princes; whether we speak of learning, of language, or of science, modern or ancient, divinity or humanity: and unto the very last year of her life she accustomed to appoint set hours for reading, scarcely any young student in an university more daily or more duly. As for her government, I assure myself, I shall not exceed, if I do affirm, that this part of the island never had forty-five years of better times; and yet not through the calmness of the season, but through the wisdom of her regiment. For if there be considered of the one side, the truth of religion established, the constant peace and security, the good administration of justice, the temperate use of the prerogative, not slackened, nor much strained, the flourishing state of learning, sortable to so excellent a patroness, the convenient estate of wealth and means, both of crown and subject, the habit of obedience, and the moderation of discontents; and there be considered on the other side the differences of religion, the troubles of neighbour countries, the ambition of Spain, and opposition of Rome; and then that she was solitary and of herself: these things I say considered, as I could not have chosen an instance so recent and so proper, so I suppose I could not have chosen one more remarkable or eminent to the purpose now in hand, which is concerning the conjunction of learning in the prince with felicity in the people.

10. Neither hath learning an influence and operation only upon civil merit and moral virtue, and the arts or temperature[124] of peace and peaceable government; but likewise it hath no less power and efficacy in enablement towards martial and military virtue and prowess; as may be notably represented in the examples of Alexander the Great and Caesar the dictator, mentioned before, but now in fit place to be resumed: of whose virtues and acts in war there needs no note or recital, having been the wonders of time in that kind: but of their affections towards learning, and perfections in learning, it is pertinent to say somewhat.

11. Alexander was bred and taught under Aristotle the great philosopher, who dedicated divers of his books of philosophy unto him; he was attended with Callisthenes[125] and divers other learned persons, that followed him in camp, throughout his journeys and conquests. What price and estimation he had learning in doth notably appear in these three particulars: first, in the envy he used to express that he bare towards Achilles, in this, that he had so good a trumpet of his praises as Homer's verses: secondly in the judgement or solution he gave touching that precious cabinet of Darius, which was found among his jewels; whereof question was made what thing was worthy to be put into it;

and he gave his opinion for Homer's works: thirdly, in his letter to Aristotle, after he had set forth his books of nature, wherein he expostulateth with them for publishing the secrets or mysteries of philosophy; and gave him to understand that himself esteemed it more to excel other men in learning and knowledge than in power and empire. And what use he had of learning doth appear, or rather shine, in all his speeches and answers, being full of science and use of science, and that in all variety.

12. And herein again it may seem a thing scholastical, and somewhat idle, to recite things that every man knoweth; but yet, since the argument I handle leadeth me thereunto, I am glad that men shall perceive I am as willing to flatter (if they will so call it) an Alexander, or a Caesar, or an Antoninus, that are dead many hundred years since, as any that now liveth; for it is the displaying of the glory of learning in sovereignty that I propound to myself, and not an humour of declaiming in any man's praises. Observe then the speech he used of Diogenes, and see if it tend not to the true state of one of the greatest questions of moral philosophy; whether the enjoying of outward things, or the contemning of them, be the greatest happiness: for when he saw Diogenes so perfectly contented with so little, he said to those that mocked at his condition, *Were I not Alexander, I would wish to be Diogenes.* But Seneca inverteth it, and saith; *Plus erat, quod hic nollet accipere, quam quod ille posset dare.* There were more things which Diogenes would have refused, than those were which Alexander could have given or enjoyed.

13. Observe again that speech which was usual with him, *That he felt his mortality chiefly in two things, sleep and lust*; and see if it were not a speech extracted out of the depth of natural philosophy, and liker to have comen out of the mouth of Aristotle or Democritus, than from Alexander.

14. See again that speech of humanity and poesy; when upon the bleeding of his wounds, he called unto him one of his flatterers, that was wont to ascribe to him divine honour, and said, *Look, this is very blood; this is not such a liquor as Homer speaketh of, which ran from Venus' hand, when it was pierced by Diomedes.*[126]

15. See likewise his readiness in reprehension of logic, in the speech he used to Cassander, upon a complaint that was made against his father Antipater: for when Alexander happed to say, *Do you think these men would have come so far to complain, except they had just cause of grief?* and Cassander answered, *Yea, that was the matter, because they thought they should not be disproved*; said Alexander laughing: *See the subtilties of Aristotle, to take a matter both ways, pro et contra, &c.*

16. But note again how well he could use the same art, which he reprehended, to serve his own humour: when bearing a secret grudge to Callisthenes, because he was against the new ceremony of his adoration, feasting one night where the same Callisthenes was at the table, it was moved by some after

supper, for entertainment sake, that Callisthenes, who was an eloquent man, might speak of some theme or purpose at his own choice; which Callisthenes did; choosing the praise of the Macedonian nation for his discourse, and performing the same with so good manner as the hearers were much ravished: whereupon Alexander, nothing pleased, said, *It was easy to be eloquent upon so good a subject*: but saith he, *Turn your style, and let us hear what you can say against us*: which Callisthenes presently undertook, and did with that sting and life, that Alexander interrupted him and said, *The goodness of the cause made him eloquent before, and despite made him eloquent then again.*

17. Consider further, for tropes of rhetoric,[127] that excellent use of a metaphor or translation, wherewith he taxed Antipater, who was an imperious and tyrannous governor: for when one of Antipater's friends commended him to Alexander for his moderation, that he did not degenerate, as his other lieutenants did, into the Persian pride, in use of purple, but kept the ancient habit of Macedon, of black; *True* (saith Alexander), *but Antipater is all purple within.* Or that other, when Parmenio came to him in the plain of Arbela, and showed him the innumerable multitude of his enemies, specially as they appeared by the infinite number of lights, as it had been a new firmament of stars, and thereupon advised him to assail them by night: whereupon he answered, *That he would not steal the victory.*

18. For matter of policy, weigh that significant distinction, so much in all ages embraced, that he made between his two friends Hephaestion and Craterus, when he said, *That the one loved Alexander, and the other loved the king*: describing the principal difference of princes' best servants, that some in affection love their person, and other in duty love their crown.

19. Weigh also that excellent taxation of an error, ordinary with counsellors of princes, that they counsel their masters according to the model of their own mind and fortune, and not of their masters'; when upon Darius' great offers Parmenio had said, *Surely I would accept these offers, were I as Alexander*; saith Alexander, *So would I were I as Parmenio.*

20. Lastly, weigh that quick and acute reply, which he made when he gave so large gifts to his friends and servants, and was asked what he did reserve for himself, and he answered, *Hope*: weigh, I say, whether he had not cast up his account aright, because *hope* must be the portion of all that resolve upon great enterprises. For this was Caesar's portion when he went first into Gaul, his estate being then utterly overthrown with largesses. And this was likewise the portion of that noble prince, howsoever transported with ambition, Henry Duke of Guise,[128] of whom it was usually said, that he was the greatest usurer in France, because he had turned all his estate into obligations.

21. To conclude therefore: as certain critics are used to say hyperbolically,

That if all sciences were lost they might be found in Virgil, so certainly this may be said truly, there are the prints and footsteps of learning in those few speeches which are reported of this prince; the admiration of whom, when I consider him not as Alexander the Great, but as Aristotle's scholar, hath carried me too far.

22. As for Julius Caesar, the excellency of his learning needeth not to be argued from his education, or his company, or his speeches; but in a further degree doth declare itself in his writings and works; whereof some are extant and permanent, and some unfortunately perished. For first, we see there is left unto us that excellent history of his own wars, which he intituled only a Commentary, wherein all succeeding times have admired the solid weight of matter, and the real passages and lively images of actions and persons, expressed in the greatest propriety of words and perspicuity of narration that ever was; which that it was not the effect of a natural gift, but of learning and precept, is well witnessed by that work of his intituled *De Analogia*,[129] being a grammatical philosophy, wherein he did labour to make this same *Vox ad placitum* to become *Vox ad licitum*, and to reduce custom of speech to congruity of speech; and took as it were the pictures of words from the life of reason.

23. So we receive from him, as a monument both of his power and learning, the then reformed computation of the year;[130] well expressing that he took it to be as great a glory to himself to observe and know the law of the heavens, as to give law to men upon the earth.

24. So likewise in that book of his, *Anti-Cato*,[131] it may easily appear that he did aspire as well to victory of wit as victory of war; undertaking therein a conflict against the greatest champion with the pen that then lived, Cicero the orator.

25. So again in his book of Apophthegms[132] which he collected, we see that he esteemed it more honour to make himself but a pair of tables, to take the wise and pithy words of others, than to have every word of his own to be made an apophthegm or an oracle; as vain princes, by custom of flattery, pretend to do. And yet if I should enumerate divers of his speeches, as I did those of Alexander, they are truly such as Salomon noteth, when he saith, *Verba sapientum tanquam aculei, et tanquam clavi in altum defixi.*[133] whereof I will only recite three, not so delectable for elegancy, but admirable for vigour and efficacy.

26. As first, it is reason he be thought a master of words, that could with one word appease a mutiny in his army, which was thus. The Romans, when their generals did speak to their army, did use the word *Milites*, but when the magistrates spake to the people, they did use the word *Quirites*.[134] The soldiers were in tumult, and seditiously prayed to be cashiered; not that they so meant,

but by expostulation thereof to draw Caesar to other conditions; wherein he being resolute not to give way, after some silence, he began his speech, *Ego, Quirites*, which did admit them already cashiered: wherewith they were so surprised, crossed, and confused, as they would not suffer him to go on in his speech, but relinquished their demands, and made it their suit to be again called by the name of *Milites*.

27. The second speech was thus: Caesar did extremely affect the name of king; and some were set on as he passed by, in popular acclamation to salute him king. Whereupon, finding the cry weak and poor, he put it off thus, in a kind of jest, as if they had mistaken his surname; *Non Rex sum, sed Caesar*;[135] a speech, that if it be searched, the life and fulness of it can scarce be expressed. For, first, it was a refusal of the name, but yet not serious: again, it did signify an infinite confidence and magnanimity, as if he presumed Caesar was the greater title; as by his worthiness it is come to pass till this day. But chiefly it was a speech of great allurement toward his own purpose; as if the state did strive with him but for a name, whereof mean families were vested; for *Rex* was a surname with the Romans, as well as *King* is with us.

28. The last speech which I will mention was used to Metellus: when Caesar, after war declared, did possess himself of the city of Rome; at which time entering into the inner treasury to take the money there accumulate, Metellus being tribune forbade him. Whereto Caesar said, *That if he did not desist, he would lay him dead in the place*. And presently taking himself up, he added, *Young man, it is harder for me to speak it than to do it; Adolescens, durius est mihi hoc dicere quam facere*. A speech compounded of the greatest terror and greatest clemency that could proceed out of the mouth of man.

29. But to return and conclude with him, it is evident himself knew well his own perfection in learning, and took it upon him; as appeared when, upon occasion that some spake what a strange resolution it was in Lucius Sylla to resign his dictature; he scoffing at him, to his own advantage, answered, *That Sylla could not skill of letters, and therefore knew not how to dictate*.

30. And here it were fit to leave this point, touching the concurrence of military virtue and learning (for what example should come with any grace after those two of Alexander and Caesar?) were it not in regard of the rareness of circumstance, that I find in one other particular, as that which did so suddenly pass from extreme scorn to extreme wonder: and it is of Xenophon the philosopher, who went from Socrates' school into Asia, in the expedition of Cyrus the younger against King Artaxerxes. This Xenophon at that time was very young, and never had seen the wars before; neither had any command in the army, but only followed the war as a voluntary, for the love and conversation of Proxenus his friend. He was present when Falinus came in message from the

great king to the Grecians, after that Cyrus was slain in the field, and they a handful of men left to themselves in the midst of the king's territories, cut off from their country by many navigable rivers, and many hundred miles. The message imported that they should deliver up their arms and submit themselves to the king's mercy. To which message before answer was made, divers of the army conferred familiarly with Falinus; and amongst the rest Xenophon[136] happened to say, *Why, Falinus, we have now but these two things left, our arms and our virtue; and if we yield up our arms, how shall we make use of our virtue?* Whereto Falinus smiling on him said, *If I be not deceived, young gentleman, you are an Athenian: and I believe you study philosophy, and it is pretty that you say: but you are much abused, if you think your virtue can withstand the king's power.* Here was the scorn; the wonder followed: which was, that this young scholar, or philosopher, after all the captains were murdered in parley by treason, conducted those ten thousand foot, through the heart of all the king's high countries, from Babylon to Grecia in safety, in despite of all the king's forces, to the astonishment of the world, and the encouragement of the Grecians in times succeeding to make invasion upon the kings of Persia; as was after purposed by Jason the Thessalian, attempted by Agesilaus the Spartan, and achieved by Alexander the Macedonian, all upon the ground of the act of that young scholar.

VIII. 1. To proceed now from imperial and military virtue to moral and private virtue; first, it is an assured truth, which is contained in the verses,

> Scilicet ingenuas didicisse fideliter artes
> Emollit mores, nec sinit esse feros.[137]

It taketh away the wildness and barbarism and fierceness of men's minds; but indeed the accent had need be upon *fideliter*: for a little superficial learning doth rather work a contrary effect. It taketh away all levity, temerity, and insolency, by copious suggestion of all doubts and difficulties, and acquainting the mind to balance reasons on both sides, and to turn back the first offers and conceits of the mind, and to accept of nothing but examined and tried. It taketh away vain admiration of anything, which is the root of all weakness. For all things are admired either because they are new, or because they are great. For novelty, no man that wadeth in learning or contemplation throughly, but will find that printed in his heart, *Nil novi super terram.*[138] Neither can any man marvel at the play of puppets, that goeth behind the curtain, and adviseth well of the motion. And for magnitude, as Alexander the Great, after that he was used to great armies, and the great conquests of the spacious provinces in Asia, when he received letters out of Greece, of some fights and services there, which were commonly for a passage, or a fort, or some walled town at the most, he said,

It seemed to him, that he was advertised of the battles of the frogs and the mice, that the old tales went of. So certainly, if a man meditate much upon the universal frame of nature, the earth with men upon it (the divineness of souls except) will not seem much other than an ant-hill, whereas some ants carry corn, and some carry their young, and some go empty, and all to and fro a little heap of dust. It taketh away or mitigateth fear of death or adverse fortune; which is one of the greatest impediments of virtue, and imperfections of manners. For if a man's mind be deeply seasoned with the consideration of the mortality and corruptible nature of things, he will easily concur with Epictetus, who went forth one day and saw a woman weeping for her pitcher of earth that was broken, and went forth the next day and saw a woman weeping for her son that was dead, and thereupon said, *Heri vidi fragilem frangi, hodie vidi mortalem mori.*[139] And therefore Virgil did excellently and profoundly couple the knowledge of causes and the conquest of all fears together, as *concomitantia.*

> Felix, qui potuit rerum cognoscere causas,
> Quique metus omnes, et inexorabile fatum
> Subjecit pedibus, strepitumque Acherontis avari.[140]

2. It were too long to go over the particular remedies which learning doth minister to all the diseases of the mind; sometimes purging the ill humours, sometimes opening the obstructions, sometimes helping digestion, sometimes increasing appetite, sometimes healing the wounds and exulcerations thereof, and the like; and therefore I will conclude with that which hath *rationem totius*;[141] which is, that it disposeth the constitution of the mind not to be fixed or settled in the defects thereof, but still to be capable and susceptible of growth and reformation. For the unlearned man knows not what it is to descend into himself, or to call himself to account, nor the pleasure of that *suavissima vita, indies sentire se fieri meliorem.*[142] The good parts he hath he will learn to show to the full, and use them dexterously, but not much to increase them. The faults he hath he will learn how to hide and colour them, but not much to amend them; like an ill mower, that mows on still, and never whets his scythe. Whereas with the learned man it fares otherwise, that he doth ever intermix the correction and amendment of his mind with the use and employment thereof. Nay further, in general and in sum, certain it is that *Veritas* and *Bonitas*[143] differ but as the seal and the print: for Truth prints Goodness, and they be the clouds of error which descend in the storms of passions and perturbations.

3. From moral virtue let us pass on to matter of power and commandment, and consider whether in right reason there be any comparable with that wherewith knowledge investeth and crowneth man's nature. We see the dignity of the commandment is according to the dignity of the commanded: to have commandment over beasts, as herdmen have, is a thing contemptible:

to have commandment over children, as schoolmasters have, is a matter of small honour: to have commandment over galley-slaves is a disparagement rather than an honour. Neither is the commandment of tyrants much better, over people which have put off the generosity of their minds: and therefore it was ever holden that honours in free monarchies and commonwealths had a sweetness more than in tyrannies, because the commandment extendeth more over the wills of men, and not only over their deeds and services. And therefore when Virgil putteth himself forth to attribute to Augustus Caesar the best of human honours, he doth it in these words:

> Victorque volentes
> Per populos dat jura, viamque affectat Olympo.[144]

But yet the commandment of knowledge is yet higher than the commandment over the will: for it is a commandment over the reason, belief, and understanding of man, which is the highest part of the mind, and giveth law to the will itself. For there is no power on earth which setteth up a throne or chair of estate in the spirits and souls of men, and in their cogitations, imaginations, opinions, and beliefs, but knowledge and learning. And therefore we see the detestable and extreme pleasure that arch-heretics, and false prophets, and imposters are transported with, when they once find in themselves that they have a superiority in the faith and conscience of men; so great as if they have once tasted of it, it is seldom seen that any torture or persecution can make them relinquish or abandon it. But as this is that which the author of the Revelation calleth the depth or profoundness of Satan, so by argument of contraries, the just and lawful sovereignty over men's understanding, by force of truth rightly interpreted, is that which approacheth nearest to the similitude of the divine rule.

4. As for fortune and advancement, the beneficence of learning is not so confined to give fortune only to states and commonwealths, as it doth not likewise give fortune to particular persons. For it was well noted long ago, that Homer hath given more men their livings, than either Sylla, or Caesar, or Augustus ever did, notwithstanding their great largesses and donatives, and distributions of lands to so many legions. And no doubt it is hard to say whether arms or learning have advanced greater numbers. And in case of sovereignty we see, that if arms or descent have carried away the kingdom, yet learning hath carried the priesthood, which ever hath been in some competition with empire.

5. Again, for the pleasure and delight of knowledge and learning, it far surpasseth all other in nature. For, shall the pleasures of the affections so exceed the pleasure of the sense, as much as the obtaining of desire or victory exceedeth a song or a dinner? and must not of consequence the pleasures of the

intellect or understanding exceed the pleasures of the affections? We see in all other pleasures there is satiety, and after they be used, their verdure departeth; which showeth well they be but deceits of pleasure, and not pleasures: and that it was the novelty which pleased, and not the quality. And therefore we see that voluptuous men turn friars, and ambitious princes turn melancholy. But of knowledge there is no satiety, but satisfaction and appetite are perpetually interchangeable; and therefore appeareth to be good in itself simply, without fallacy or accident. Neither is that pleasure of small efficacy and contentment to the mind of man, which the poet Lucretius describeth elegantly,

Suave mari magno, turbantibus aequora ventis, &c.[145]

It is a view of delight (saith he) to stand or walk upon the shore side, and to see a ship tossed with tempest upon the sea; or to be in a fortified tower, and to see two battles join upon a plain. But it is a pleasure incomparable, for the mind of man to be settled, landed, and fortified in the certainty of truth; and from thence to descry and behold the errors, perturbations, labours, and wanderings up and down of other men.

6. Lastly, leaving the vulgar arguments, that by learning man excelleth man in that wherein man excelleth beasts; that by learning man ascendeth to the heavens and their motions, where in body he cannot come; and the like; let us conclude with the dignity and excellency of knowledge and learning in that whereunto man's nature doth most aspire, which is immortality or continuance; for to this tendeth generation, and raising of houses and families; to this tend buildings, foundations, and monuments; to this tendeth the desire of memory, fame, and celebration; and in effect the strength of all other human desires. We see then how far the monuments of wit and learning are more durable than the monuments of power or of the hands. For have not the verses of Homer continued twenty-five hundred years, or more, without the loss of a syllable or letter; during which time infinite palaces, temples, castles, cities, have been decayed and demolished? It is not possible to have the true pictures or statues of Cyrus, Alexander, Caesar, no nor of the kings or great personages of much later years; for the originals cannot last, and the copies cannot but leese of the life and truth. But the images of men's wits and knowledges remain in books, exempted from the wrong of time and capable of perpetual renovation. Neither are they fitly to be called images, because they generate still, and cast their seeds in the minds of others, provoking and causing infinite actions and opinions in succeeding ages. So that if the invention of the ship was thought so noble, which carrieth riches and commodities from place to place, and consociateth the most remote regions in participation of their fruits, how much more are letters to be magnified, which as ships pass through the vast seas of time, and make ages so distant to participate of the wisdom, illuminations, and inventions, the one of

the other? Nay further, we see some of the philosophers which were least divine,[146] and most immersed in the senses, and denied generally the immortality of the soul, yet came to this point, that whatsoever motions the spirit of man could act and perform without the organs of the body, they thought might remain after death; which were only those of the understanding, and not of the affection; so immortal and incorruptible a thing did knowledge seem unto them to be. But we, that know by divine revelation that not only the understanding but the affections purified, not only the spirit but the body changed, shall be advanced to immortality, do disclaim in these rudiments of the senses. But it must be remembered, both in this last point, and so it may likewise be needful in other places, that in probation of the dignity of knowledge or learning, I did in the beginning separate divine testimony from human, which method I have pursued, and so handled them both apart.

7. Nevertheless I do not pretend, and I know it will be impossible for me, by any pleading of mine, to reverse the judgement, either of Aesop's cock, that preferred the barley-corn before the gem; or of Midas, that being chosen judge between Apollo, president of the Muses, and Pan, god of the flocks, judged for plenty; or of Paris, that judged for beauty and love against wisdom and power; or of Agrippina, *occidat matrem, modo imperet*,[147] that preferred empire with any condition never so detestable; or of Ulysses, *qui vetulam praetulit immortalitati*,[148] being a figure of those which prefer custom and habit before all excellency; or of a number of the like popular judgements. For these things must continue as they have been: but so will that also continue whereupon learning hath ever relied, and which faileth not: *Justificata est sapientia a filiis suis.*[149]

Second Book of Francis Bacon
Of the Proficience and
Advancement of Learning
Divine and Human

To the King

1. It might seem to have more convenience, though it come often otherwise to pass (excellent king), that those which are fruitful in their generations, and have in themselves the foresight of immortality in their descendants, should likewise be more careful of the good estate of future times, unto which they know they must transmit and commend over their dearest pledges.[1] Queen Elizabeth was a sojourner in the world in respect of her unmarried life, and was a blessing to her own times; and yet so as the impression of her good government, besides her happy memory, is not without some effect which doth survive her. But to your Majesty, whom God hath already blessed with so much royal issue, worthy to continue and represent you for ever, and whose youthful and fruitful bed doth yet promise many the like renovations, it is proper and agreeable to be conversant not only in the transitory parts of good government, but in those acts also which are in their nature permanent and perpetual. Amongst the which (if affection do not transport me) there is not any more worthy than the further endowment of the world with sound and fruitful knowledge. For why should a few received authors stand up like Hercules' columns,[2] beyond which there should be no sailing or discovering, since we have so bright and benign a star as your Majesty to conduct and prosper us? To return therefore where we left, it remaineth to consider of what kind those acts are which have been undertaken and performed by kings and others for the increase and advancement of learning: wherein I purpose to speak actively without digressing or dilating.

2. Let this ground therefore be laid, that all works are overcommen[3] by amplitude of reward, by soundness of direction, and by the conjunction of labours. The first multiplieth endeavour, the second preventeth error, and the third supplieth the frailty of man. But the principal of these is direction: for *claudus in via antevertit cursorem extra viam*;[4] and Salomon excellently setteth it down, *If the iron be not sharp, it requireth more strength; but wisdom is that which prevaileth*; signifying that the invention or election of the mean is more effectual than any inforcement or accumulation of endeavours. This I am induced to speak, for that (not derogating from the noble intention of any that have

been deservers towards the state of learning) I do observe nevertheless that their works and acts are rather matters of magnificence and memory, than of progression and proficience, and tend rather to augment the mass of learning in the multitude of learned men, than to rectify or raise the sciences themselves.

3. The works or acts of merit towards learning are conversant about three objects: the places of learning, the books of learning, and the persons of the learned. For as water, whether it be the dew of heaven, or the springs of the earth, doth scatter and leese itself in the ground, except it be collected into some receptacle, where it may by union comfort and sustain itself: and for that cause the industry of man hath made and framed spring-heads, conduits, cisterns, and pools, which men have accustomed likewise to beautify and adorn with accomplishments of magnificence and state, as well as of use and necessity: so this excellent liquor of knowledge, whether it descend from divine inspiration, or spring from human sense, would soon perish and vanish to oblivion, if it were not preserved in books, traditions, conferences, and places appointed, as universities, colleges, and schools, for the receipt and comforting of the same.

4. The works which concern the seats and places of learning are four: foundations and buildings, endowments with revenues, endowments with franchises and privileges, institutions and ordinances for government; all tending to quietness and privateness of life, and discharge of cares and troubles; much like the stations which Virgil prescribeth for the hiving of bees:

> Principio sedes apibus statioque petenda,
> Quo neque sit ventis aditus, &c.[5]

5. The works touching books are two: first, libraries which are as the shrines where all the relics of the ancient saints, full of true virtue, and that without delusion or imposture, are preserved and reposed; secondly, new editions of authors, with more correct impressions, more faithful translations, more profitable glosses, more diligent annotations, and the like.

6. The works pertaining to the persons of learned men (besides the advancement and countenancing of them in general) are two: the reward and designation of readers in sciences already extant and invented; and the reward and designation of writers and inquirers concerning any parts of learning not sufficiently laboured and prosecuted.

7. These are summarily the works and acts, wherein the merits of many excellent princes and other worthy personages have been conversant. As for any particular commemorations, I call to mind what Cicero said, when he gave general thanks: *Difficile non aliquem, ingratum quenquam praeterire.*[6] Let us

rather, according to the scriptures, look unto that part of the race which is before us, than look back to that which is already attained.

8. First therefore, amongst so many great foundations of colleges in Europe, I find strange that they are all dedicated to professions, and none left free to arts and sciences at large. For if men judge that learning should be referred to action, they judge well; but in this they fall into the error described in the ancient fable,[7] in which the other parts of the body did suppose the stomach had been idle, because it neither performed the office of motion, as the limbs do, nor of sense, as the head doth: but yet notwithstanding it is the stomach that digesteth and distributeth to all the rest. So if any man think philosophy and universality to be idle studies, he doth not consider that all professions are from thence served and supplied. And this I take to be a great cause that hath hindered the progression of learning, because these fundamental knowledges have been studied but in passage. For if you will have a tree bear more fruit than it hath used to do, it is not anything you can do to the boughs, but it is the stirring of the earth and putting new mould about the roots that must work it. Neither is it to be forgotten, that this dedicating of foundations and dotations to profes- sory learning hath not only had a malign aspect and influence upon the growth of sciences, but hath also been prejudicial to states and governments. For hence it proceedeth that princes find a solitude in regard of able men to serve them in causes of estate, because there is no education collegiate which is free; where such as were so disposed mought give themselves to histories, modern lang- uages, books of policy and civil discourse, and other the like enablements unto service of estate.

9. And because founders of colleges do plant, and founders of lectures do water, it followeth well in order to speak of the defect which is in public lectures; namely, in the smallness and meanness of the salary or reward which in most places is assigned unto them; whether they be lectures of arts, or of professions. For it is necessary to the progression of sciences that readers be of the most able and sufficient men; ast hose which are ordained for generating and propagating of sciences, and not for transitory use. This cannot be, except their condition and endowment be such as may content the ablest man to appropriate his whole labour and continue his whole age in that function and attendance; and therefore must have a proportion answerable to that medio- crity or competency of advancement, which may be expected from a profession or the practice of a profession. So as, if you will have sciences flourish, you must observe David's military law, which was, *That those which staid with the carriage should have equal part with those which were in the action*; else will the carriages be ill attended. So readers in sciences are indeed the guardians of the stores and provisions of sciences, whence men in active courses are furnished,

and therefore ought to have equal entertainment with them; otherwise if the fathers in sciences be of the weakest sort or be ill maintained,

Et patrum invalidi referent jejunia nati.[8]

10. Another defect I note, wherein I shall need some alchemist to help me, who call upon men to sell their books, and to build furnaces; quitting and forsaking Minerva and the Muses as barren virgins, and relying upon Vulcan. But certain it is, that unto the deep, fruitful, and operative study of many sciences, specially natural philosophy and physic, books be not only the instrumentals; wherein also the beneficence of men hath not been altogether wanting. For we see spheres, globes, astrolabes, maps, and the like, have been provided as appurtenances to astronomy and cosmography, as well as books. We see likewise that some places instituted for physic[9] have annexed the commodity of gardens for simples of all sorts, and do likewise command the use of dead bodies for anatomies. But these do respect but a few things. In general, there will hardly be any main proficience in the disclosing of nature, except there be some allowance for expenses about experiments; whether they be experiments appertaining to Vulcanus or Daedalus, furnace or engine, or any other kind. And therefore as secretaries and spials of princes and states bring in bills for intelligence, so you must allow the spials and intelligencers of nature to bring in their bills; or else you shall be ill advertised.

11. And if Alexander[10] made such a liberal assignation to Aristotle of treasure for the allowance of hunters, fowlers, fishers, and the like, that he mought compile an history of nature, much better do they deserve it that travail in arts of nature.

12. Another defect which I note, is an intermission or neglect, in those which are governors in universities, of consultation, and in princes or superior persons, of visitation: to enter into account and consideration, whether the readings, exercises, and other customs appertaining unto learning, anciently begun and since continued, be well instituted or no; and thereupon to ground an amendment or reformation in that which shall be found inconvenient. For it is one of your Majesty's own most wise and princely maxims, *That in all usages and precedents, the times be considered wherein they first began; which if they were weak or ignorant, it derogateth from the authority of the usage, and leaveth it for suspect.* And therefore inasmuch as most of the usages and orders of the universities were derived from more obscure times, it is the more requisite they be re-examined. In this kind I will give an instance or two, for example sake, of things that are the most obvious and familiar. The one is a matter, which though it be ancient and general, yet I hold to be an error; which is, that scholars in universities come too soon and too unripe to logic and rhetoric,[11] arts fitter for graduates

than children and novices. For these two rightly taken, are the gravest of sciences, being the arts of arts; the one for judgement, the other for ornament. And they be the rules and directions how to set forth and dispose matter: and therefore for minds empty and unfraught with matter, and which have not gathered that which Cicero[12] calleth *sylva* and *supellex*, stuff and variety, to begin with those arts (as if one should learn to weigh, or to measure, or to paint the wind) doth work but this effect, that the wisdom of those arts, which is great and universal, is almost made contemptible, and is degenerate into childish sophistry and ridiculous affectation. And further, the untimely learning of them hath drawn on by consequence the superficial and unprofitable teaching and writing of them, as fitteth indeed to the capacity of children. Another is a lack I find in the exercises used in the universities, which do make too great a divorce between invention and memory. For their speeches are either premeditate, in *verbis conceptis*, where nothing is left to invention; or merely extemporal, where little is left to memory. Whereas in life and action there is least use of either of these, but rather of intermixtures of premeditation and invention, notes and memory. So as the exercise fitteth not the practice, nor the image the life; and it is ever a true rule in exercises, that they be framed as near as may be to the life of practice; for otherwise they do pervert the motions and faculties of the mind, and not prepare them. The truth whereof is not obscure, when scholars come to the practices of professions, or other actions of civil life; which when they set into, this want is soon found by themselves, and sooner by others. But this part, touching the amendment of the institutions and orders of universities, I will conclude with the clause of Caesar's letter to Oppius and Balbus, *Hoc quemadmodum fieri possit, nonnulla mihi in mentem veniunt, et multa reperiri possunt; de iis rebus rogo vos ut cogitationem suscipiatis.*[13]

13. Another defect which I note, ascendeth a little higher than the precedent. For as the proficience of learning consisteth much in the orders and institutions of universities in the same states and kingdoms, so it would be yet more advanced, if there were more intelligence mutual between the universities of Europe than now there is. We see there be many orders and foundations,[14] which though they be divided under several sovereignties and territories, yet they take themselves to have a kind of contract, fraternity, and correspondence one with the other, insomuch as they have provincials and generals. And surely as nature createth brotherhood in families, and arts mechanical contract brotherhoods in communalties, and the anointment of God superinduceth a brotherhood in kings and bishops, so in like manner there cannot but be a fraternity in learning and illumination, relating to that paternity which is attributed to God, who is called the Father of Illuminations or Lights.[15]

14. The last defect which I will note is, that there hath not been, or very

rarely been, any public designation of writers or inquirers, concerning such parts of knowledge as may appear not to have been already sufficiently laboured or undertaken; unto which point it is an inducement to enter into a view and examination what parts of learning have been prosecuted and what omitted. For the opinion of plenty is amongst the causes of want,[16] and the great quantity of books maketh a show rather of superfluity than lack; which surcharge nevertheless is not to be remedied by making no more books, but by making more good books, which, as the serpent of Moses,[17] mought devour the serpents of the enchanters.

15. The removing of all the defects formerly enumerate, except the last, and of the active part also of the last (which is the designation of writers), are *opera basilica*;[18] towards which the endeavours of a private man may be but as an image in a crossway, that may point at the way, but cannot go it. But the inducing[19] part of the latter (which is the survey of learning) may be set forward by private travail. Wherefore I will now attempt to make a general and faithful perambulation of learning, with an inquiry what parts thereof lie fresh and waste, and not improved and converted by the industry of man; to the end that such a plot made and recorded to memory, may both minister light to any public designation, and also serve to excite voluntary endeavours. . . .

On the Method and
Illustration of Tradition

XVII. 1. For the method of tradition,[1] I see it hath moved a controversy in our time. But as in civil business, if there be a meeting, and men fall at words, there is commonly an end of the matter for that time, and no proceeding at all; so in learning, where there is much controversy, there is many times little inquiry. For this part of knowledge of method seemeth to me so weakly inquired as I shall report it deficient.

2. Method hath been placed and that not amiss, in logic, as a part of judgement.[2] For as the doctrine of syllogisms comprehendeth the rules of judgement upon that which is invented, so the doctrine of method containeth the rules of judgement upon that which is to be delivered; for judgement precedeth delivery, as it followeth invention[3]. Neither is the method or the nature of the tradition material only to the use of knowledge, but likewise to the progression of knowledge: for since the labour and life of one man cannot attain to perfection of knowledge, the wisdom of the tradition is that which inspireth the felicity of continuance and proceeding. And therefore the most real diversity of method is of method referred to use, and method referred to progression: whereof the one may be termed magistral, and the other of probation.[4]

3. The latter whereof seemeth to be *via deserta et interclusa*.[5] For as knowledges are now delivered, there is a kind of contract of error between the deliverer and the receiver. For he that delivereth knowledge, desireth to deliver it in such form as may be best believed, and not as may be best examined; and he that receiveth knowledge, desireth rather present satisfaction, than expectant inquiry; and so rather not to doubt, than not to err: glory making the author not to lay open his weakness, and sloth making the disciple not to know his strength.

4. But knowledge that is delivered as a thread to be spun on, ought to be delivered and intimated, if it were possible, in the same method wherein it was invented: and so is it possible of knowledge induced.[6] But in this same anticipated and prevented[7] knowledge, no man knoweth how he came to the knowledge which he hath obtained. But yet nevertheless, *secundum majus et minus*,[8] a man may revisit and descend unto the foundations of his knowledge and consent; and so transplant it into another, as it grew in his own mind.

For it is in knowledges as it is in plants: if you mean to use the plant, it is no matter for the roots; but if you mean to remove it to grow, then it is more assured to rest upon roots than slips:[9] so the delivery of knowledges (as it is now used) is as of fair bodies of trees without the roots; good for the carpenter, but not for the planter. But if you will have sciences grow, it is less matter for the shaft or body of the tree, so you look well to the taking up of the roots. Of which kind of delivery the method of the mathematics, in that subject, hath some shadow: but generally I see it neither put in use nor put in inquisition, and therefore note it for deficient.

5. Another diversity of method there is, which hath some affinity with the former, used in some cases by the discretion of the ancients, but disgraced since by the impostures of many vain persons, who have made it as a false light for their counterfeit merchandises; and that is, enigmatical and disclosed.[10] The pretence whereof is, to remove the vulgar capacities from being admitted to the secrets of knowledges, and to reserve them to selected auditors, or wits of such sharpness as can pierce the veil.

6. Another diversity of method, whereof the consequence is great, is the delivery of knowledge in aphorisms, or in methods;[11] wherein we may observe that it hath been too much taken into custom, out of a few axioms or observations upon any subject, to make a solemn and formal art, filling it with some discourses, and illustrating it with examples, and digesting it into a sensible method. But the writing in aphorisms hath many excellent virtues, whereto the writing in method doth not approach.

7. For first, it trieth the writer, whether he be superficial or solid: for aphorisms, except they should be ridiculous, cannot be made but of the pith and heart of sciences; for discourse of illustration is cut off; recitals of examples are cut off; discourse of connexion and order is cut off; descriptions of practice are cut off. So there remaineth nothing to fill the aphorisms but some good quantity of observation: and therefore no man can suffice, nor in reason will attempt, to write aphorisms, but he that is sound and grounded. But in methods,

Tantum series juncturaque pollet,
Tantum de medio sumptis accedit honoris,[12]

as a man shall make a great show of an art, which, if it were disjointed, would come to little. Secondly, methods are more fit to win consent or belief, but less fit to point to action; for they carry a kind of demonstration in orb or circle, one part illuminating another, and therefore satisfy. But particulars being dispersed do best agree with dispersed directions.[13] And lastly, aphorisms, representing a knowledge broken,[14] do invite men to inquire further; whereas methods, carrying the show of a total, do secure men, as if they were at furthest.

8. Another diversity of method, which is likewise of great weight, is the handling of knowledge by assertions and their proofs, or by questions and their determinations. The latter kind whereof, if it be immoderately followed, is as prejudicial to the proceeding of learning, as it is to the proceeding of an army to go about to besiege every little fort or hold. For if the field be kept, and the sum of the enterprise pursued, those smaller things will come in of themselves: indeed a man would not leave some important piece[15] enemy at his back. In like manner, the use of confutation in the delivery of sciences ought to be very sparing; and to serve to remove strong preoccupations and prejudgements, and not to minister and excite disputations and doubts.

9. Another diversity of methods is, according to the subject or matter which is handled. For there is a great difference in delivery of the mathematics, which are the most abstracted of knowledges, and policy, which is the most immersed.[16] And howsoever contention hath been moved, touching an uniformity of method in multiformity of matter, yet we see how that opinion, besides the weakness of it, hath been of ill desert towards learning, as that which taketh the way to reduce learning to certain empty and barren generalities; being but the very husks and shells of sciences, all the kernel being forced out and expulsed with the torture and press of the method. And therefore as I did allow well of particular topics for invention, so I do allow likewise of particular methods of tradition.

10. Another diversity of judgement[17] in the delivery and teaching of knowledge is, according unto the light and presuppositions of that which is delivered. For that knowledge which is new, and foreign from opinions received, is to be delivered in another form than that that is agreeable and familiar; and therefore Aristotle, when he thinks to tax Democritus, doth in truth commend him, where he saith, *If we shall indeed dispute, and not follow after similitudes, &c.* For those whose conceits are seated in popular opinions, need only but to prove or dispute; but those whose conceits are beyond popular opinions, have a double labour; the one to make themselves conceived, and the other to prove and demonstrate. So that it is of necessity with them to have recourse to similitudes and translations to express themselves. And therefore in the infancy of learning, and in rude times, when those conceits which are now trivial were then new, the world was full of parables and similitudes;[18] for else would men either have passed over without mark, or else rejected for paradoxes that which was offered, before they had understood or judged. So in divine learning, we see how frequent parables and tropes are: for it is a rule, that whatsoever science is not consonant to presuppositions, must pray in aid of similitudes.

11. There be also other diversities of methods[19] vulgar and received: as that of resolution or analysis, of constitution or systasis, of concealment or

cryptic &c., which I do allow well of, though I have stood upon those which are least handled and observed. All which I have remembered to this purpose, because I would erect and constitute one general inquiry (which seems to me deficient) touching the wisdom of tradition.

12. But unto this part of knowledge, concerning method, doth further belong not only the architecture of the whole frame of a work, but also the several beams and columns thereof; not as to their stuff, but as to their quantity and figure. And therefore method considereth not only the disposition of the argument or subject, but likewise the propositions: not as to their truth or matter, but as to their limitation and manner. For herein Ramus[20] merited better a great deal in reviving the good rules of propositions, $Ka\theta \delta \lambda o \upsilon \pi \rho \hat{\omega} \tau o \nu$, $\kappa \alpha \tau \grave{\alpha} \pi \alpha \nu \tau \delta s$, &c., than he did in introducing the canker of epitomes;[21] and yet (as it is the condition of human things that, according to the ancient fables, *the most precious things have the most pernicious keepers*) it was so, that the attempt of the one made him fall upon the other. For he had need be well conducted that should design to make axioms convertible, if he make them not withal circular, and non-promovent,[22] or incurring into themselves; but yet the intention was excellent.

13. The other considerations of method, concerning propositions, are chiefly touching the utmost propositions, which limit the dimensions of sciences: for every knowledge may be fitly said, besides the profundity (which is the truth and substance of it, that makes it solid), to have a longitude and a latitude; accounting the latitude towards other sciences, and the longitude towards action; that is, from the greatest generality to the most particular precept. The one giveth rule how far one knowledge ought to intermeddle within the province of another, which is the rule they call $Ka\theta \alpha \upsilon \tau \delta$;[23] the other giveth rule unto what degree of particularity a knowledge should descend: which latter I find passed over in silence, being in my judgement the more material. For certainly there must be somewhat left to practice; but how much is worthy the inquiry. We see remote and superficial generalities do but offer knowledge to scorn of practical men; and are no more aiding to practice, than an Ortelius' universal map[24] is to direct the way between London and York. The better sort of rules have been not unfitly compared to glasses of steel unpolished, where you may see the images of things, but first they must be filed: so the rules will help, if they be laboured and polished by practice. But how crystalline they may be made at the first, and how far forth they may be polished aforehand is the question; the inquiry whereof seemeth to me deficient.

14. There hath been also laboured and put in practice a method, which is not a lawful method, but a method of imposture; which is, to deliver knowledges in such manner, as men may speedily come to make a show of learning

who have it not. Such was the travail of Raymundus Lullius, [25] in making that art which bears his name: not unlike to some books of typocosmy, which have been made since; being nothing but a mass of words of all arts, to give men countenance, that those which use the terms might be thought to understand the art; which collections are much like a fripper's or broker's shop, that hath ends of everything, but nothing of worth.

XVIII. 1. Now we descend to that part which concerneth the illustration of tradition, comprehended in that science which we call rhetoric, or art of eloquence; a science excellent, and excellently well laboured. For although in true value it is inferior to wisdom, as it is said by God to Moses, when he disabled himself for want of this faculty, *Aaron shall be thy speaker, and thou shalt be to him as God*; yet with people it is the more mighty: for so Salomon saith, *Sapiens corde appellabitur prudens, sed dulcis eloquio majora reperiet*;[26] signifying that profoundness of wisdom will help a man to a name or admiration, but that it is eloquence that prevaileth in an active life. And as to the labouring of it, the emulation of Aristotle with the rhetoricians of his time, and the experience of Cicero, hath made them in their works of rhetorics exceed themselves. Again, the excellency of examples of eloquence in the orations of Demosthenes and Cicero, added to the perfection of the precepts of eloquence, hath doubled the progression in this art; and therefore the deficiences which I shall note will rather be in some collections, which may as handmaids attend the art, than in the rules or use of the art itself.

2. Notwithstanding, to stir the earth a little about the roots of this science, as we have done of the rest; the duty and office of rhetoric is to apply reason to imagination[27] for the better moving of the will. For we see reason is disturbed in the administration thereof by three means; by illaqueation or sophism, which pertains to logic; by imagination or impression, which pertains to rhetoric; and by passion or affection, which pertains to morality. And as in negotiation with others, men are wrought by cunning, by importunity, and by vehemency; so in this negotiation within ourselves, men are undermined by inconsequences, solicited and importuned by impressions or observations, and transported by passions. Neither is the nature of man so unfortunately built, as that those powers and arts should have force to disturb reason, and not to establish and advance it. For the end of logic is to teach a form of argument to secure reason, and not to entrap it. The end of morality is to procure the affections to obey reason, and not to invade it. The end of rhetoric is to fill the imagination to second reason, and not to oppress it: for these abuses of arts come in but *ex obliquo*, for caution.

3. And therefore it was great injustice in Plato,[28] though springing out of a just hatred to the rhetoricians of his time, to esteem of rhetoric but as a

voluptuary art, resembling it to cookery, that did mar wholesome meats, and help unwholesome by variety of sauces to the pleasure of the taste. For we see that speech is much more conversant in adorning that which is good, than in colouring that which is evil; for there is no man but speaketh more honestly than he can do or think: and it was excellently noted by Thucydides in Cleon, that because he used to hold on the bad side in causes of estate, therefore he was ever inveighing against eloquence and good speech; knowing that no man can speak fair of courses sordid and base. And therefore as Plato said elegantly, *That virtue, if she could be seen, would move great love and affection;*[29] so seeing that she cannot be showed to the sense by corporal shape, the next degree is to show her to the imagination in lively representation: for to show her to reason only in subtility of argument was a thing ever derided in Chrysippus and many of the Stoics, who thought to thrust virtue upon men by sharp disputations and conclusions, which have no sympathy with the will of man.

4. Again, if the affections in themselves were pliant and obedient to reason, it were true there should be no great use of persuasions and insinuations to the will, more than of naked proposition and proofs; but in regard of the continual mutinies and seditions of the affections,

> Video meliora, proboque,
> Deteriora sequor,[20]

reason would become captive and servile, if eloquence of persuasions did not practise and win the imagination from the affections' part, and contract a confederacy between the reason and imagination against the affections; for the affections themselves carry ever an appetite to good, as reason doth. The difference is, that the affection beholdeth merely the present; reason beholdeth the future and sum of time. And therefore the present filling the imagination more, reason is commonly vanquished; but after that force of eloquence and persuasion hath made things future and remote appear as present, then upon the revolt of the imagination reason prevaileth.

5. We conclude therefore that rhetoric can be no more charged with the colouring of the worse part, than logic with sophistry, or morality with vice. For we know the doctrines of contraries are the same, though the use be opposite. It appeareth also that logic differeth from rhetoric, not only as the fist from the palm,[31] the one close, the other at large; but much more in this, that logic handleth reason exact and in truth, and rhetoric handleth it as it is planted in popular opinions and manners. And therefore Aristotle doth wisely place rhetoric as between logic on the one side and moral or civil knowledge on the other, as participating of both: for the proofs and demonstrations of logic are

toward all men indifferent and the same; but the proofs and persuasions of rhetoric ought to differ according to the auditors:

Orpheus in sylvis, inter delphinas Arion.[32]

Which application, in perfection of idea, ought to extend so far, that if a man should speak of the same thing to several persons, he should speak to them all respectively and several ways: though this politic part of eloquence in private speech it is easy for the greatest orators to want; whilst, by the observing their well-graced forms of speech, they leese the volubility of application: and therefore it shall not be amiss to recommend this to better inquiry, not being curious whether we place it here, or in that part which concerneth policy.

Novum Organum
The Doctrine of Idols

The *Novum Organum* (The New Method) was written in Latin and published in 1620 with a mass of preliminary material which explained Bacon's plan of the Great Instauration. It was the final form of a work which had occupied Bacon for about 17 years, the busy years of his political career. Some of the ideas he had cast into other moulds, which survive in incomplete works with such titles as *Valerius Terminus, Partis instaurationis secundae delineatio et argumentum, Filum labyrinthi, Cogitata et Visa, Aphorismi et Consilia.* The New Method was itself not finished. As published it contains 130 aphorisms in the first Book and 52 in the second, but breaks off after promising to go on to other aspects of Induction. What Bacon's new 'Method' was, has, therefore, been the subject of discussion ever since.

'The name *Organon* was applied to the works of Aristotle which treated of logic, that is, of the method of establishing and proving knowledge, and of refuting error, by means of Syllogisms' (Whewell, *Novum Organum Renovatum*). Bacon's *New Organon,* or New Method was thus offered as a text-book of Logic, but of Inductive instead of Deductive Logic. He described his work as 'a kind of logic', contriving and preparing 'helps and guards for the Understanding', but differing from the old logic 'in the end aimed at, in the order of demonstration, and in the starting point of the inquiry'. By its means Bacon hoped to emancipate the understandings of men, 'whence there cannot but follow an improvement in man's estates, and an enlargement of his power over nature'.

The Great Instauration (Bacon's title for his magnificent plan for the renovation or renewal of the sciences or learning) was divided into six parts. The first was to contain a survey of the present state of knowledge. This he had, in a fashion, already made in the *Advancement of Learning,* where the second book is a classification of all branches of knowledge together with assessments of the deficiencies of each. In

1623 Bacon published a Latin version of the *Advancement*, called *De Augmentis Scientiarum*, in which the survey of knowledge is expanded and distributed into Books II to IX. The second part of the Instauration was the New Method, represented here by the opening aphorisms of Book I on the Idols. Part three was to have been a treasure house of all the phenomena of the universe, a Natural History, on which the New Method was to be employed. It is represented here by extracts from the *Sylva Sylvarum*. Part four, of which only the preface (*Scala Intellectus*) was written, was to contain examples of the method applied to phenomena, with the results to which it led. Part five (again only a preface, *Prodromi sive anticipationes*, exists) was to contain what Bacon had discovered in natural philosophy without the aid of his new method. The last part was to have set forth the New Philosophy—the result of the application of the method to all the phenomena of the universe. The whole scheme is thus not only incomplete, but could only have been finished in the distant future. A vision of the society that the successful pursuit of his ideals might have produced is given in the (also incomplete) *New Atlantis*.

The outstanding characteristics of Bacon's method of inquiring into Nature are two—its results would be certain, and it would have the power of placing 'all wits and understandings nearly on a level' (I. 61), as a ruler enables all men to draw a straight line. He is more successful, however, in showing what are the hindrances to the advancement of learning than in expounding a new method of induction, and most writers on Bacon have considered his doctrine of Idols as his most valuable contribution to philosophy. The Idols are not images of false gods worshipped by men, but are the illusions or false appearances that have taken possession of men's minds and hindered the approach to new knowledge. The doctrine is expounded in the *Advancement* (II. xiv. 9–11) and in the *De Augmentis* (V. iv). In these discussions, Bacon is at his best, combining the acuteness of psychological insight, the understanding of previous philosophies, and the cool and deep analysis of the thinker, with the passion, the verbal inventiveness and the imaginative understanding of the poet. He understood man's 'natural, though corrupt, love of the *Lie* itself', and longed to bring others to dwell with him in 'naked, and open daylight'. 'For the mind of man is far from the nature of a clear and equal glass wherein the beams of things

77

should reflect according to their true incidence; nay, it is rather like an enchanted glass, full of superstition and imposture, if it be not delivered and reduced.'

The Doctrine of Idols

Aphorisms Concerning the Interpretation of Nature and the Kingdom of Man

BOOK I

I

Man, being the servant and interpreter of Nature, can do and understand so much and so much only as he has observed in fact or in thought of the course of nature: beyond this he neither knows anything nor can do anything.

II

Neither the naked hand nor the understanding left to itself can effect much. It is by instruments and helps that the work is done, which are as much wanted for the understanding as for the hand. And as the instruments of the hand either give motion or guide it, so the instruments of the mind supply either suggestions for the understanding or cautions.

III

Human knowledge and human power meet in one; for where the cause is not known the effect cannot be produced. Nature to be commanded must be obeyed; and that which in contemplation is as the cause is in operation as the rule.

IV

Towards the effecting of works, all that man can do is to put together or put asunder natural bodies. The rest is done by nature working within.

V

The study of nature with a view to works is engaged in by the mechanic, the mathematician, the physician, the alchemist, and the magician;[1] but by all (as things now are) with slight endeavour and scanty success.

VI

It would be an unsound fancy and self-contradictory to expect that things which have never yet been done can be done except by means which have never yet been tried.

VII

The productions of the mind and hand seem very numerous in books and manufactures. But all this variety lies in an exquisite subtlety and derivations from a few things already known; not in the number of axioms.[2]

VIII

Moreover the works already known are due to chance and experiment[3] rather than to sciences; for the sciences we now possess are merely systems for the nice ordering and setting forth of things already invented; not methods of invention or directions for new work.

IX

The cause and root of nearly all evils in the sciences is this—that while we falsely admire and extol the powers of the human mind we neglect to seek for its true helps.

X

The subtlety of nature is greater many times over than the subtlety of the senses and understanding; so that all those specious meditations, speculations, and glosses in which men indulge are quite from the purpose, only there is no one by to observe it.

XI

As the sciences which we now have do not help us in finding out new works, so neither does the logic[4] which we now have help us in finding out new sciences.

XII

The logic now in use serves rather to fix and give stability to the errors which have their foundation in commonly received notions than to help the search after truth. So it does more harm than good.

XIII

The syllogism is not applied to the first principles of sciences, and is applied in vain to intermediate axioms; being no match for the subtlety of nature. It commands assent therefore to the proposition, but does not take hold of the thing.

XIV

The syllogism consists of propositions, propositions consist of words, words are symbols of notions. Therefore if the notions themselves (which is the root of the matter) are confused and over-hastily abstracted from the facts, there can be no firmness in the superstructure. Our only hope therefore lies in a true induction.[5]

XV

There is no soundness in our notions whether logical or physical. Substance, Quality, Action, Passion, Essence itself, are not sound notions: much less are Heavy, Light, Dense, Rare, Moist, Dry, Generation, Corruption, Attraction, Repulsion, Element, Matter, Form, and the like; but all are fantastical and ill defined.

XVI

Our notions of less general species, as Man, Dog, Dove, and of the immediate perceptions of the sense, as Hot, Cold, Black, White, do not materially mislead us; yet even these are sometimes confused by the flux and alteration of matter and the mixing of one thing with another. All the others which men have hitherto adopted are but wanderings, not being abstracted and formed from things by proper methods.

XVII

Nor is there less of wilfulness and wandering in the construction of axioms than in the formation of notions; not excepting even those very principles which are obtained by common induction;[6] but much more in the axioms and lower propositions educed by the syllogism.

XVIII

The discoveries which have hitherto been made in the sciences are such as lie close to vulgar notions, scarcely beneath the surface. In order to penetrate into the inner and further recesses of nature, it is necessary that both notions and axioms be derived from things by a more sure and guarded way; and that a method of intellectual operation be introduced altogether better and more certain.

XIX

There are and can be only two ways of searching into and discovering truth. The one flies from the senses and particulars to the most general axioms, and from these principles, the truth of which it takes for settled and immoveable, proceeds to judgment and to the discovery of middle axioms. And this way is now in fashion. The other derives axioms from the senses and particulars, rising by a gradual and unbroken ascent, so that it arrives at the most general axioms last of all. This is the true way, but as yet untried.[7]

XX

The understanding left to itself takes the same course (namely, the former) which it takes in accordance with logical order. For the mind longs to spring up to positions of higher generality, that it may find rest there; and so after a little while wearies of experiment. But this evil is increased by logic, because of the order and solemnity of its disputations.

XXI

The understanding left to itself, in a sober, patient and grave mind, especially if it be not hindered by received doctrines, tries a little that other way, which is the right one, but with little progress; since the understanding, unless directed and assisted, is a thing unequal, and quite unfit to contend with the obscurity of things.

XXII

Both ways set out from the senses and particulars, and rest in the highest generalities; but the difference between them is infinite. For the one just glances at experiment and particulars in passing, the other dwells duly and orderly among them. The one, again, begins at once by establishing certain abstract and useless generalities,[8] the other rises by gradual steps to that which is prior and better known in the order of nature.

XXIII

There is a great difference between the idols[9] of the human mind and the ideas of the divine. That is to say, between certain empty dogmas, and the true signatures and marks set upon the works of creation as they are found in nature.

XXIV

It cannot be that axioms established by argumentation should avail for the discovery of new works; since the subtlety of nature is greater many times over than the subtlety of argument. But axioms duly and orderly formed from particulars easily discover the way to new particulars, and thus render sciences active.

*   *   *

XXXI

It is idle to expect any great advancement in science from the superinducing and engrafting of new things upon old. We must begin anew from the very foundations, unless we would revolve for ever in a circle with mean and contemptible progress.[10]

XXXII

The honour of the ancient authors, and indeed of all, remains untouched; since the comparison I challenge is not of wits[11] or faculties, but of ways and methods, and the part I take upon myself is not that of a judge, but of a guide.

XXXIII

This must be plainly avowed: no judgment can be rightly formed either of my method or of the discoveries to which it leads, by means of anticipations (that is to say, of the reasoning which is now in use); since I cannot be called on to abide by the sentence of a tribunal which is itself on its trial.

XXXIV

Even to deliver and explain what I bring forward is no easy matter; for things in themselves new will yet be apprehended with reference to what is old.

XXXV

It was said by Borgia of the expedition of the French into Italy, that they came with chalk in their hands to mark out their lodgings, not with arms to force their way in.[12] I in like manner would have my doctrine enter quietly into the minds that are fit and capable of receiving it; for confutations cannot be employed, when the difference is upon first principles and very notions and even upon forms of demonstration.

XXXVI

One method of delivery alone remains to us; which is simply this: we must lead men to the particulars themselves, and their series and order; while men on their side must force themselves for awhile to lay their notions by and begin to familiarise themselves with facts.

XXXVII

The doctrine of those who have denied that certainty could be attained at all,[13] has some agreement with my way of proceeding at the first setting out; but they end in being infinitely separated and opposed. For the holders of that doctrine assert simply that nothing can be known; I also assert that not much can be known in nature by the way which is now in use. But then they go on to destroy the authority of the senses and understanding; whereas I proceed to devise and supply helps for the same.

XXXVIII

The Idols and false notions which are now in possession of the human under-standing, and have taken deep root therein, not only so beset men's minds that truth can hardly find entrance, but even after entrance obtained, they will again in the very instauration of the sciences meet and trouble us, unless men being forewarned of the danger fortify themselves as far as may be against their assaults.

XXXIX

There are four classes of Idols which beset men's minds. To these for distinc-tion's sake I have assigned names—calling the first class *Idols of the Tribe*; the second, *Idols of the Cave*; the third, *Idols of the Market-place*; the fourth, *Idols of the Theatre*.

XL

The formation of ideas and axioms by true induction is no doubt the proper remedy to be applied for the keeping off and clearing away of idols. To point them out, however, is of great use; for the doctrine of Idols is to the Interpretation of Nature what the doctrine of the refutation of Sophisms[14] is to common Logic.

XLI

The Idols of the Tribe[15] have their foundation in human nature itself, and in the tribe or race of men. For it is a false assertion that the sense of man is the measure of things.[16] On the contrary, all perceptions as well of the sense as of the mind are according to the measure of the individual and not according to the measure of the universe. And the human understanding is like a false mirror, which, receiving rays irregularly, distorts and discolours the nature of things by mingling it own nature with it.

XLII

The Idols of the Cave are the Idols of the individual man. For every one (besides the errors common to human nature in general) has a cave or den of his own, which refracts and discolours the light of nature; owing either to his own proper and peculiar nature; or to his education and conversation with others; or to the reading of books, and the authority of those whom he esteems and admires; or to the differences of impressions, accordingly as they take place in a mind preoccupied and predisposed or in a mind indifferent and settled; or the like. So that the spirit of man (according as it is meted out to different individuals)[17] is in fact a thing variable and full of perturbation, and governed as it were by chance. Whence it was well observed by Heraclitus that men look for sciences in their own lesser worlds, and not in the greater or common world.

XLIII

There are also Idols formed by the intercourse and association of men with each other, which I call Idols of the Market-place, on account of the commerce and consort of men there. For it is by discourse that men associate; and words are imposed according to the apprehension of the vulgar. And therefore the ill and unfit choice of words wonderfully obstructs the understanding. Nor do the definitions or explanations wherewith in some things learned men are wont to guard and defend themselves, by any means set the matter right. But words plainly force and overrule the understanding, and throw all into confusion, and lead men away into numberless empty controversies and idle fancies.

XLIV

Lastly, there are Idols which have immigrated into men's minds from the various dogmas of philosophies, and also from wrong laws of demonstration. These I call Idols of the Theatre; because in my judgment all the received systems are but so many stage-plays, representing worlds of their own creation after an unreal and scenic fashion. Nor is it only of the systems now in vogue, or only of the ancient sects and philosophies, that I speak; for many more plays of the same kind may yet be composed and in like artificial manner set forth; seeing that errors the most widely different have nevertheless causes for the most part alike. Neither again do I mean this only of entire systems, but also of many principles and axioms in science, which by tradition, credulity, and negligence have come to be received.

But of these several kinds of Idols I must speak more largely and exactly, that the understanding may be duly cautioned.

XLV

The human understanding is of its own nature prone to suppose the existence of more order and regularity in the world than it finds. And though there be many things in nature which are singular and unmatched, yet it devises for them parallels and conjugates and relatives which do not exist. Hence the fiction that all celestial bodies move in perfect circles; spirals and dragons being (except in name) utterly rejected. Hence too the element of Fire with its orb is brought in, to make up the square with the other three which the sense perceives. Hence also the ratio of density of the so-called elements is arbitrarily fixed at ten to one. And so on of other dreams. And these fancies affect not dogmas only, but simple notions also.[18]

XLVI

The human understanding when it has once adopted an opinion (either as being the received opinion or as being agreeable to itself) draws all things else to support and agree with it. And though there be a greater number and weight of instances to be found on the other side, yet these it either neglects and despises, or else by some distinction sets aside and rejects; in order that by this great and pernicious pre-determination the authority of its former conclusions may remain inviolate. And therefore it was a good answer that was made by one who when they showed him hanging in a temple a picture of those who had paid their vows as having escaped shipwreck, and would have him say whether he did not now acknowledge the power of the gods—'Aye,' asked he again, 'but where are they painted that were drowned after their vows?' And such is the way of all superstition, whether in astrology, dreams, omens, divine judgments, or the like; wherein men having a delight in such vanities, mark the events where they are fulfilled, but where they fail, though this happen much oftener, neglect and pass them by. But with far more subtlety does this mischief insinuate itself into philosophy and the sciences; in which the first conclusion colours and brings into conformity with itself all that come after, though far sounder and better. Besides, independently of that delight and vanity which I have described, it is the peculiar and perpetual error of the human intellect to be more moved and excited by affirmatives than by negatives; whereas it ought properly to hold itself indifferently disposed towards both alike. Indeed in the establishment of any true axiom, the negative instance is the more forcible of the two.

XLVII

The human understanding is moved by those things most which strike and enter the mind simultaneously and suddenly, and so fill the imagination; and then it feigns and supposes all other things to be somehow, though it cannot see how, similar to those few things by which it is surrounded. But for that going to and fro to remote and heterogeneous instances, by which axioms are tried as in the fire, the intellect is altogether slow and unfit, unless it be forced thereto by severe laws and overruling authority.

XLVIII

The human understanding is unquiet; it cannot stop or rest, and still presses onward, but in vain. Therefore it is that we cannot conceive of any end or limit to the world; but always as of necessity it occurs to us that there is something beyond. Neither again can it be conceived how eternity has flowed down to the present day; for that distinction which is commonly received of infinity in time past and in time to come can by no means hold; for it would thence follow that one infinity is greater than another, and that infinity is wasting away and tending to become finite. The like subtlety arises touching the infinite divisibility of lines, from the same inability of thought to stop. But this inability interferes more mischievously in the discovery of causes: for although the most general principles in nature ought to be held merely positive, as they are discovered, and cannot with truth be referred to a cause; nevertheless the human understanding being unable to rest still seeks something prior in the order of nature. And then it is that in struggling towards that which is further off it falls back upon that which is more nigh at hand; namely, on final causes: which have relation clearly to the nature of man rather than to the nature of the universe, and from this source have strangely defiled philosophy. But he is no less an unskilled and shallow philosopher who seeks causes of that which is most general, than he who in things subordinate and subaltern omits to do so.

XLIX

The human understanding is no dry light,[19] but receives an infusion from the will and affections; whence proceed sciences which may be called 'sciences as one would'. For what a man had rather were true he more readily believes. Therefore he rejects difficult things from impatience of research; sober things, because they narrow hope; the deeper things of nature, from superstition; the light of experience, from arrogance and pride, lest his mind should seem to be occupied with things mean and transitory; things not commonly believed, out of deference to the opinion of the vulgar. Numberless in short are the ways, and sometimes imperceptible, in which the affections colour and infect the understanding.

L

But by far the greatest hindrance and aberration of the human understanding proceeds from the dullness, incompetency, and deceptions of the senses; in that things which strike the sense outweigh things which do not immediately strike it, though they be more important. Hence it is that speculation commonly ceases where sight ceases; insomuch that of things invisible there is little or no observation. Hence all the working of the spirits inclosed in tangible bodies[20] lies hid and unobserved of men. So also all the more subtle changes of form in the parts of coarser substances (which they commonly call alteration, though it is in truth local motion through exceedingly small spaces) is in like manner unobserved. And yet unless these two things just mentioned be searched out and brought to light, nothing great can be achieved in nature, as far as the production of works is concerned. So again the essential nature of our common air, and of all bodies less dense than air (which are very many), is almost unknown. For the sense by itself is a thing infirm and erring; neither can instruments for enlarging or sharpening the senses do much; but all the truer kind of interpretation of nature is effected by instances and experiments fit and apposite; wherein the sense decides touching the experiment only, and the experiment touching the point in nature and the thing itself.

LI

The human understanding is of its own nature prone to abstractions and gives a substance and reality to things which are fleeting. But to resolve nature into abstractions is less to our purpose than to dissect her into parts; as did the school of Democritus, which went further into nature than the rest. Matter rather than forms should be the object of our attention, its configurations and changes of configuration, and simple action, and law of action or motion; for forms are figments of the human mind, unless you will call those laws of action forms.

LII

Such then are the idols which I call *Idols of the Tribe*: and which take their rise either from the homogeneity of the substance of the human spirit, or from its preoccupation, or from its narrowness, or from its restless motion, or from an infusion of the affections, or from the incompetency of the senses, or from the mode of impression.

LIII

The *Idols of the Cave* take their rise in the peculiar constitution, mental or bodily, of each individual; and also in education, habit, and accident. Of this kind there is a great number and variety; but I will instance those the pointing out of which contains the most important caution, and which have most effect in disturbing the clearness of the understanding.

LIV

Men become attached to certain particular sciences and speculations, either because they fancy themselves the authors and inventors thereof, or because they have bestowed the greatest pains upon them and become most habituated to them. But men of this kind, if they betake themselves to philosophy and contemplations of a general character, distort and colour them in obedience to their former fancies; a thing especially to be noticed in Aristotle, who made his natural philosophy a mere bond-servant to his logic, thereby rendering it contentious and well nigh useless. The race of chemists[12] again out of a few experiments of the furnace have built up a fantastic philosophy, framed with reference to a few things; and Gilbert[22] also, after he had employed himself most laboriously in the study and observation of the loadstone, proceeded at once to construct an entire system in accordance with his favourite subject.

LV

There is one principle and as it were radical distinction between different minds, in respect of philosophy and the sciences; which is this: that some minds are stronger and apter to mark the differences of things, others to mark their resemblances.[23] The steady and acute mind can fix its contemplations and dwell and fasten on the subtlest distinctions: the lofty and discursive mind recognizes and puts together the finest and most general resemblances. Both kinds, however, easily err in excess, by catching the one at gradations the other at shadows.

LVI

There are found some minds given to an extreme admiration of antiquity, others to an extreme love and appetite for novelty; but few so duly tempered that they can hold the mean, neither carping at what has been well laid down by the ancients, nor despising what is well introduced by the moderns. This, however, turns to the great injury of the sciences and philosophy; since these affectations of antiquity and novelty are the humours of partisans rather than judgements; and truth is to be sought for not in the felicity of any age, which is an unstable thing, but in the light of nature and experience, which is eternal. These factions therefore must be abjured, and care must be taken that the intellect be not hurried by them into assent.[24]

LVII

Contemplations of nature and of bodies in their simple form break up and distract the understanding, while contemplations of nature and bodies in their composition and configuration overpower and dissolve the understanding: a distinction well seen in the school of Leucippus and Democritus as compared with the other philosophies. For that school is so busied with the particles that it hardly attends to the structure; while the others are so lost in admiration of the structure that they do not penetrate to the simplicity of nature. These kinds of contemplation should therefore be alternated and taken by turns; that so the understanding may be rendered at once penetrating and comprehensive, and the inconveniences above mentioned, with the idols which proceed from them, may be avoided.

LVIII

Let such then be our provision and contemplative prudence for keeping off and dislodging the *Idols of the Cave*, which grow for the most part either out of the predominance of a favourite subject, or out of an excessive tendency to compare or to distinguish or out of partiality for particular ages, or out of the largeness or minuteness of the objects contemplated. And generally let every student of nature take this as a rule—that whatever his mind seizes and dwells upon with peculiar satisfaction is to be held in suspicion, and that so much the more care is to be taken in dealing with such questions to keep the understanding even and clear.

LIX

But the *Idols of the Market-place* are the most troublesome of all: idols which have crept into the understanding through the alliances of words and names. For men believe that their reason governs words; but it is also true that words react on the understanding; and this it is that has rendered philosophy and the sciences sophistical and inactive. Now words, being commonly framed and applied according to the capacity of the vulgar, follow those lines of division which are most obvious to the vulgar understanding. And whenever an understanding of greater acuteness or a more diligent observation would alter those lines to suit the true divisions of nature, words stand in the way and resist the change. Whence it comes to pass that the high and formal discussions of learned men end oftentimes in disputes about words and names; with which (according to the use and wisdom of the mathematicians) it would be more prudent to begin, and so by means of definitions reduce them to order. Yet even definitions cannot cure this evil in dealing with natural and material things; since the definitions themselves consist of words, and those words beget others: so that it is necessary to recur to individual instances, and those in due series and order; as I shall say presently when I come to the method and scheme for the formation of notions and axioms.

LX

The idols imposed by words on the understanding are of two kinds. They are either names of things which do not exist (for as there are things left unnamed through lack of observation, so likewise are there names which result from fantastic suppositions and to which nothing in reality corresponds), or they are names of things which exist, but yet confused and ill defined, and hastily and irregularly derived from realities. Of the former kind are Fortune, the Prime Mover, Planetary Orbits, Element of Fire, and like fictions which owe their origin to false and idle theories. And this class of idols is more easily expelled, because to get rid of them it is only necessary that all theories should be steadily rejected and dismissed as obsolete.

But the other class, which springs out of a faulty and unskilful abstraction, is intricate and deeply rooted. Let us take for example such a word as *humid*; and see how far the several things which the word is used to signify agree with each other; and we shall find the word *humid* to be nothing else than a mark loosely and confusedly applied to denote a variety of actions which will not bear to be reduced to any constant meaning. For it both signifies that which easily spreads itself round any other body; and that which in itself is indeterminate and cannot solidise; and that which readily yields in every direction; and that which easily divides and scatters itself; and that which easily unites and collects itself; and that which readily flows and is put in motion; and that which readily clings to another body and wets it; and that which is easily reduced to a liquid, or being solid easily melts. Accordingly when you come to apply the word—if you take it in one sense, flame is humid; if in another, air is not humid; if in another, fine dust is humid; if in another, glass is humid. So that it is easy to see that the notion is taken by abstraction only from water and common and ordinary liquids, without any due verification.

There are, however, in words certain degrees of distortion and error. One of the least faulty kinds is that of names of substances, especially of lowest species and well deduced (for the notion of *chalk* and of *mud* is good, of *earth* bad); a more faulty kind is that of actions, as *to generate, to corrupt, to alter*; the most faulty is of qualities (except such as are the immediate objects of the sense) as *heavy, light, rare, dense*, and the like. Yet in all these cases some notions are of necessity a little better than others, in proportion to the greater variety of subjects that fall within the range of the human sense.

LXI

But the *Idols of the Theatre* are not innate, nor do they steal into the understanding secretly, but are plainly impressed and received into the mind from the play-books of philosophical systems and the perverted rules of demonstration. To attempt refutations in this case would be merely inconsistent with what I have already said: for since we agree neither upon principles nor upon demonstrations there is no place for argument. And this is so far well, inasmuch as it leaves the honour of the ancients untouched. For they are no wise disparaged—

the question between them and me being only as to the way. For as the saying is, the lame man who keeps the right road outstrips the runner who takes a wrong one. Nay it is obvious that when a man runs the wrong way, the more active and swift he is the further he will go astray.

But the course I propose for the discovery of sciences is such as leaves but little to the acuteness and strength of wits, but places all wits and understandings nearly on a level.[25] For as in the drawing of a straight line or perfect circle, much depends on the steadiness and practice of the hand, if it be done by aim of hand only, but if with the aid of rule or compass, little or nothing; so is it exactly with my plan. But though particular confutations would be of no avail, yet touching the sects and general divisions of such systems I must say something; something also touching the external signs which show that they are unsound; and finally something touching the causes of such great infelicity and of such lasting and general agreement in error; that so the access to truth may be made less difficult, and the human understanding may the more willingly submit to its purgation and dismiss its idols.

LXII

Idols of the Theatre, or of Systems, are many, and there can be and perhaps will be yet many more. For were it not that now for many ages men's minds have been busied with religion and theology; and were it not that civil governments, especially monarchies, have been averse to such novelties, even in matters speculative; so that men labour therein to the peril and harming of their fortunes, not only unrewarded, but exposed also to contempt and envy; doubtless there would have arisen many other philosophical sects like to those which in great variety flourished once among the Greeks. For as on the phenomena of the heavens many hypotheses may be constructed, so likewise (and more also) many various dogmas may be set up and established on the phenomena of philosophy. And in the plays of this philosophical theatre you may observe the same thing which is found in the theatre of the poets, that stories invented for the stage are more compact and elegant, and more as one would wish them to be, than true stories out of history.

In general, however, there is taken for the material of philosophy either a great deal out of a few things, or a very little out of many things; so that on both sides philosophy is based on too narrow a foundation of experiment and natural history, and decides on the authority of too few cases. For the Rational School of philosophers snatches from experience a variety of common instances neither duly ascertained nor diligently examined and weighed, and leaves all the rest to meditation and agitation of wit.

There is also another class of philosophers, who having bestowed much diligent and careful labour on a few experiments, have thence made bold to educe and construct systems; wresting all other facts in a strange fashion to conformity therewith.

And there is yet a third class, consisting of those who out of faith and veneration mix their philosophy with theology and traditions; among whom the vanity of some has gone so far aside as to seek the origin of sciences among spirits and genii. So that this parent stock of errors—this false philosophy—is of three kinds; the Sophistical, the Empirical, and the Superstitious.

LXIII

The most conspicuous example of the first class was Aristotle, who corrupted natural philosophy by his logic; fashioning the world out of categories; assigning to the human soul, the noblest of substances, a genus from words of the second intention;[26] doing the business of density and rarity (which is to make bodies of greater or less dimensions, that is, occupy greater or less spaces), by the frigid distinction of act and power; asserting that single bodies have each a single and proper motion, and that if they participate in any other, then this results from an external cause; and imposing countless other arbitrary restrictions on the nature of things; being always more solicitous to provide an answer to the question and affirm something positive in words, than about the inner truth of things; a failing best shown when his philosophy is compared with other systems of note among the Greeks. For the Homoeomera of Anaxagoras;[27] the Atoms of Leucippus and Democritus; the Heaven and Earth of Parmenides; the Strife and Friendship of Empedocles; Heraclitus's doctrine how bodies are resolved into the indifferent nature of fire, and remoulded into solids; have all of them some taste of the natural philosopher—some savour of the nature of things, and experience, and bodies; whereas in the physics of Aristotle you hear hardly anything but the words of logic; which in his metaphysics also, under a more imposing name, and more forsooth as a realist than a nominalist,[28] he has handled over again. Nor let any weight be given to the fact, that in his books on animals and his problems, and other of his treatises, there is frequent dealing with experiments. For he had come to his conclusion before; he did not consult experience, as he should have done, in order to the framing of his decisions and axioms; but having first determined the question according to his will, he then resorts to experience, and bending her into conformity with his placets leads her about like a captive in a procession; so that even on this count he is more guilty than his modern followers, the Schoolmen, who have abandoned experience altogether.

LXIV

But the Empirical school of philosophy gives birth to dogmas more deformed and monstrous than the Sophistical or Rational school. For it has its foundations not in the light of common notions (which though it be a faint and superficial light, is yet in a manner universal, and has reference to many things), but in the narrowness and darkness of a few experiments. To those therefore who are daily busied with these experiments, and have infected their imagination with them, such a philosophy seems probable and all but certain; to all men else incredible and vain. Of this there is a notable instance in the alchemists and their dogmas; though it is hardly to be found elsewhere in these times, except perhaps in the philosophy of Gilbert. Nevertheless with regard to philosophies of this kind there is one caution not to be omitted; for I foresee that if ever men are roused by my admonitions to betake themselves seriously to experiment and bid farewell to sophistical doctrines, then indeed through the premature hurry of the understanding to leap or fly to universals and principles of things, great danger may be apprehended from philosophies of this kind; against which evil we ought even now to prepare.

LXV

But the corruption of philosophy by superstition and an admixture of theology is far more widely spread, and does the greatest harm, whether to entire systems or to their parts. For the human understanding is obnoxious to the influence of the imagination no less than to the influence of common notions. For the contentious and sophistical kind of philosophy ensnares the understanding; but this kind, being fanciful and tumid and half poetical, misleads it more by flattery. For there is in man an ambition of the understanding, no less than of the will, especially in high and lofty spirits.

Of this kind we have among the Greeks a striking example in Pythagoras, though he united with it a coarser and more cumbrous superstition; another in Plato and his school, more dangerous and subtle. It shows itself likewise in parts of other philosophies, in the introduction of abstract forms and final causes and first causes, with the omission in most cases of causes intermediate, and the like. Upon this point the greatest caution should be used. For nothing is so mischievous as the apotheosis of error; and it is a very plague of the understanding for vanity to become the object of veneration. Yet in this vanity some of the moderns have with extreme levity indulged so far as to attempt to found a system of natural philosophy on the first chapter of Genesis, on the book of Job, and other parts of the sacred writings; seeking for the dead among the

living:[29] which also makes the inhibition and repression of it the more important, because from this unwholesome mixture of things human and divine there
arises not only a fantastic philosophy but also an heretical religion. Very meet
it is therefore that we be sober-minded, and give to faith that only which is
faith's.

★   ★   ★

LXVIII

So much concerning the several classes of Idols, and their equipage: all of which
must be renounced and put away with a fixed and solemn determination, and
the understanding thoroughly freed and cleansed; the entrance into the kingdom
of man, founded on the sciences, being not much other than the entrance into
the kingdom of heaven, whereinto none may enter except as a little child.

Essays

The first ten essays printed in 1597 are collections of statements of what Bacon regarded as facts; statements such as 'Costly followers are not to be liked', 'Riches are for spending', 'Discrete followers help much to reputation.' They merge imperceptibly with the two or three proverbs that are quoted, 'Light gains make heavy purses', 'Lookers on many times see more than gamesters.' Occasionally the statements are linked in simple argument, by such words as 'therefore', 'because', 'but', and 'if'. But mostly they simply follow each other. They are the results of Bacon's observation of the behaviour of politicians at Elizabeth's court: 'There is little friendship in the world, and least of all between equals.' His observation does not issue in anecdote or personal tales, but in general axioms that are abstracted from particulars. The result is a valuable collection of politic aphorisms, different from those uttered by Polonius only because they are much better.

There are three surprising interlopers, in the observations *Of Studie*, *Of Expence* and *Of Regiment of health*. Here the Bacon who is always at his book and always not very well and always in debt, puts down what he has observed about his personal obsessions. And the result is just as cool and distant a series of aphorisms as those on political behaviour.

During the next 15 years Bacon added to the essays already written, and wrote 29 new ones. Some of the latter are expansions of the discussions, in the second book of the *Advancement*, of the deficiencies in civil knowledge. They fill gaps in the study of practical psychology, ethics and sociology. They go on in the same way as the original seven politic essays, stating what men *do* rather than what they ought to do. But others deal with more general topics—death, love, friendship, beauty, superstition. And to the lists of pregnantly expressed observations, Bacon now adds illustrative anecdotes from history, quotations, and sometimes a pithy opening and conclusion, with linked argument in between. He does not exhort the reader, but he sometimes adopts a lofty moral tone which pushes an essay away from observation of what

actually happens towards a fervent statement of what should happen—
as in the account of the duties of a Judge.

This process of expansion continued in the edition of 1625, which
has 58 essays. During the years, Bacon had put down his ideas on
subjects that he was not a little pleased to notice 'come home to men's
business and bosoms'. They were subjects 'whereof a man shall find
much in experience, little in books', and he treated each one briefly
and pithily. He valued them for the ideas—he believed that the Latin
translation would 'last as long as Books last'. The ideas had been
collected over a long period. For some of the essays he had gone to
his collection of *Antitheta* (maxims arranged pro and contra some
topic such as Boldness), and expanded both sides of the arguments
locked up in his brief sentences. Sometimes he had clearly gone to his
commonplace-book where he had jotted down ideas, his own and
other people's, under headings. The ideas in the essays are good, and
most of them, when Bacon wrote them down, were being written
down for the first time. But had he written the essays in Latin they
would not have survived. And this he must have realized. For he did
in fact write them in English, and took care to mould and polish each
sentence. The idea may sometimes have been suggested by a Latin
source, as Lucretius suggested to Bacon 'Men fear death as children
fear to go in the dark.' But the idea has been thought and felt in English.
One might say that when Bacon is writing at his best he does not even
quote Latin. In *Of Revenge*, for example, he translates his quotations
without giving the original Latin. In *Of Adversity* he quotes Seneca only
to show that his translation is a match for him in balance, brevity and
rhyme. In *Of Truth* the only Latin is *Vinum Daemonum*, and one can
imagine Bacon trying many English equivalents before deciding that
it lost its power in translation.

The *Essays* are not written in any one style, though the styles all
tend towards Senecan 'pointed expressions and short periods'. The
growing popularity of Senecan prose in English at the end of Bacon's
life led him to condemn this style as 'no more than a jingle, or peculiar
quaint affectation of words'. His own example justifies this—*It is true
greatnesse, to haue in one, the Frailty of a Man, & the Security of a God.
Vere magnum, habere Fragilitatem Hominis, Securitatem Dei.*

Both Seneca and Bacon are able to balance ideas as well as words.

But Bacon's pursuit of brevity and epigrammatic point is only part of his style. The *Essays* are just as full of such sentences as 'The vices of *Authoritie* are chiefly foure . . .' and 'Now to speake of Publique Envy', sentences busy organizing the material. Or one meets great lists, in *Of Travel* and *Of Gardens*. Sometimes the style is no more than colloquial rudeness, 'Let the Songs be *Loud*, and *Cheerefull*, and not *Chirpings*, or *Pulings*', or colloquial ease, 'There is a Toy, which I have heard, and I would not have it given over, but waited upon a little.' It is the opening sentences of the *Essays* that are memorable because they are startling, shrewd, simple, rhythmically pleasing. No matter how familiar they become they never lose the air of newness with which Bacon has invested them.

The following selection represents the range of styles—the list of aphorisms in the 1597 version of the essay *Of Studies*, the slightly looser aphoristic form of the 1625 *Of Adversity*, the noble exposition in *Of Judicature*, the demonstrative balance of the essay *Of Cunning*, and so on. The topics also suggest Bacon's range in the *Essays*, and show him writing on matters near to his heart, (as Truth, Studies, Great Place, Judicature), on politics (Cunning, Simulation), on light relaxation (Masques), and on topics such as Marriage, Revenge, Death, on which every man may be expected to have ideas.

Each of the three editions of the *Essays* has its own dedication, but in addition is the one printed below, a dedication of the 1612 edition to Prince Henry, whose death prevented its being used. It tells one more about the essays than the three more familiar dedications.

Dedication (intended for 1612 edition)

To the most high and excellent Prince Henry, Prince of Wales,
Duke of Cornwall and Earl of Chester.
It may please your Highness
Having divided my life into the contemplative and active part, I
am desirous to give his Majesty, and your Highness of the fruit of both, simple
though they be. To write just treatises requireth leisure in the writer, and
leisure in the reader, and therefore are not so fit, neither in regard of your
Highness' princely affairs, nor in regard of my continual service, which is the
cause, that hath made me choose to write certain brief notes, set down rather
significantly, than curiously, which I have called Essays. The word is late, but
the thing is ancient. For Seneca's *Epistles to Lucilius*, if one mark them well, are
but Essays—That is dispersed meditations, though conveyed in the form of
epistles. These labours of mine I know cannot be worthy of your Highness, for
what can be worthy of you. But my hope is, they may be as grains of salt, that
will rather give you an appetite than offend you with satiety. And although
they handle those things wherein both men's lives and their pens are most
conversant, yet (what I have attained I know not) but I have endeavoured to
make them not vulgar; but of a nature, whereof a man shall find much in
experience, little in books; so as they are neither repetitions nor fancies. But
howsoever, I shall most humbly desire your Highness to accept them in gracious
part, and so contrive that if I cannot rest, but must show my dutiful and
devoted affection to your Highness in these things which proceed from my
self, I shall be much more ready to do it, in performance of your princely
commandment; And so wishing your Highness all princely felicity I rest.
Your Highness' most humble
Servant.

Of Studies

STudies serue for pastimes, for ornaments & for abilities.[1] Their chiefe vse for pastime is in priuatenes and retiring;[2] for ornamente is in discourse, and for abilitie is in iudgement. For expert men[3] can execute, but learned men are fittest to iudge or censure.

To spend too much time in them is slouth, to vse them too much for ornament is affectation: to make iudgement wholly by their rules, is the humour[4] of a Scholler.

They perfect *Nature*, and are perfected by experience.

Craftie men[5] contemne them, simple men admire them, wise men vse them: For they teach not their owne vse, but that is a wisedome without them: and aboue them wonne by obseruation.

Reade not to contradict, nor to belieue, but to waigh and consider. Some bookes are to bee tasted, others to bee swallowed, and some few to bee chewed and digested: That is, some bookes are to be read only in partes; others to be read, but cursorily, and some few to be read wholly and with diligence and attention.

Reading maketh a full man, conference[6] a readye man, and writing[7] an exacte man. And therefore if a man write little, he had neede haue a great memorie, if he conferre little, he had neede haue a present wit, and if he reade little, he had neede haue much cunning, to seeme to know that he doth not.

Histories make men wise, Poets wittie:[8] the Mathematickes subtle, naturall Phylosophie deepe: Morall graue, Logicke and Rhetoricke able to contend.

Of Truth

WHAT is *Truth*; said jesting *Pilate*;[1] And would not stay for an Answer. Certainly there be, that delight in Giddinesse;[2] And count it a Bondage, to fix a Beleefe; Affecting Free-will in Thinking, as well as in Acting. And though the Sects of Philosophers of that Kinde be gone, yet there remaine certaine discoursing Wits,[3] which are of the same veines, though there be not so much Bloud in them, as was in those of the Ancients. But it is not onely the Difficultie, and Labour, which Men take in finding out of *Truth*; Nor againe, that when it is found, it imposeth[4] vpon mens Thoughts; that doth bring *Lies* in fauour: But a naturall, though corrupt Loue, of the *Lie* it selfe. One of the later Schoole of the Grecians,[5] examineth the matter, and is at a stand, to thinke what should be in it, that men should loue *Lies*; Where neither they make for Pleasure, as with Poets; Nor for Aduantage, as with the Merchant; but for the *Lies* sake. But I cannot tell: This same *Truth*, is a Naked, and Open day light,[6] that doth not shew, the Masques, and Mummeries, and Triumphs of the world, halfe so Stately, and daintily, as Candlelights. *Truth* may perhaps come to the price of a Pearle, that sheweth best by day: But it will not rise, to the price of a Diamond, or Carbuncle, that sheweth best in varied lights. A mixture of a *Lie* doth euer adde Pleasure. Doth any man doubt, that if there were taken out of Mens Mindes, Vaine Opinions, Flattering Hopes, False valuations, Imaginations as one would, and the like; but it would leaue the Mindes, of a Number of Men, poore shrunken Things; full of Melancholy, and Indisposition, and vnpleasing to themselues? One of the Fathers,[7] in great Seuerity, called Poesie, *Vinum Daemonum*; because it filleth the Imagination, and yet it is, but with the shadow of a *Lie*. But it is not the *Lie*, that passeth through the Minde, but the *Lie* that sinketh in, and setleth in it, that doth the hurt, such as we spake of before. But howsoeuer these things are thus, in mens depraued Iudgements, and Affections, yet *Truth*, which only doth iudge it selfe, teacheth, that the Inquirie of *Truth*, which is the Loue-making, or Wooing of it; The knowledge of *Truth*, which is the Presence of it; and the Beleefe of *Truth*, which is the Enioying of it; is the Soueraigne Good of humane Nature. The first Creature of God, in the workes of the Dayes, was the Light of the Sense; The last, was the Light of Reason; and his Sabbath Worke, euer since, is the Illumination of his Spirit.

First he breathed Light, vpon the Face, of the Matter or Chaos; Then he breathed Light, into the Face of Man; and still he breathed and inspireth Light, into the Face of his Chosen. The Poet,[8] that beautified the Sect, that was otherwise inferiour to the rest, saith yet excellently well: *It is a pleasure to stand vpon the shore, and to see ships tost vpon the Sea: A pleasure to stand in the window of a Castle, and to see a Battaile, and the Adventures thereof, below: But no pleasure is comparable, to the standing, vpon the vantage ground of Truth*: (a hill not to be commanded,[9] and where the Ayre is alwaies cleare and serene;) *And to see the Errours, and Wandrings, and Mists, and Tempests, in the vale below:* So alwaies, that this prospect, be with Pitty,[10] and not with Swelling, or Pride. Certainly, it is Heauen vpon Earth, to haue a Mans Minde Moue in Charitie,[11] Rest in Prouidence, and Turne vpon the Poles of *Truth*.

To passe from Theologicall, and Philosophicall *Truth*, to the *Truth* of ciuill Businesse;[12] It will be acknowledged, euen by those, that practize it not, that cleare and Round dealing, is the Honour of Mans Nature; and that Mixture of Falshood, is like Allay in Coyne of Gold and Siluer; which may make the Metall worke the better, but it embaseth it. For these winding, and crooked courses, are the Goings of the Serpent; which goeth basely vpon the belly, and not vpon the Feet. There is no Vice, that doth so couer a Man with Shame, as to be found false, and perfidious. And therefore *Mountaigny*[13] saith prettily, when he enquired the reason, why the word of the *Lie*, should be such a Disgrace, and such an Odious Charge? Saith he, *If it be well weighed, To say that a man lieth, is as much to say, as that he is braue towards God, and a Coward towards Men.* For a *Lie* faces God, and shrinkes from Man. Surely the Wickednesse of Falshood, and Breach of Faith, cannot possibly be so highly expressed, as in that it shall be the last Peale, to call the Iudgements of God, vpon the Generations of Men, It being fore-told, that when Christ commeth, *He shall not finde Faith vpon the Earth.*[14]

REuenge is a kinde of Wilde[1] Iustice; which the more Mans Nature runs to, the more ought Law to weed it out. For as for the first Wrong, it doth but offend the Law; but the *Reuenge* of that wrong, putteth the Law out of Office. Certainly, in taking *Reuenge*, A Man is but euen with his Enemy; But in passing it ouer, he is Superiour: For it is a Princes part to Pardon. And *Salomon*,[2] I am sure, saith, *It is the Glory of a Man to passe by an offence*. That which is past, is gone, and Irreuocable; And wise Men haue Enough to doe, with things present, and to come: Therefore, they doe but trifle with themselues, that labour in past matters. There is no man, doth a wrong, for the wrongs sake; But therby to purchase himselfe, Profit, or Pleasure, or Honour, or the like. Therfore why should I be angry with a Man, for louing himselfe better then mee? And if any Man should do wrong, meerely out of ill nature, why? yet it is but like the Thorn, or Bryar, which prick, and scratch, because they can doe no other. The most Tolerable Sort of *Reuenge*, is for those wrongs which there is no Law to remedy: But then, let a man take heed, the *Reuenge* be such as there is no law to punish: Else, a Mans Enemy, is still before hand, And it is two for one. Some, when they take *Reuenge*, are Desirous the party should know, whence it commeth: This is the more Generous. For the Delight seemeth to be, not so much in doing the Hurt, as in Making the Party repent: But Base and Crafty Cowards, are like the Arrow,[3] that flyeth in the Darke. *Cosmus* Duke of *Florence*,[4] had a Desperate Saying, against Perfidious or Neglecting Friends, as if those wrongs were vnpardonable: *You shall reade* (saith he) *that we are commanded to forgiue our Enemies; But you neuer read, that wee are commanded, to forgiue our Friends*. But yet the Spirit of *Iob*,[5] was in a better tune; *Shall wee* (saith he) *take good at Gods Hands, and not be content to take euill also*? And so of Friends in a proportion.[6] This is certaine; That a Man that studieth *Reuenge*, keepes his owne Wounds greene, which otherwise would heale, and doe well. Publique *Reuenges*, are, for the most part, Fortunate;[7] As that for the Death of *Caesar*; For the Death of *Pertinax*; for the Death of *Henry* the Third of France; And many more. But in priuate *Reuenges* it is not so. Nay rather, Vindicatiue Persons liue the Life of Witches; who as they are Mischieuous, So end they Infortunate.

Of Aduersitie

IT was an high speech[1] of *Seneca* (after the manner of the Stoickes) *That the good things, which belong to Prosperity, are to be wished; but the good things, that belong to Aduersity, are to be admired. Bona Rerum Secundarum, Optabilia; Aduersarum, Mirabilia.* Certainly if Miracles, be the Command ouer Nature, they appeare most in Aduersity. It is yet a higher speech of his, then the other, (much too high[2] for a Heathen) *It is true greatnesse, to haue in one, the Frailty of a Man, & the Security[3] of a God. Vere magnum, habere Fragilitatem Hominis, Securitatem Dei.* This would haue done better in Poesy; where Transcendences[4] are more allowed. And the Poets indeed, haue beene busy with it; For it is, in effect, the thing, which is figured in that Strange Fiction,[5] of the Ancient Poets, which seemeth not to be without mystery; Nay, and to haue some approach, to the State of a Christian: That *Hercules, when hee went to vnbinde Prometheus* (by whom Humane Nature is represented) *sailed the length of the great Ocean, in an Earthen Pot, or Pitcher*: Liuely describing Christian Resolution;[6] that saileth, in the fraile Barke of the Flesh, thorow the Waues of the World, But to speake in a Meane.[7] The Vertue of *Prosperitie*, is Temperance; The Vertue of *Aduersity*, is Fortitude: which in Morals is the more Heroicall Vertue. *Prosperity* is the Blessing of the Old Testament; *Aduersity*[8] is the Blessing of the New; which carrieth the greater Benediction, and the Clearer Reuelation of Gods Fauour. Yet, euen in the old Testament, if you Listen to *Dauids* Harpe, you shall heare as many Herselike Ayres, as Carols: and the Pencill of the holy Ghost, hath laboured more, in describing, the Afflictions of *Iob*, then the Felicities of *Salomon*. *Prosperity* is not without many Feares and Distastes; and *Aduersity* is not without Comforts and Hopes. Wee see in Needleworkes, and Imbroideries, It is more pleasing, to haue a Liuely Worke, vpon a Sad and Solemne Ground; then to haue a Darke and Melancholy Worke, vpon a Lightsome Ground: Iudge therfore, of the Pleasure of the Heart, by the Pleasure of the Eye. Certainly, Vertue is like pretious Odours, most fragrant, when they are incensed, or crushed: For *Prosperity* doth best discouer Vice; but *Aduersity* doth best discouer Vertue.

Of Iudicature

IUdges ought to remember, that their Office is *Ius dicere*, and not *Ius dare; To Interpret Law*, and not to *Make Law*, or *Giue Law*. Else will it be like the Authority, claimed by the *Church* of *Rome;* which vnder pretext of Exposition of Scripture, doth not sticke to Adde and Alter; And to Pronounce[1] that, which they doe not Finde; and by *Shew*[2] of *Antiquitie*, to introduce *Noueltie. Iudges* ought to be more Learned, then Wittie;[3] More Reuerend, then Plausible;[4] And more Aduised,[5] then Confident. Aboue all Things, Integritie is their Portion, and Proper Vertue. *Cursed* (saith the Law) *is hee that remoueth the Landmarke.*[6] The Mislaier of a *Meere Stone*[7] is to blame. But it is the Vniust *Iudge,* that is the Capitall Remouer of Land-markes, when he Defineth amisse of Lands and Propertie. One Foule Sentence, doth more Hurt, then many Foule Examples. For these doe but Corrupt the Streame; The other Corrupteth the Fountaine. So saith *Salomon; Fons turbatus, & Vena corrupta, est Iustus cadens in causâ suâ coram Aduersario.*[8] The Office of *Iudges*, may haue Reference, Vnto the *Parties that sue;* Vnto the *Aduocates that Plead;* Vnto the *Clerkes* and *Ministers of Iustice* vnderneath them; And to the *Soueraigne* or *State* aboue them.

First, for the *Causes* or *Parties that Sue. There be* (saith the Scripture[9]) *that turne Iudgement into Worme-wood;* And surely, there be also, that turne it into *Vinegar;* For Iniustice maketh it Bitter, and Delaies make it Soure. The Principall Dutie of a *Iudge*, is to suppresse Force and Fraud; whereof Force is the more Pernicious, when it is Open; and Fraud, when it is Close and Disguised. Adde thereto Contentious Suits, which ought to be spewed out, as the Surfet of Courts. A *Iudge* ought to prepare his Way to a Iust Sentence, as *God* vseth to prepare his Way, by *Raising Valleys*, and *Taking downe Hills:*[10] So when there appeareth on either side, an High Hand; Violent Prosecution, Cunning Aduantages taken, Combination, Power, Great Counsell, then is the Vertue of a *Iudge* seene, to make Inequalitie Equall; That he may plant his *Iudgement*, as vpon an Euen Ground. *Qui fortiter emungit, elicit sanguinem;*[11] And where the Wine-Presse is hard wrought, it yeelds a harsh Wine, that tastes of the Grapestone. *Iudges* must beware of Hard Constructions, and Strained Inferences; For there is no Worse Torture, then the Torture of Lawes, Specially in case of Lawes Penall, they ought to haue Care, that that which was meant for Terrour,[12] be not turned into Rigour; And that they bring not vpon the People, that Shower, whereof the Scripture speaketh; *Pluet super eos Laqueos*:[13] For Penall Lawes Pressed, are a *Shower of Snares* vpon the People. Therefore, let *Penall Lawes*, if they haue beene Sleepers of long, or if they be growne vnfit for the present Time, be by Wise *Iudges* confined in the Execution; *Iudicis Officium est, vt Res, ita Tempora Rerum, &c.*[14] In *Causes* of *Life* and *Death: Iudges* ought (as farre as the Law permitteth) in Iustice to remember Mercy; And to Cast a Seuere Eye vpon the Example, but a Mercifull Eye vpon the Person.

Secondly, for the *Aduocates* and *Counsell that Plead: Patience* and Grauitie of Hearing, is an Essential Part of Iustice; And an Ouerspeaking *Iudge* is no *well tuned Cymball*.[15] It is no Grace to a *Iudge*, first to finde that, which hee might haue heard, in due time, from the Barre; or to shew Quickness of Conceit in Cutting off Euidence or Counsell too short; Or to preuent Information, by Questions though Pertinent. The Parts of a *Iudge* in Hearing are Foure: To direct the Euidence; To Moderate Length, Repetition, or Impertinency of Speech; to Recapitulate, Select, and Collate, the Materiall Points of that, which hath beene said; And to Giue the Rule or Sentence. Whatsoeuer is aboue these, is too much; and proceedeth, Either of Glory and willingness to Speake; or of Impatience to Heare; Or of Shortnesses of Memorie; Or of Want of a Staid and Equall Attention. It is a Strange Thing to see, that the Boldness of *Aduocates*, should preuaile with *Iudges*; Whereas they should imitate *God*, in whose Seat they sit; who *represseth the Presumptuous*,[16] and *giueth Grace to the Modest*. But it is more Strange, that *Iudges* should haue Noted Fauourites; Which cannot but Cause Multiplication of Fees, and Suspicion of By-waies.[17] There is due from the *Iudge*, to the *Aduocate*, some Commendation and Gracing, where *Causes* are well Handled, and faire Pleaded; Especially towards the Side which obtaineth not; For that vpholds, in the *Client*, the Reputation of his *Counsell*, and beats downe, in him, the Conceit of his *Cause*. There is likewise due to the *Publique*, a Ciuill Reprehension of *Aduocates*, where there appeareth Cunning Counsel, Grosse Neglect, Slight Information, Indiscreet Pressing, or an Ouer-bold Defence. And let not the *Counsell* at the Barre, chop[18] with the *Iudge*, nor winde himselfe into the handling of the *Cause* anew, after the *Iudge* hath Declared his Sentence: But on the other side, Let not the *Iudge* meet the *Cause* halfe Way; Nor giue Occasion to the Partie to say; *His Counsell or Proofes were not heard*.

Thirdly, for that that concernes *Clerkes*, and *Ministers*. The Place of *Iustice*, is an Hallowed Place; And therefore, not only the Bench, but the Foot-pace,[19] and Precincts, and Purprise thereof, ought to be preserued without Scandall and Corruption. For certainly, *Grapes* (as the *Scripture* saith) *will not be gathered of Thornes or Thistles*:[29] Neither can *Iustice* yeeld her Fruit with Sweetnesse, amongst the Briars and Brambles, of Catching and Poling[21] *Clerkes* and

Ministers. The Attendance of Courts is subiect to Foure bad Instruments. First, Certaine Persons, that are the Sowers of Suits; which make the Court swell, and the Country pine. The Second Sort is of those, that ingage Courts, in Quarells of Iurisdiction, and are not truly *Amici Curiae*,[22] but *Parasiti Curiae*; in puffing a Court vp beyond her Bounds, for their owne Scraps, and Aduantage. The Third Sort is of those, that may be accounted, the Left Hands of Courts; Persons that are full of Nimble and Sinister Trickes and Shifts, whereby they peruert the Plaine and Direct Courses of *Courts*, and bring *Iustice* into Oblique Lines and Labyrinths. And the Fourth is, the Poler[23] and Exacter of Fees; which iustifies the Common Resemblance of the *Courts* of *Iustice*, to the *Bush*, whereunto while the Sheepe flies for defence in Wether,[24] hee is sure to loose Part of his Fleece. On the other side, an *Ancient Clerke*, skilfull in Presidents, Wary in Proceeding, and Vnderstanding in the *Businesse* of the *Court*, is an excellent Finger of a *Court*; And doth many times point the way to the *Iudge* himselfe.

Fourthly, for that which may concerne the *Soueraigne* and *Estate*. *Iudges* ought aboue all to remember the Conclusion of the *Roman Twelve Tables; Salus Populi Suprema Lex;*[25] And to know, that Lawes, except they bee in Order to that End, are but Things Captious, and Oracles not well Inspired. Therefore it is an Happie Thing in a *State*, when *Kings* and *States* doe often Consult[26] with *Iudges*; And againe, when *Iudges* doe often Consult with the *King* and *State*: The one, when there is Matter of Law, interuenient[27] in Businesse of State; the other, when there is some Consideration of State, interuenient in Matter of Law. For many times, the Things Deduced to *Iudgement*, may bee *Meum* and *Tuum*, when the Reason and Consequence thereof, may Trench to[28] Point of Estate: I call Matter of Estate, not onely the parts of *Soueraigntie*, but whatsoeuer introduceth any Great Alteration, or Dangerous president; Or Concerneth manifestly any great Portion of People. And let no Man weakly conceiue, that Iust Laws, and True Policie, haue any *Antipathie*: For they are like the Spirits, and Sinewes, that One moues with the Other. Let *Iudges* also remember, that *Salomons Throne*,[29] was supported by Lions, on both Sides; Let them be Lions, but yet Lions vnder the Throne; Being circumspect, that they doe not checke, or oppose any Points of *Soueraigntie*. Let not *Iudges* also, be so Ignorant of their owne Right, as to thinke, there is not left to them, as a Principall Part of their Office, a Wise Vse, and application of Lawes. For they may remember, what the *Apostle*[30] saith, of a Greater *Law*, then theirs; *Nos scimus quia Lex bona est, modò quis eâ vtatur Legitimè.*

Of Marriage and Single Life

HE that hath *Wife* and *Children*, hath giuen Hostages to Fortune; For they are Impediments, to great Enterprises, either of Vertue, or Mischiefe. Certainly, the best workes, and of greatest Merit for the Publike, haue proceeded from the *vnmarried*, or *Childlesse Men*; which, both in Affection, and Meanes, haue married and endowed the Publike. Yet it were great Reason, that those that haue *Children*, should haue greatest care of future times;[1] vnto which, they know, they must transmit, their dearest pledges. Some there are, who though they lead a *Single Life*, yet their Thoughts doe end with themselues, and account future Times, Impertinences.[2] Nay, there are some other, that account *Wife* and *Children*, but as Bills of charges. Nay more, there are some foolish rich couetous Men, that take a pride in hauing no *Children*, because they may be thought, so much the richer. For perhaps, they haue heard some talke; *Such an one is a great rich Man*; And another except to it; *Yea, but he hath a great charge of Children*: As if it were an Abatement to his Riches. But the most ordinary cause of a *Single Life*, is Liberty; especially, in certaine Selfe-pleasing, and humorous[3] Mindes, which are so sensible of euery restraint, as they will goe neare, to think their Girdles, and Garters, to be Bonds and Shackles. *Vnmarried Men* are best Friends; best Masters; best Seruants; but not alwayes best Subiects; For they are light to runne away; And almost all Fugitiues are of that Condition. A *Single Life* doth well with Church men; For Charity will hardly water the Ground, where it must first fill a Poole. It is indifferent for Iudges and Magistrates: For if they be facile, and corrupt, you shall haue a Seruant, fiue times worse than a *Wife*. For Souldiers, I finde the Generalls commonly in their Hortatiues, put Men in minde of their *Wiues and Children*: And I thinke the Despising of *Marriage*, amongst the Turkes, maketh the vulgar souldier more base. Certainly, *Wife* and *Children*, are a kinde of Discipline of Humanity: And *single Men*, though they be many times more Charitable, because their Meanes are lesse exhaust; yet, on the other side, they are more cruell, and hard hearted, (good to make seuere Inquisitors) because their Tendernesse, is not so oft called vpon. Graue Natures, led by Custome, and therefore constant, are commonly louing *Husbands*; As was said of *Vlysses; Vetulam suam praetulit Immortalitati*.[4] Chast Women are often Proud, and froward, as Presuming vpon the Merit of their Chastity. It is one of the best Bonds, both of Chastity and Obedience, in the *Wife,* if She thinke her *Husband* Wise; which She will neuer doe, if she finde him *Iealous. Wiues* are young Mens Mistresses; Companions for middle Age; and old Mens Nurses. So as a Man may haue a Quarrell[5] to marry, when he will. But yet, he was reputed one of the wise Men,[6] that made Answer to the Question; When a Man should marry? *A young Man not yet, an Elder Man not at all.* It is often seene, that bad *Husbands,* haue very good *Wiues;* whether it be, that it rayseth[7] the Price of their *Husbands* Kindnesse, when it comes; Or that the *Wiues* take a Pride, in their Patience. But this neuer fails, if the bad *Husbands* were of their owne choosing, against their Friends consent; For then, they will be sure, to make good their owne Folly.

Of Loue

THe Stage is more beholding to *Loue*, then the Life of Man.[1] For as to the Stage, *Loue* is euer matter of Comedies, and now and then of Tragedies: But in Life, it doth much mischiefe: Sometimes like a *Syren*; Sometimes like a *Fury*. You may obserue, that amongst all the great and worthy Persons, (whereof the memory remaineth, either Ancient or Recent) there is not One, that hath been transported, to the mad degree of *Loue*: which shewes, that great Spirits,[2] and great Businesse, doe keepe out this weake Passion. You must except, neuerthelesse, *Marcus Antonius*, the halfe Partner of the Empire of *Rome;* and *Appius Claudius*[3] the *Decemuir*, and Lawgiuer: Whereof the former, was indeed a Voluptuous Man, and Inordinate; but the latter, was an Austere, and wise man: And therefore it seemes (though rarely) that *Loue* can finde entrance, not only into an open Heart; but also into a Heart well fortified; if watch be not well kept. It is a poore Saying of *Epicurus; Satis magnum Alter Alteri Theatrum sumus:*[4] As if Man, made for the contemplation of Heauen, and all Noble Obiects, should doe nothing, but kneele before a little Idoll,[5] and make himselfe subiect, though not of the Mouth (as Beasts are) yet of the Eye; which was giuen him for higher Purposes. It is a strange Thing, to note the Excesse of this Passion; And how it braues,[6] the Nature, and value of things; by this, that the Speaking in a perpetuall *Hyperbole*, is comely in nothing, but in *Loue*. Neither is it meerely in the Phrase;[7] For whereas it hath beene well said, that the Arch-flatterer,[8] with whom all the petty Flatterers haue Intelligence, is a Mans Selfe; Certainly, the *Louer* is more. For there was neuer Proud Man, thought so absurdly well of himselfe, as the *Louer* doth of the Person *loued*: And therefore, it was well said; *That it is impossible to loue, and to be wise.*[9] Neither doth this weaknesse appeare to others onely, and not to the Party *Loued*; But to the *Loued*, most of all: except the *Loue* be reciproque.[10] For, it is a true Rule, that *Loue* is ever rewarded, either with the Reciproque, or with an inward, and secret Contempt. By how much the more, Men ought to beware of this Passion, which loseth not only other things but it selfe. As for the other losses, the Poets Relation,[11] doth well figure them; That he that preferred *Helena*, quitted the Gifts of *Iuno*, and *Pallas*. For whosoeuer esteemeth too much of Amorous Affection, quitteth both *Riches*, and *Wisedome*. This Passion, hath his Flouds, in the very times of Weaknesse; which are, great *Prosperitie*; and great *Aduersitie*; though this latter hath beene lesse obserued. Both which times kindle *Loue*, and make it more feruent, and therefore shew it to be the Childe of Folly. They doe best, who, if they cannot but admit *Loue*, yet make it keepe Quarter: And seuer it wholly, from their serious Affaires, and Actions of Life: For if it checke[12] once with Businesse, it troubleth Mens Fortunes, and maketh Men, that they can, no wayes be true, to their owne Ends. I know not how, but Martiall Men, are giuen to *Loue*: I thinke it is, but as they are giuen to *Wine*; For *Perils*, commonly aske, to be paid in *Pleasures*. There is in Mans Nature, a secret Inclination, and Motion, towards *loue* of others; which, if it be not spent, vpon some one, or a few, doth naturally spread it selfe, towards many; and maketh men become Humane, and Charitable; As it is seene sometime in Friars. Nuptiall *loue* maketh Mankinde; Friendly *loue* perfecteth it; but Wanton *loue* Corrupteth, and Imbaseth it.

MEn feare *Death*, as Children feare to goe in the darke:[1] And as that Natural Feare in Children, is increased with Tales,[2] so is the other. Certainly, the Contemplation of *Death*, as the *wages of sinne*, and Passage to another world, is Holy, and Religious; But the Feare of it, as a Tribute due vnto Nature, is weake. Yet in Religious Meditations, there is sometimes, Mixture of Vanitie, and of Superstition. You shal reade, in some of the Friars Books of *Mortification*,[3] that a man should thinke with himselfe, what the Paine is, if he haue but his Fingers end Pressed, or Tortured; And thereby imagine, what the Paines of *Death* are, when the whole Body, is corrupted and dissolued; when many times, *Death* passeth with lesse paine, then the Torture of a Limme: For the most vitall parts, are not the quickest of Sense. And by him, that spake onely as a Philosopher, and Naturall Man,[4] it was well said; *Pompa Mortis magis terret, quam Mors ipsa.* Groanes and Conuulsions, and a discoloured Face, and Friends weeping, and Blackes,[5] and Obsequies, and the like, shew *Death* Terrible. It is worthy the obseruing, that there is no passion in the minde of man, so weake, but it Mates,[6] and Masters, the Feare of *Death*: And therefore Death, is no such terrible Enemie, when a man hath so many Attendants, about him, that can winne the combat of him. *Reuenge* triumphs ouer *Death*; *Loue* slights it; *Honour* aspireth to it; *Griefe* flieth to it; *Feare* pre-occupateth it;[7] Nay we reade, after *Otho*[8] the Emperour had slaine himselfe, *Pitty* (which is the tenderest of Affections) prouoked many to die, out of meere compassion to their Soueraigne, and as the truest sort of Followers. Nay *Seneca* addes *Nicenesse*[9] *& Saciety; Cogita quam diù eadem feceris; Mori velle, non tantùm Fortis, aut Miser, sed etiam Fastidiosus potest.* A man would die, though he were neither valiant, nor miserable, onely vpon a wearinesse to doe the same thing, so oft ouer and ouer. It is no lesse worthy to obserue, how little Alteration, in good Spirits, the Approaches of *Death* make; For they appeare, to be the same Men, till the last Instant. *Augustus Caesar* died in a Complement; *Liuia, Coniugij nostri memor, viue & vale.*[10] *Tiberius* in dissimulation; As *Tacitus* saith of him; *Iam Tiberium Vires, & Corpus, non Dissimulatio, deserebant.*[11] *Vespasian* in a Iest; Sitting vpon the Stoole, *Vt puto Deus fio.*[12] *Galba* with a Sentence; *Feri, si ex re sit populi Romani;*[13] Holding forth his Necke. *Septimius Seuerus* in dispatch; *Adeste, si* *quid mihi restat agendum.*[14] And the like. Certainly, the *Stoikes*[15] bestowed too much cost vpon *Death*, and by their great preparations, made it appeare more fearefull. Better saith he, *Qui Finem Vitae extremum inter Munera ponat Naturae.*[16] It is as Naturall to die, as to be borne; And to a little Infant, perhaps, the one, is as painfull, as the other. He that dies in an earnest Pursuit, is like one that is wounded in hot Bloud; who, for the time, scarce feeles the Hurt; and therefore, a Minde fixt, and bent vpon somewhat, that is good, doth auert the Dolors of *Death*: But aboue all, beleeue it, the sweetest Canticle is, *Nunc dimittis*;[17] when a Man hath obtained worthy Ends, and Expectations. *Death* hath this also; That it openeth the Gate, to good Fame, and extinguisheth Enuie.

—Extinctus amabitur idem.[18]

Of Great Place

MEn in *Great Place*,[1] are thrice *Seruants*: Seruants of the Soueraigne or State; Seruants of Fame; and Seruants of Businesse. So as they haue no Freedome; neither in their Persons; nor in their Actions; nor in their Times. It is a strange desire, to seeke Power, and to lose Libertie; Or to seeke Power ouer others, and to loose Power ouer a Mans Selfe. The Rising vnto *Place* is Laborious; And by Paines Men come to greater Paines; And it is sometimes base; And by Indignities, Men come to Dignities. The standing is slippery, and the Regresse, is either a downfall, or at least an Eclipse, which is a Melancholy Thing. *Cum non sis, qui fueris, non esse, cur velis viuere.*[2] Nay, retire Men cannot, when they would; neither will they, when it were Reason: But are impatient of priuatenesse,[3] euen in Age, and Sicknesse, which require the Shadow: Like old Townesmen, that will be still sitting at their Street doore; though thereby they offer Age to Scorne. Certainly Great Persons, had need to borrow other Mens Opinions; to thinke themselues happy; For if they iudge by their owne Feeling; they cannot finde it: But if they thinke with themselues, what other men thinke of them, and that other men would faine be as they are, then they are happy, as it were by report; When perhaps they finde the Contrary within. For they are the first, that finde their owne Griefs; though they be the last, that finde their owne Faults. Certainly, Men in Great Fortunes, are strangers to themselues, and while they are in the pulse[4] of businesse, they haue no time to tend their Health, either of Body, or Minde. *Illi Mors grauis incubat, qui notus nimis omnibus, ignotus moritur sibi.*[5] In *Place*, There is License to doe Good, and Euill; wherof the latter is a Curse; For in Euill, the best condition is, not to will; The Second, not to Can.[6] But Power to doe good, is the true and lawfull End of Aspiring. For good Thoughts (though God accept them,) yet towards men, are little better then good Dreames; Except they be put in Act; And that cannot be without Power, and Place; As the Vantage, and Commanding Ground. Merit, and good Works, is the End of Mans Motion; And Conscience[7] of the same, is the Accomplishment of Mans Rest. For if a Man, can be Partaker of Gods Theater,[8] he shall likewise be Partaker of Gods Rest. *Et conuersus Deus, vt aspiceret Opera, quae fecerunt manus suae, vidit quod omnia essent bona nimis;*[9] And then the Sabbath. In the Discharge of thy *Place*, set before thee the best Examples; For Imitation, is a Globe of Precepts.[10] And after a time, set before thee, thine owne Example; And examine thy selfe strictly, whether thou didst not best at first. Neglect not also the Examples of those, that haue carried themselues ill, in the same *Place*: Not to set off thy selfe, by taxing[11] their Memory: but to direct thy selfe, what to auoid. Reforme therfore, without Brauerie, or Scandall,[12] of former Times, and Persons; but yet set it downe to[13] thy selfe, as well to create good Presidents, as to follow them. Reduce things, to the first Institution, and obserue, wherein, and how, they haue degenerate; but yet aske Counsell of both Times; Of the Ancient Time, what is best; and of the Latter Time, what is fittest.[14] Seeke to make thy Course Regular; that Men may know before hand what they may expect: But be not too positiue, and peremptorie; And expresse thy selfe well,[15] when thou digressest from thy Rule. Preserue the Right of thy *Place*; but stirre not questions of Iurisdiction:[16] And rather assume thy Right, in Silence, and *de facto*, then voice it, with Claimes, and Challenges. Preserue likewise, the Rights of Inferiour *Places*; And thinke it more Honour to direct in chiefe, then to be busie in all. Embrace, and inuite Helps, and Aduices, touching the Execution of thy Place; And do not driue away such, as bring thee Information, as Medlers; but accept of them in good part. The vices of *Authoritie* are chiefly foure: *Delaies*; *Corruption*; *Roughnesse*; and *Facilitie*. For *Delaies*; Giue easie Accesse; Keepe times appointed; Goe through with that which is in hand; And interlace[17] not businesse, but of necessitie. For *Corruption*; Doe not onely binde thine owne Hands, or thy Seruants hands, from taking; but binde the hands of Sutours also from offring.[18] For Integritie vsed doth the one; but Integritie professed, and with a manifest detestation of Bribery, doth the other. And auoid not onely the Fault, but the Suspicion. Whosoeuer is found variable, and changeth manifestly, without manifest Cause, giueth Suspicion of *Corruption*. Therefore, alwayes, when thou changest thine Opinion, or Course, professe it plainly, and declare it, together with the Reasons, that moue thee to change; And doe not thinke to steale it.[19] A Seruant, or a Fauorite, if hee be inward,[20] and no other apparent Cause of Esteeme, is commonly thought but a By-way, to close *Corruption*. For *Roughnesse*; It is a needlesse cause of *Discontent; Seueritie* breedeth Feare, but *Roughnesse* breedeth Hate. Euen Reproofes from Authoritie, ought to be Graue, and not Taunting. As for *Facilitie*; It is worse then Bribery.[21] For *Bribes* come but now and then; But if Importunitie, or Idle Respects lead a Man, he shall neuer be without. As *Salomon* saith; *To respect Persons, is not good; For such a man will transgresse for a peece of Bread.*[22] It is most true, that was anciently spoken: *A place sheweth the Man*: And it sheweth some to the better, and some to the worse: *Omnium consensu, capax Imperij, nisi imperasset;* saith *Tacitus Galba;* but of *Vespasian* he saith; *Solus Imperantium Vespasianus mutatus in melius.*[23] Though the one was meant of Sufficiencie, the other of Manners, and Affection.[24] It is an assured Signe, of a worthy and generous Spirit, whom *Honour* amends. For *Honour* is, or should be, the Place of Vertue: And as in Nature, Things moue violently to their Place, and calmely in their Place: So Vertue in Ambition is violent, in Authoritie setled and calme. All Rising to *Great Place*, is by a winding Staire; And if there be Factions, it is good, to side a Mans selfe, whilest hee is in the Rising; and to ballance Himselfe, when hee is placed. Vse the Memory of thy Predecessour fairely, and tenderly; For if thou dost not, it is a Debt, will sure be paid, when thou art gone. If thou haue Colleagues, respect them, and rather call them, when they looke not for it, then exclude them, when they haue reason to looke to be called. Be not too sensible,[25] or too remembering, of thy Place, in Conuersation, and priuate Answers to Suitors; But let it rather be said; *When he sits in Place, he is another Man.*

Of Simulation *And* Dissimulation

DIssimulation is but a faint kind of Policy, or Wisdome; For it asketh a strong Wit, and a strong Heart, to know, when to tell Truth, and to doe it. Therfore it is the weaker Sort of Politicks, that are the great Dissemblers.

Tacitus saith: *Liuia sorted well, with the Arts of her Husband, & Dissimulation of her Sonne:*[1] Attributing *Arts* or *Policy* to *Augustus*, and *Dissimulation* to *Tiberius*. And againe, when *Mucianus* encourageth *Vespasian*, to take Arms against *Vitellius*, he saith; *We rise not, against the Piercing Iudgment of Augustus, nor the Extreme Caution or Closenesse of Tiberius.* These Properties of *Arts* or *Policy*, and *Dissimulation* or *Closenesse*, are indeed Habits and Faculties, seuerall,[2] and to be distinguished. For if a Man, haue that Penetration of Iudgement, as he can discerne, what Things are to be laid open, and what to be secretted, and what to be shewed at Halfe lights, and to whom, and when, (which indeed are Arts of State, and Arts of Life, as *Tacitus* well calleth them) to him, A Habit of *Dissimulation*, is a Hinderance, and a Poorenesse.[3] But if a Man cannot obtaine to that Iudgment, then it is left to him, generally,[4] to be Close, and a *Dissembler.* For where a Man cannot choose, or vary in Particulars, there it is good to take the safest and wariest Way in generall; Like the Going softly by one that cannot well see. Certainly the ablest Men, that euer were, haue had all an Opennesse, and Francknesse of dealing; And a name of Certainty, and Veracity; But then they were like Horses, well mannaged;[5] For they could tell passing well, when to stop, or turne: And at such times, when they thought the Case indeed, required *Dissimulation*, if then they vsed it, it came to passe, that the former Opinion, spred abroad of their good Faith, and Clearnesse of dealing, made them almost Inuisible.

There be three degrees, of this Hiding, and Vailing of a Mans Selfe. The first *Closenesse, Reseruation,* and *Secrecy*; when a Man leaueth himselfe without Obseruation, or without Hold to be taken, what he is.[6] The second *Dissimulation*, in the *Negatiue*; when a man lets fall Signes, and Arguments, that he is not, that he is. And the third *Simulation*, in the Affirmatiue; when a Man industriously,[7] and expressely, faigns, and pretends to be, that he is not.

For the first of these, *Secrecy*: It is indeed, the Vertue of a Confessour; And assuredly, the *Secret* Man, heareth many Confessions; For who will open

himselfe, to a Blab or a Babler? But if a Man be thought *Secret*, it inuiteth
Discouerie; As the more Close Aire, sucketh in the more Open:[8] And as in
Confession, the Reuealing is not for worldly vse, but for the Ease of a Mans
Heart, so *Secret* Men come to the Knowledge of Many Things, in that kinde;[9]
while Men rather discharge their Mindes, then impart their Mindes. In few
words, Mysteries are due to *Secrecy*.[10] Besides (to say Truth) *Nakednesse* is
vncomely, as well in Minde, as Body; and it addeth no small Reuerence, to
Mens Manners, and Actions, if they be not altogether Open. As for Talkers, and
Futile Persons, they are commonly Vaine, and Credulous withall.[11] For He that
talketh, what he knoweth, will also talke, what he knoweth not. Therfore set
it downe; *That an Habit of Secrecy, is both Politick, and Morall.*[12] And in this Part,
it is good, that a Mans Face, giue his Tongue, leaue to Speake.[13] For the
Discouery, of a Mans Selfe, by the Tracts of his Countenance, is a great Weaknesse, and Betraying; By how much, it is many times, more marked and
beleeued, then a Mans words.

For the Second, which is *Dissimulation*. It followeth many times vpon *Secrecy*,
by a necessity: So that, he that will be *Secret*, must be a *Dissembler*, in some
degree. For Men are too cunning, to suffer a Man, to keepe an indifferent[14]
carriage, betweene both, and to be *Secret*, without Swaying the Ballance, on
either side. They will so beset a man with Questions, and draw him on, and
picke it out of him, that without an absurd Silence, he must shew an Inclination,
one way; Or if he doe not, they will gather as much by his Silence, as by his
Speech. As for Equiuocations, or Oraculous[15] Speeches, they cannot hold out
long. So that no man can be *secret*, except he giue himselfe a little Scope of
Dissimulation; which is, as it were, but the Skirts or Traine of *Secrecy*.

But for the third Degree, which is *Simulation*, and false Profession; That I
hold more culpable, and lesse politicke; except it be in great and rare Matters.
And therefore a generall Custome of *Simulation* (which is this last Degree) is a
Vice, rising, either of a naturall Falsenesse, or Fearefulnesse; Or of a Minde,
that hath some maine Faults; which because a man must needs disguise, it
maketh him practise *Simulation*, in other things, lest his Hand should be out
of vse.[16]

The great *Aduantages* of *Simulation* and *Dissimulation* are three. First to lay
asleepe Opposition, and to Surprize. For where a Mans Intentions, are published,
it is an Alarum, to call vp, all that are against them. The second is, to reserue to a
Mans Selfe, a faire Retreat: For if a man engage himselfe, by a manifest
Declaration, he must goe through, or take a Fall. The third is, the better to
discouer the Minde of another. For to him that opens himselfe, Men will
hardly shew themselues aduerse; but will (faire)[17] let him goe on, and turne
their Freedome of Speech, to Freedome of thought. And therefore, it is a good

shrewd Prouerbe of the Spaniard; *Tell a lye, and finde a Troth*.[18] As if there were no way of Discouery, but by *Simulation*. There be also three *Disaduantages*, to set it euen. The first, That *Simulation* and *Dissimulation*, commonly carry with them, a Shew of Fearfulnesse, which in any Businesse, doth spoile the Feathers,[19] of round flying vp to the Mark. The second, that it pusleth & perplexeth the Conceits of many; that perhaps would otherwise co-operate with him; and makes a Man walke, almost alone, to his owne Ends. The third, and greatest is, that it depriueth a Man, of one, of the most principall Instruments for Action; which is *Trust* and *Beleefe*. The best Composition, and Temperature[20] is, to haue *Opennesse* in Fame and Opinion;[21] *Secrecy* in Habit; *Dissimulation* in seasonable vse; And a Power to faigne, if there be no Remedy.

Of Cunning

WE take *Cunning*[1] for a Sinister or Crooked Wisedome. And certainly, there is great difference between a *Cunning* Man, and a *Wise* Man; Not onely in Point of Honesty, but in point of Ability. There be that can packe the Cards, and yet cannot play well; So there are some, that are good in Canuasses, and Factions,[2] that are otherwise Weake Men. Againe, it is one thing to vnderstand Persons, and another thing to vnderstand Matters; For many are perfect in Mens Humours, that are not greatly Capable of the Reall Part of Businesse;[3] Which is the Constitution of one, that hath studied Men, more then Bookes. Such Men are fitter for Practise, then for Counsell; And they are good but in their own Alley:[4] Turne them to New Men, and they haue lost their Ayme; So as the old Rule, to know a Foole from a Wise Man; *Mitte ambos nudos ad ignotos, & videbis*;[5] doth scarce hold for them. And because these *Cunning Men*, are like Haberdashers of Small Wares, it is not amisse to set forth their Shop.

It is a point of *Cunning*; to wait vpon[6] him, with whom you speake, with your eye; As the Iesuites giue it in precept: For there be many Wise Men, that haue Secret Hearts, and Transparant Countenances. Yet this would be done, with a demure Abasing of your Eye sometimes, as the Iesuites also doe vse.

Another is, that when you haue any thing to obtaine of present dispatch,[7] you entertaine, and amuse the party, with whom you deale, with some other Discourse; That he be not too much awake, to make Obiections. I knew a *Counsellor* and *Secretary*, that neuer came to *Queene Elizabeth* of *England*, with Bills to signe, but he would alwaies first put her into some discourse of Estate, that she mought the lesse minde the Bills.

The like Surprize, may be made, by Mouing things, when the Party is in haste, and cannot stay, to consider aduisedly, of that is moued.

If a man would crosse a Businesse, that he doubts[8] some other would handsomely and effectually moue, let him pretend to wish it well, and moue it himselfe, in such sort, as may foile it.

The breaking off, in the midst of that, one was about to say, as if he tooke himselfe vp, breeds a greater Appetite in him, with whom you conferre, to know more.

And because it workes better, when any thing seemeth to be gotten from you by Question, then if you offer it of your selfe, you may lay a Bait for a Question, by shewing another Visage and Countenance, then you are wont; To the end, to giue Occasion, for the party to aske, what the Matter is of the Change? As *Nehemias* did; *And I had not before that time been sad before the King*.[9]

In Things, that are tender[10] and vnpleasing, it is good to breake the Ice, by some whose Words are of lesse weight, and to reserue the more weighty Voice, to come in, as by chance, so that he may be asked the Question vpon the others Speech. As *Narcissus* did, in relating to *Claudius*, the Marriage of *Messalina* and *Silius*.[11]

In things, that a Man would not be seen in, himselfe; It is a Point of *Cunning*, to borrow the Name of the World; As to say; *The World sayes*, Or, *There is a speech abroad*.

I knew one, that when he wrote a Letter, he would put that which was most Materiall, in the *Post-script*, as if it had been a Bye-matter.

I knew another, that when he came to haue Speech, he would passe ouer that, that he intended most, and goe forth, and come backe againe, and speake of it, as of a Thing, that he had almost forgot.

Some procure themselues, to be surprized, at such times, as it is like, the party that they work vpon, will suddenly come vpon them; And to be found with a Letter in their hand,[12] or doing somewhat which they are not accustomed; To the end, they may be apposed of those things, which of themselues they are desirous to vtter.

It is a Point of *Cunning*, to let fall those Words, in a Mans owne Name, which he would haue another Man learne, and vse, and thereupon take Aduantage. I knew two, that were Competitors, for the Secretaries Place,[13] in *Queene Elizabeths* time, and yet kept good Quarter betweene themselues; And would conferre, one with another, vpon the Businesse; And the one of them said, That to be a Secretary, in the *Declination of a Monarchy*, was a Ticklish Thing, and that he did not affect it: The other, straight caught vp those Words, and discoursed with diuers of his Friends, that he had no reason to desire to be Secretary, in the *Declination of a Monarchy*. The first Man tooke hold of it, and found Meanes, it was told the *Queene*; Who hearing of a *Declination of a Monarchy*, tooke it so ill, as she would neuer after heare of the others Suit.

There is a *Cunning*, which we in *England* call, *The Turning of the Cat in the Pan*;[14] which is, when that which a Man sayes to another, he laies it, as if Another had said it to him. And to say Truth, it is not easie, when such a Matter passed between two, to make it appeare, from which of them, it first moued and began.

It is a way, that some men haue, to glaunce and dart at Others, by Iustifying themselues, by Negatiues; As to say, *This I doe not*: As *Tigillinus* did towards *Burrhus*; *Se non diuersas spes, sed Incolumitatem Imperatoris simpliciter spectare.*[15]

Some haue in readinesse, so many Tales and Stories, as there is Nothing, they would insinuate, but they can wrap it into a Tale; which serueth both to keepe themselues more in Guard, and to make others carry it, with more Pleasure.

It is a good Point of *Cunning*, for a Man, to shape the Answer he would haue, in his owne Words, and Propositions; For it makes the other Party sticke the lesse.

It is strange, how long some Men will lie in wait, to speake somewhat, they desire to say; And how farre about they will fetch;[16] And how many other Matters they will beat ouer, to come neare it. It is a Thing of great Patience, but yet of much Vse.

A sudden, bold, and vnexpected Question, doth many times surprise a **Man**, and lay him open. Like to him, that hauing changed his Name, and walking in *Pauls*, Another suddenly came behind him, and called him by his true Name, whereat straightwaies he looked backe.

But these Small Wares, and Petty Points of *Cunning*, are infinite: And it were a good deed, to make a List of them: For that nothing doth more hurt in a State, then that *Cunning Men* passe for *Wise*.

But certainly, some there are, that know the Resorts and Falls of Businesse,[17] that cannot sinke into the Maine of it: Like a House, that hath conuenient Staires, and Entries, but neuer a faire Roome. Therfore, you shall see them finde out pretty Looses in the Conclusion,[18] but are no waies able to Examine, or debate Matters. And yet commonly they take aduantage of their Inability and would be thought Wits of direction.[19] Some build rather upon the Abusing of others, and (as we now say;) *Putting Tricks vpon them*; Then vpon Soundnesse of their own proceedings. But *Salomon* saith; *Prudens aduertit ad Gressus suos: Stultus diuertit ad Dolos.*[20]

Of Masques and Triumphs[1]

THese Things are but Toyes, to come amongst such Serious Obseruations. But yet, since Princes will haue such Things, it is better, they should be Graced with Elegancy, then Daubed[2] with Cost. *Dancing to Song*,[3] is a Thing of great State, and Pleasure. I vnderstand it, that the Song be in Quire, placed aloft, and accompanied with some broken Musicke:[4] And the Ditty fitted to the Deuice. *Acting in Song*, especially in *Dialogues*, hath an extreme Good Grace: I say *Acting*, not *Dancing*, (For that is a Meane and Vulgar Thing;) and the *Voices* of the *Dialogue*, would be Strong and Manly, (A Base, and a Tenour; No Treble;) and the *Ditty* High and Tragicall; Not nice or Dainty.[5] *Seuerall Quires*, placed one ouer against another, and taking the Voice by Catches, *Antheme* wise, giue great Pleasure. *Turning Dances* into *Figure*, is a childish Curiosity. And generally, let it be noted, that those Things, which I here set downe, are such, as doe naturally take the Sense, and not respect Petty Wonderments. It is true, the *Alterations of Scenes*, so it be quietly, and without Noise, are Things of great Beauty, and Pleasure: For they feed and relieue the Eye, before it be full of the same Obiect. Let the *Scenes* abound with *Light*, specially *Coloured* and *Varied*: And let the Masquers, or any other, that are to come down from the *Scene*, haue some Motions,[6] vpon the *Scene* it selfe, before their Comming down: For it drawes the Eye strangely, & makes it with great pleasure, to desire to see that, it cannot perfectly discerne. Let the *Songs* be Loud, and *Cheerefull*, and not *Chirpings*, or *Pulings*. Let the *Musicke* likewise, be *Sharpe*, and *Loud*, and *Well Placed*. The *Colours*, that shew best by Candlelight, are; White, Carnation, and a Kinde of Sea-Water-Greene; and *Oes*,[7] or *Spangs*, as they are of no great Cost, so they are of most Glory. As for *Rich Embroidery*, it is lost, and not Discerned. Let the *Sutes* of the *Masquers*, be Gracefull, and such as become the Person, when the Vizars[8] are off: Not after Examples of Knowne Attires; Turks, Soldiers, Mariners, and the like. Let *Antimasques*[9] not be long; They haue been commonly of Fooles, Satyres, Baboones, Wilde-Men, Antiques,[10] Beasts, Sprites, Witches, Ethiopes, Pigmies, Turquets,[11] Nimphs, Rusticks, Cupids, Statua's Mouing, and the like. As for *Angels*, it is not Comicall enough, to put them in *Anti-Masques*; And any Thing that is hideous, as Deuils, Giants, is on the other side as vnfit. But chiefly, let the *Musicke* of them, be

Recreatiue, and with some strange Changes. Some *Sweet Odours*, suddenly comming forth, without any drops falling, are, in such a Company, as there is Steame and Heate, Things of great Pleasure; & Refreshment. *Double Masques*, one of Men, another of Ladies, addeth State, and Variety. But All is Nothing, except the *Roome* be kept Cleare, and Neat.

For *Iusts*,[12] and *Tourneys*, and *Barriers*; The Glories of them, are chiefly in the Chariots, wherein the Challengers make their Entry; Especially if they be drawne with Strange Beasts; As Lions, Beares, Cammels, and the like: Or in the Deuices of their Entrance; Or in the Brauery of their Liueries; Or in the Goodly Furniture of their Horses, and Armour. But enough of these Toyes.

De Augmentis Scientiarum
On Poetry and the Wisdom of the Ancients

The following extract is a translation of chapter 13 of Book II of *De Augmentis Scientiarum* (1623), being an expanded version of the *Advancement of Learning*, II.iv. Bacon divides human learning into History, Poesy and Philosophy, and this is all he has to say of Poetry. The function of the Imagination, for Bacon, is 'to second reason', not to provide knowledge. Of the three faculties of the Understanding (Memory, Imagination and Reason) it is the only one that, by itself, cannot lead to the advancement of learning. History (which pertains to Memory), he says at the beginning of Book III of the *De Augmentis*, 'walks upon the earth, and performs the office rather of a guide than of a light'. Poesy (which pertains to Imagination), however, 'is as a dream of learning; a thing sweet and varied, and that would be thought to have in it something divine; a character which dreams likewise effect'. Poetry, then, is merely 'feigned history', and while it 'serveth and conferreth to magnanimity, morality and delectation', has no function in the advancement of learning. It is the product of dreams and desires, not of close observation of things. The only poetry he takes seriously is myth, and the only myths he recognizes are those of the Greeks. For him *The Faerie Queene* is allegory concerned with teaching, and therefore not so interesting as the myths of Pan or Prometheus, where the mysteries of philosophy are bodied forth in narrative.

Bacon is therefore brief on the subject of poetry because he feels that he need only fit it into his categories, subdivide it and characterize each genre, and then report that there is no noticeable deficiency in this branch of learning. Narrative, Dramatic and Allegorical poetry relate easily to the branch of learning called History, and so occupy Bacon's attention. But he does not notice that allegory is a mode, whereas narrative and drama are 'kinds', of literature. For allegory fascinates him, and while he sees no deficiency in imaginative literature, he does find a lack of adequate critical interpretation of mythology. This lack he did not notice in 1605 when he was writing the *Advancement*. But in 1609 he published *De Sapientia Veterum* (translated by Sir Arthur Gorges, as *The Wisdom of the Ancients* in 1619). In this he takes 31 classical myths and interprets each one allegorically. When reporting the inadequacy of this type of criticism in 1623 he used three of his fables, slightly expanded, to indicate how the deficiency could be supplied.

The modern reader will be surprised by Bacon's fanciful interpretations of Pan as Nature, and of the story of Perseus and Medusa as an account of how to conduct wars. In fact the tradition of such interpretations was well established and Charles W. Lemmi (*The Classical Deities in Bacon*, 1933) has shown that Bacon is indebted to Macrobius, Boccaccio, Fulgentius and Natalis Comes. Nevertheless the wisdom which Bacon extracts is pure Bacon. All that he tells us of Nature as Pan, or of the state of man as Prometheus, reads like a résumé of his basic ideas. He wavered between thinking that the myths were so ancient, and sometimes so odd, that they must contain hidden meanings such as he discovered, and believing that the allegories were foisted upon them. Certainly, as he said, 'the wisdom of the ancients, it was either much or happy'. Bacon expresses *his* ideas by ingenious interpretations of familiar myths. His delight in finding similitudes conveys itself to the reader, and the enthusiastic wit with which myth and idea are made to coincide is a powerful device for persuading the reader to accept the ideas.

De Augmentis Scientiarum

BOOK II

Chapter XIII

On the second principal part of Learning, namely, Poesy. The Division of Poesy into Narrative, Dramatic, and Parabolical.[1] Three Examples of Parabolical Poesy are propounded.

I now come to Poesy, which is a part of learning in measure of words for the most part restrained,[2] but in all other points extremely free and licensed; and therefore (as I said at first) it is referred to the imagination,[3] which may at pleasure make unlawful matches and divorces of things. Now Poesy, as I have already observed, is taken in two senses: in respect of words or matter.[4] In the first sense it is but a character of speech; for verse is only a kind of style and a certain form of elocution, and has nothing to do with the matter; for both true history may be written in verse and feigned history in prose. But in the latter sense, I have set it down from the first as one of the principal branches of learning, and placed it by the side of history; being indeed nothing else but an imitation of history at pleasure. And therefore, endeavouring as I do in these divisions to trace out and pursue the true veins of learning, without (in many points) following customs and the divisions which are received, I dismiss from the present discourse Satires, Elegies, Epigrams, Odes and the like; and refer them to philosophy and arts of speech. And under the name of Poesy, I treat only of feigned history.[5]

The division of Poesy which is aptest and most according to the propriety thereof, besides those divisions which it has in common with History (for there are feigned Chronicles, feigned Lives, and feigned Relations[6]), is into Poesy *Narrative, Dramatic,* and *Parabolical.* Narrative Poesy is a mere imitation of History, such as might pass for real, only that it commonly exaggerates things beyond probability. Dramatic Poesy is as History made visible; for it represents actions as if they were present, whereas History represents them as past. Parabolical Poesy is typical History,[7] by which ideas that are objects of the intellect are represented in forms that are objects of the sense.

As for Narrative Poesy—or Heroical,[8] if you like so to call it (understanding it of the matter, not of the verse)—the foundation of it is truly noble, and has a special relation to the dignity of human nature. For as the sensible world is inferior in dignity to the rational soul, Poesy seems to bestow upon human nature those things which history denies to it; and to satisfy the mind with the shadows of things when the substance cannot be obtained.[9] For if the matter be attentively considered, a sound argument may be drawn from Poesy, to show that there is agreeable to the spirit of man a more ample greatness, a more perfect order,[10] and a more beautiful variety than it can anywhere (since the Fall) find in nature. And therefore, since the acts and events which are the subjects of real history are not of sufficient grandeur to satisfy the human mind, Poesy is at hand to feign acts more heroical; since the successes and issues of actions as related in true history are far from being agreeable to the merits of virtue and vice, Poesy corrects it, exhibiting events and fortunes as according to merit and the law of providence; since true history wearies the mind with satiety of ordinary events, one like another, Poesy refreshes it, by reciting things unexpected and various and full of vicissitudes. So that this Poesy conduces not only to delight but also to magnanimity and morality. Whence it may be fairly thought to partake somewhat of a divine nature; because it raises the mind and carries it aloft, accommodating the shows of things to the desires of the mind, not (like reason and history) buckling and bowing down the mind to the nature of things.[11] And by these charms, and that agreeable congruity which it has with man's nature, accompanied also with music, to gain more sweet access, it has so won its way as to have been held in honour even in the rudest ages and among barbarous peoples, when other kinds of learning were utterly excluded.

Dramatic Poesy, which has the theatre for its world, would be of excellent use if well directed. For the stage is capable of no small influence both of discipline and of corruption. Now of corruptions in this kind we have enough; but the discipline has in our times been plainly neglected. And though in modern states play-acting is esteemed but as a toy,[12] except when it is too satirical and biting; yet among the ancients it was used as a means of educating men's minds to virtue. Nay, it has been regarded by learned men and great philosophers as a kind of musician's bow by which men's minds may be played upon. And certainly it is most true, and one of the great secrets of nature, that the minds of men are more open to impressions and affections when many are gathered together than when they are alone.

But Parabolical Poesy[13] is of a higher character than the others, and appears to be something sacred and venerable; especially as religion itself commonly uses its aid as a means of communication between divinity and humanity. But this too is corrupted by the levity and idleness of wits in dealing with allegory. It is of double use and serves for contrary purposes; for it serves for an infoldment; and it likewise serves for illustration. In the latter case the object is a certain method of teaching, in the former an artifice for concealment. Now this method of teaching, used for illustration, was very much in use in the ancient times. For the inventions and conclusions of human reason (even those that are now common and trite) being then new and strange, the minds of men were hardly subtle enough to conceive them, unless they were brought nearer to the sense by this kind of resemblances and examples. And hence the ancient times are full of all kinds of fables, parables, enigmas, and similitudes; as may appear by the numbers of Pythagoras, the enigmas of the Sphinx, the fables of Aesop, and the like.[14] The Apophthegms[15] too of the ancient sages commonly explained the matter by similitudes. Thus Menenius Agrippa among the Romans (a nation at that time by no means learned) quelled a sedition by a fable. In a word, as hieroglyphics were before letters, so parables were before arguments. And even now, and at all times, the force of parables is and has been excellent; because arguments cannot be made so perspicuous nor true examples so apt.

But there remains yet another use of Poesy Parabolical, opposite to the former; wherein it serves (as I said) for an infoldment; for such things, I mean, the dignity whereof requires that they should be seen as it were through a veil; that is when the secrets and mysteries of religion, policy, and philosophy are involved in fables or parables. Now whether any mystic meaning be concealed beneath the fables of the ancient poets is a matter of some doubt. For my own part I must confess that I am inclined to think that a mystery is involved in no small number of them. Nor does the fact that they are left commonly to boys and grammarians, and held in slight repute, make me despise them; but rather, since it is evident that the writings in which these fables are related are, next to sacred story, the most ancient of human writings and the fables themselves still more ancient (for they are related not as being invented by the writers, but as things believed and received from of old), I take them to be a kind of breath from the traditions of more ancient nations, which fell into the pipes of the Greeks. But since that which has hitherto been done in the interpretation of these parables, being the work of unskilful men,[16] not learned beyond commonplaces, does not by any means satisfy me, I think fit to set down Philosophy according to the Ancient Parables among the *desiderata*.[17] Of which work I will subjoin one or two examples; not so much perhaps for the value of the thing as for the sake of carrying out my principle; which is this; whenever I set down a work among the desiderata (if there be anything obscure about it), I intend always to set forth either instructions for the execution of it, or an example of the thing; else it might be thought that it was merely some light notion that had glanced through my mind; or that I am like an auger measuring countries in thought, without knowing the way to enter them. I can report no other deficiency in Poesy; for being as a plant which comes from the lust of the earth without a formal seed, it has sprung up and spread abroad more than any other kind of learning. But I will now propound the examples, only three in number;

one taken from things Natural, one from things Political, and one from things Moral.

The First Example of Philosophy according to the Fables of the Ancients, in Natural Philosophy. Of the Universe, *according to the Fable* of Pan.[18]

The ancients leave the parentage of Pan[19] uncertain. Some call him the son of Mercury; others attribute to him a very different mode of generation, affirming that he sprang from the promiscuous intercourse of Penelope with all the suitors. There is also a third account, which must not be omitted; for some have declared that he was the son of Jupiter and Hybris (which signifies Contumely). Whatever his origin, the Fates are said to have been his sisters; who dwelt in a cave underground; while he himself lived in the open air. The person of Pan is described by ancient tradition as follows:—horns on his head, rising to a point and reaching up to heaven; his whole body rough and shaggy; his beard especially long; his figure biform, the upper part human, the lower part like a beast and ending in goat's feet. He carried as insignia of his office, in his left hand a pipe compact of seven reeds, in his right a shepherd's crook or staff, curved and bent at the upper end. His dress was a mantle of leopard's skin. The titles and offices attributed to him were these; he was the god of hunters; also of shepherds, and of all persons dwelling in the country; the president likewise of mountains. He was moreover next to Mercury the messenger of the Gods. He was regarded as the leader and commander of the Nymphs, who were always wont to dance and frisk around him. The Satyrs and their elders the Sileni were also of his company. He had besides the power to inspire sudden terrors, such especially as were vain and superstitious, which received the name of *Panics*. Not many actions are recorded of him. The chief one is that he challenged Cupid at wrestling and was overcome in the contest. He also caught the giant Typhon in nets and held him fast. They say likewise that when Ceres, in sorrow and passion for the rape of Proserpine, had hid herself, and all the gods were eagerly engaged in seeking her, and had dispersed themselves in different paths for the pursuit, it was reserved for Pan to meet with her by a happy accident as he was hunting, and inform the rest of her hiding-place. He presumed also to contend in music with Apollo, and in the judgment of Midas was pronounced victor; for which judgment Midas had to wear the ears of an ass, but not so as to be seen. No amours, or at least very few, are related of Pan; a strange thing for one of a crowd of Gods so profusely amorous. It is only said of him that he was the lover of Echo, who was also esteemed his wife; and of one other nymph besides, named Syringa; with desire for whom he was inflamed by the revengeful anger of Cupid, whom he had not scrupled to challenge to the wrestling. He is also said on one occasion to have drawn the

Moon apart into deep woods. Moreover he had no issue (which is likewise a marvel, when the gods, especially those of the male kind, were so prolific), unless it were one daughter, a little handmaid named Iambe, who used to amuse strangers with ridiculous stories; and was supposed by some to be Pan's daughter by his wife Echo. The parable may be thus explained.

Pan (as the name itself imports) represents and denotes the Universe, or the All of Things. Concerning his origin there are only two opinions, nor can there indeed be more. For he either sprang from Mercury, that is, the Word of God (which the Holy Scripture places beyond question, and which was perceived also by those of the philosophers themselves who have been accounted most divine), or else from the seeds of things mixed and confused together. For some philosophers have set down the seeds of things as infinite in their substance; whence arose the doctrine of *Homoeomerae*, which Anaxagoras[20] either invented or brought into repute. Some with greater penetration and judgment thought that the variety of things would be sufficiently explained, if the seeds were supposed to be in substance the same, but to take various, though certain and definite, figures; accounting for the rest by the position and connexion of the seeds one with the other; from which opinion emanated the doctrine of Atoms[21] invented by Leucippus, and sedulously followed out by Democritus. Others, though they asserted one principle of things (as Thales, Water; Anaximenes, Air; Heraclitus, Fire),[22] yet maintained that principle itself to be actually one, but potentially various and dispensable, as that which had latent within it the seeds of all things. But those who (like Plato and Aristotle)[23] have represented Matter as entirely despoiled, shapeless, and indifferent to forms, have approached much nearer to the figure of the parable. For they have made Matter as a common harlot, and Forms as suitors; so that all the opinions about the origins of things return to this point, and may be reduced to this distribution—that the universe proceeds either from Mercury, or from Penelope and all her suitors.[24] From the third story of Pan's origin, it would seem as if the Greeks, either by intercourse with the Egyptians or otherwise, had heard something of the Hebrew mysteries. For it relates to the state of the world, not at its very birth, but after the fall of Adam; exposed and made subject to death and corruption. For that state was and is the offspring of God and Sin (or Contumely). For the sin of Adam, when he wished to 'become like God', was a kind of contumely. Therefore the three-fold account of the birth of Pan may be allowed as true, if rightly distinguished with respect to facts and times. For this Pan (as we now view and understand him) is the offspring of the *Divine Word*, through the medium of *confused matter* (which itself, however, was the work of God), and with the help of *Sin*, and by Sin Corruption, entering in.[25]

To the Nature of things, the *Fates*[26] or Destinies of things are truly represented as sisters. For the beginnings, durations, and ends of things, as also their fallings, risings, labours, felicities, and in a word whatever may happen to an individual, are termed Fates; which, however, except it be in some noble individual (as a man, or a city, or a people), are commonly not observed and recognised. Now it is *Pan*, that is, the nature of things, that reduces these separate individuals to such various conditions; insomuch that the chain of nature and the thread of the Fates are (so far as individuals are concerned) the same thing. In addition to this the ancients feigned that Pan lived always in the open air, but the Fates in a huge subterranean cave, whence they suddenly flew to men with exceeding swiftness; because nature and the face of the universe is open and visible, whereas the fates of individuals are secret and rapid. But if Fate be taken in a wider acceptation,[27] so as to signify every event of any kind, and not the more noble only, yet in this sense too it excellently answers to the universal frame of things; seeing that there is nothing in the order of nature so small as to be without a cause, nor again anything so great but it depends on something else; so that the fabric of nature contains in her own lap and bosom every event whatever, both small and great, and develops them in due season by a fixed law. Therefore no wonder that the Parcae are represented as sisters of Pan, and certainly legitimate. For Fortune[28] is the child of the vulgar,[29] and has only found favour with the lighter kind of philosophers. Indeed Epicurus[30] seems not only to be profane, but also foolish, when he says 'That it is better to believe in the fable of the gods, than to assert the power of fate'; as if anything in the universe could be like an island, separated from connexion with the rest. But Epicurus, accommodating and subjecting his natural to his moral philosophy (as appears from his own words), would not willingly admit any opinion that depressed or hurt the mind, and troubled or disturbed that *Euthumia*[31] of his, which he had adopted from Democritus. And so being more fond of enjoying the sweets of thought than patient of the truth, he fairly threw off the yoke, and rejected both the necessity of Fate and the fear of the gods. And so much for the relationship of Pan to the Fates.

Horns[32] are attributed to the Universe, broad at the base and pointed at the top. For all nature rises to a point, the top like a pyramid. Individuals, which lie at the base of nature, are infinite in number; these are collected into Species, which are themselves manifold; the Species rise again into Genera; which also by continual gradations are contracted into more universal generalities, so that at last nature seems to end as it were in unity; as is signified by the pyramidal form of the horns of Pan. Nor need we wonder if the horns of Pan reach even to the heaven, seeing that the transcendentals of nature, or universal ideas, do in a manner reach up to divinity. And hence the famous chain of Homer[33] (that is, the chain of natural causes) was said to be fastened to the foot of Jupiter's throne; and we see that no one has handled metaphysics and the eternal and immovable in nature, and withdrawn his mind for awhile from the variable succession of things, without falling at once on Natural Theology; so easy and near a passage is it from the top of the pyramid to matters divine.[34]

The body of nature is elegantly and truly represented as covered with hair; in allusion to the rays of things. For rays are as the hairs or bristles of nature, nor is there anything which is not more or less radiant. This is seen most evidently in the faculty of sight, and no less in all magnetic virtue, and every effect which takes place at a distance. For whatever produces an effect at a distance may be truly said to emit rays.[35] But Pan's hair is especially long in the beard; because the rays of celestial bodies, especially of the sun, operate and pierce from a greater distance than any other; so that not only the surface, but even the interior of the Earth for some distance, is changed, wrought, and filled with spirit by them.[36] And that figure of Pan's beard is the more elegant, because the sun himself, when the upper part is obscured by a cloud and his rays break out below, appears to the eye as bearded.

The body of nature is likewise most aptly described as biform, on account of the difference between bodies of the upper and lower world; whereof the former, from their beauty and regularity and constancy of motion, as well as their influence over the Earth and earthly things, are properly represented by the human figure, human nature participating of order and dominion. But the latter, by reason of their perturbation and irregular movements, and because they are for the most part ruled by the heavenly bodies, may be content with the figure of a brute beast. Moreover this same description of a biform body has reference to the participation of species; for there is no natural species which can be regarded as simple; every one seeming to participate and be made up of two. Thus man has somewhat of the brute, the brute somewhat of the plant, the plant somewhat of the body inanimate; so that all things are indeed biform, being compounded of a superior and inferior species. And it is a very acute allegory, that of the goat's feet; which refers to the upward motion of earthly bodies towards the regions of the air and heaven; where also they remain hanging, and whence they are rather forced down than descend of themselves. For the goat is a climbing animal, and loves to hang from rocks and cling to the sides of precipices; a tendency which is also exhibited in a wonderful manner by substances which belong properly to the lower world; as appears most plainly in clouds and meteors.[37] Nay a question was raised not without reason by Gilbert, who has written upon the magnet most laboriously, and after the experimental method, whether heavy bodies may not, when removed to a great distance from the earth, gradually lose their downward tendency?

Of the two insignia which Pan bears in his hands, the one represents harmony, the other empire. For the pipe of seven reeds plainly denotes the consent and harmony of things, or concord mixed with discord (which is caused by the motion of the seven planets).[38] For there are not found any other wanderings or manifest expatiations in the heavens, besides those of the planets, such as when combined and tempered with the regularity of the fixed stars and their eternal and invariable distance one from the other, may keep up and set in motion at once the constancy of species and the continual change of individuals. And if there be any lesser planets which are not visible, or any greater change in the heaven (as in some superlunary comets),[39] it seems they are as pipes either entirely mute or vocal only for a season; inasmuch as their influences either do not approach so low as ourselves, or do not long interrupt the harmony of the seven pipes of Pan.[40] That sheep-hook also representing empire contains a noble metaphor, alluding to the mixture of straight and crooked in the ways of nature. And this rod or staff is crooked principally in the upper part; because all the works of Divine Providence in the world are mostly brought about in a mysterious and circuitous manner, so that while one thing appears to be doing another is doing really; as the selling of Joseph into Egypt and the like. Moreover in all wise human governments, those who sit at the helm can introduce and insinuate what they desire for the good of the people more successfully by pretexts and indirect ways than directly. Nay (which perchance may seem strange), even in mere natural things you may deceive nature sooner than force her; so ineffectual and self-impeding are all things which are done directly; whereas on the other hand the indirect and insinuating way proceeds smoothly and gains its end.[41] The cloak or mantle of Pan is ingeniously feigned to be the skin of a leopard; because it is full of spots. For the heavens are spotted with stars,[42] the seas with islands, the earth with flowers; and even particular objects are commonly variegated on the surface, which may be regarded as their mantle.

The office of Pan could in no other way be so lively set forth and expressed, as by terming him the god of hunters.[43] For every natural action, and indeed every motion and progression, is but a hunting. Arts and sciences hunt after their works; human counsels hunt after their ends; and all natural things hunt either after their food to preserve them, or after their pleasures and delights to perfect them (for all hunting is for the sake either of prey or pleasure); and this too by methods expert and sagacious:

> Torva leaena lupum sequitur, lupus ipse capellam:
> Florentem cytisum sequitur lasciva capella.[44]

Pan is also the god of all dwellers in the country,[45] because such men live more according to nature than in cities and courts, where nature is corrupted by too much cultivation; so that what the poet says of his mistress is by reason of such arts of luxury true likewise of nature,

Pars minima est ipsa puella sui.[46]

Pan is likewise termed the president of the mountains, because in mountains and high places nature is more open and exposed to sight and study. That Pan next to Mercury is the messenger of the gods is plainly a divine allegory; for next to the word of God, the image of the world is the herald of divine power and wisdom. *The Heavens* (says the Psalmist) *declare the glory of God, and the firmament showeth his handiwork.*[47]

Pan delights in the nymphs, that is in spirits;[48] for the spirits of living creatures are the delight of the world. And with reason is he styled their leader, for each of them follows its own nature as a guide, round which after their own fashion they leap and frisk in endless variety and constant motion. And therefore one of the moderns has ingeniously referred all the powers of the soul to motion,[49] and remarked on the conceit and precipitancy of some of the ancients, who in too eagerly fixing their eyes and thoughts on the memory, imagination, and reason, have neglected the Thinking Faculty, which holds the first place. For he who remembers or recollects, thinks; he who imagines, thinks; he who reasons, thinks; and in a word the spirit of man, whether prompted by sense or left to itself, whether in the functions of the intellect, or of the will and affections, dances to the tune of the thoughts;[50] and this is the frisking of the Nymphs. And in their company are ever found the Satyrs and Sileni, that is old age and youth. For all things have their merry and dancing time, and again their heavy and tippling time; and to one who truly considers them the pursuits of either age may appear perhaps ridiculous and deformed, like a Satyr or Silenus. As for the Panic terrors, a most wise doctrine is therein propounded. For nature has implanted in every living creature apprehension and fear, as the means of preserving its own life and essence, and avoiding and repelling the attacks of things hurtful. And yet this same nature knows not how to keep a mean, but is always intermixing vain and useless fears with such as are salutary; so that all things (if they might be seen within) are full of panic terrors; especially things human; and most of all among the common people, who are exceedingly troubled and agitated by superstition (which is nothing else but a panic terror), especially in hard and anxious and adverse times. Nor is this superstition confined to the vulgar, but it passes occasionally from them to the wiser sort; as Epicurus has said divinely (if only his other doctrines concerning the gods had breathed the same spirit), *It is not profane to deny the gods of the vulgar, but to apply the ideas of the vulgar to the gods.*[51]

With regard to the presumption of Pan, and his challenging Cupid to wrestle, the meaning is that Matter is not devoid of an appetite and inclination to dissolve the world and fall back into the old Chaos, but that its force and malice is restrained and kept in order by the prevailing concord of things (which is signified by Love or Cupid). And therefore it falls out most luckily (or say rather by the infinite goodness of God) for man and the world, that Pan has the worst of that contest and goes away defeated. The same thing is alluded to in that other circumstance of catching Typhon in a net; because however it be that vast and strange swellings (for that is the meaning of Typhon) take place occasionally in nature—whether of the sea or the clouds or the earth or any other body—nevertheless all such exuberances and irregularities are by the nature of things caught and confined in an inextricable net, and bound down as with a chain of adamant.

As for the tale that the discovery of Ceres was reserved for this god, and that while he was hunting, and denied to the rest of the gods, though diligently and specially engaged in seeking her, it contains a very true and wise admonition, which is, not to look for the invention of things useful for life and civilisation from abstract philosophies, which are as it were the greater gods, even though they devote all their strength to the purpose; but only from Pan, that is from sagacious experience and the universal knowledge of nature; which oftentimes, by a kind of chance, and while engaged as it were in hunting, stumbles upon such discoveries. For the most useful inventions are due to experience, and have come to men like windfalls.[52]

Again that contest in music and the issue of it exhibits a wholesome doctrine, and one which may well restrain and reduce to sobriety the pride and over-weening confidence of human reason and judgment. For it seems that there are two kinds of harmony and music; one of divine wisdom, the other of human reason. And to the human judgment, and the ears as it were of mortals, the government of the world and the more secret judgments of God sound some-what harsh and untunable; and though this be ignorance, such as deserves to be distinguished with the ears of an ass, yet those ears are worn secretly and not in the face of the world; for it is not a thing observed or noticed as a deformity by the vulgar.

Lastly it is no marvel if no loves are attributed to Pan, besides his marriage with Echo. For the world enjoys itself, and in itself all things that are. Now he who is in love wants something; and where there is plenty of everything there is no room for want. The world therefore can have no loves, nor any want (being content with itself), unless it be of *discourse*. Such is the nymph Echo, a thing not substantial but only a voice; or if it be of the more exact and delicate kind, *Syringa*[53]—when the words and voices are regulated and modulated by numbers, whether poetical or oratorical. But it is well devised that of all words and voices Echo alone should be chosen for the world's wife; for that is the true philosophy which echoes most faithfully the voices of the world itself, and is written as it were at the world's own dictation; being nothing else than the image and reflexion thereof,[54] to which it adds nothing of its own, but only iterates and gives it back.

The story that Pan once drew the Moon apart into deep woods, seems to have reference to the intercourse of sense with heavenly or divine things. For the case of Endymion is different from that of Pan. To Endymion the Moon descended of her own accord as he slept; for divine influences sometimes steal spontaneously into the understanding when at rest, and withdrawn from the senses; but if they are invoked and solicited by the sense, as by Pan, then they afford no other light but that,

> Quale per incertam lunam sub luce maligna
> Est iter in silvis.[55]

That the world has no issue is another allusion to the sufficiency and perfection of it in itself. Generation goes on among the parts of the world; but how can the whole generate, when no body exists out of itself? As for that little woman, Iambe, Pan's putative daughter, it is an addition to the fable with a great deal of wisdom in it; for by her are represented those vain babbling doctrines about the nature of things, which wander abroad in all times and fill the world; doctrines barren in fact, counterfeit in breed, but by reason of their garrulity sometimes entertaining, and sometimes again troublesome and annoying.

Another example of Philosophy according to the Ancient Parables, in Politics. Of War according to the story of Perseus.[56]

Perseus, an Eastern man, was sent, it is said, by Pallas to destroy Medusa, who was a grievous plague to many nations of the West in the furthest parts of Spain. She was a monster, otherwise huge and savage, and of an aspect so foul and hideous that her look alone turned men into stones. Now Medusa was one of the Gorgons, and the only mortal amongst them, the others not being subject to death. Perseus then, equipping himself for so noble an enterprise, borrowed arms as presents from three of the gods; from Mercury wings—fitted to the ankles, not the shoulders; from Pluto a helmet; from Pallas[57] a shield and mirror. Nevertheless (though he was now so well furnished) he did not go direct to Medusa, but turned aside to the Graeae. These were the half-sisters of the Gorgons; and were grey-headed from their birth, and like old women. They had but one eye and one tooth among them all; which, as they had occasion to go abroad, each wore by turns and put off again when she came back. This eye and this tooth they lent to Perseus. And now judging himself sufficiently armed to effect his purpose, he went against Medusa with all haste, flying. Her he found sleeping; but not daring to meet her gaze (in case she should wake), he turned his face away, and looking into the mirror of Pallas to direct his blow, cut off her head. From her blood spilt upon the ground immediately sprang forth Pegasus the winged horse. But the severed head Perseus transferred to the shield of Pallas, and fixed it there; where it still retained its former virtue, that whoever gazed upon it became as it were thunder or planet struck.

This fable seems to have been devised with reference to method and prudence in making war. And first, the undertaking of every war ought to be as a mission from Pallas; not from Venus (as the Trojan war was), or for any other slight motive; for resolutions respecting wars ought to be based on solid counsels. Secondly, with regard to the kind of war to be chosen, the fable propounds three very wholesome and important precepts. The first is, not to make too great a point of subjugating the neighbouring nations. For the method of enlarging a patrimony and an empire is not the same. In private estates contiguity of lands is taken into account, but in the extension of empire, occasion and facility for making war and fruit of conquest ought to be regarded in place of contiguity. And therefore Perseus, though in the East, did not shrink from an expedition even to the far West. Of this there is a notable instance in the different modes of war practised by Philip and Alexander, father and son. The former, engaging in wars with neighbouring countries, after much exertion and danger (for both at other times and especially at Chaeronea[58] he was reduced to extreme peril), added a few cities to his empire; whereas Alexander, with wise boldness undertaking a distant expedition into Persia, subjugated an infinite number of nations, and suffered more by his marches than his battles. But perhaps this difference is shown still more clearly in the increase of the empire of the Romans, who while they had scarce penetrated westward beyond Liguria,[59] had already conquered and included within their empire eastern provinces as far off as Mount Taurus.[60] So Charles the Eighth, King of France,[61] having found the war with Bretagne (afterwards arranged by marriage) no easy matter, undertook that distant enterprise against Naples, which he effected with wonderful ease and success. Certainly wars made upon distant nations have this advantage, that the invaders have to fight with those who have no experience of their mode of warfare and arms; whereas in a war with neighbours it is otherwise. Moreover the equipment of such expeditions is generally more perfect and better appointed, and the very boldness and confidence of the aggressor inspires greater terror into the enemy. Nor does it often happen in these distant expeditions that the enemy to whom the war is brought from such a distance can make diversions or counter-invasions, as is the case in wars between neighbours. But the chief point is that in subduing neighbouring states there is only a small choice of opportunities; whereas in distant enterprises the aggressor may carry the war at pleasure, either where military discipline is most relaxed, or the strength of a people is most weakened and impaired, or the rise of civil dissension and other like opportunities present themselves. The second precept is, that there must ever be a cause of war, just, pious, honourable, and popular. For this begets alacrity as well in the soldiers, as in those who provide the funds, opens the way to alliances, and conciliates friends, and has many other advantages. Now among the causes of war few are more popular than the putting down of tyrannies, beneath whose yoke the spirit and energy of the people are worn down and prostrated, as by the head of Medusa; a thing which gained Hercules divine honours.[62] Certainly the Romans made it a great point of duty to hasten with all speed to succour their allies when in any way attacked. Wars also undertaken for a just revenge have almost always been successful; as the war against Brutus and Cassius to avenge the murder of Caesar;[63] of Severus to avenge the death of Pertinax;[64] of Junius Brutus to avenge the death of Lucretia.[65] In a word, whosoever either relieves or avenges by war the calamities and injuries of men, bears arms under Perseus. The third precept is, that in every war a true estimate of strength must be taken, and it must be duly considered whether the war be such as can be carried through and brought to an issue; so that one may not engage in pursuit of vast and boundless projects. For of the Gorgons (which are the representatives of war) Perseus wisely chose her alone who was of mortal nature, nor did he attempt impossibilities. Such then is the advice which the fable gives touching the things that require deliberation in undertaking war; the rest relates to the carrying it on.

In war those three gifts of the gods are of all things the most important; insomuch that they commonly command and carry with them fortune itself. For Perseus received speed from Mercury, secrecy of counsels from Orcus, and foresight from Pallas. And it is not without allegory, and that of the wisest sort, that those wings of speed (seeing speed is of much avail in war) were attached to the feet and not to the shoulders; because celerity is required not so much in the first onsets of war as in the pursuit and following up thereof. For no error in war is more common than this, that the prosecutions and subsidiary actions correspond not to the energy of the first commencements. And the helmet of Pluto (which used to render men invisible) is a manifest parable. For next to speed in war secrecy of counsels is of the greatest moment; of which indeed speed itself is a great part; for speed anticipates the disclosures of counsels. To the helmet of Pluto belongs also this: that there should be one commander in a war, with free instructions; for consultations held with many savour more of the crests of Mars than the helmet of Pluto. Variety of pretexts, ambiguous directions, rumours spread abroad, which either blind or avert men's eyes and involve the real design in obscurity, refer to the same. So also diligent and suspicious precautions respecting despatches, ambassadors, deserters, and many like matters, are wreathed round the helmet of Pluto. But it is of no less importance to discover the counsels of the enemy than to conceal our own. To the helmet of Pluto therefore must be added the mirror of Pallas, whereby to discern the strength or weakness of the enemy, their secret partisans, their discords and factions, their movements and designs. But since there is so much of chance in war, that no great confidence can be placed either in discovering the designs of the enemy, or in concealing our own, or even in speed itself, we must take special care to be armed with the shield of Pallas, that is, of foresight, so as to leave as little as possible to fortune. To this belong the exploring of roads before a march, the careful fortification of the camp (which in modern warfare has fallen almost into disuse, whereas the camps of the Romans were like a fortified town, to fall back upon in case of defeat), a firm and well drawn up line of battle, not trusting too much to light troops, or even to cavalry; in a word, everything which relates to a sound and careful system of defensive war; for the shield of Pallas is generally of more avail in war than the sword of Mars itself. But Perseus, however furnished with forces and courage, has still need of one thing more, of the greatest possible importance, before he commences the campaign; he must turn aside to the Graeae. Now the Graeae are Treasons, which are the Sisters of War, though not indeed our own sisters, but as it were of less noble birth. For wars are noble and generous; treasons degenerate and base. They are portrayed appropriately as being grey-headed from their birth, and like old women, by reason of the perpetual cares and anxieties attending traitors. Their power (before they openly desert) is in the eye or tooth; for all faction, when discontented and inclined to treason, is both watchful and biting. Moreover this eye and tooth are, as it were, common to them all; for whatever they learn and discover is handed from one to another, and circulates through the whole party. And with regard to the tooth, they all bite as it were with one mouth, and utter the same scandals; so that if you hear one, you hear all. Wherefore Perseus must conciliate these Graeae, and bring them into alliance with him, especially that they may lend him their eye and tooth; the eye to gain information; the tooth to spread rumours, raise envy,[66] and gain over the minds of men. But when everything has been arranged in order for war, we must take special care, like Perseus, to find Medusa asleep; for he who undertakes a war wisely will almost always attack his enemy unprepared and in security. Lastly, in the very actions and onsets of war the mirror of Pallas must be resorted to; for there are many who before the time of danger can take a clear and accurate survey of the position of the enemy, but in the very moment of peril they are either stupefied with terror, or look their dangers too rashly in the face; and so rush madly into them, bent on overcoming, not on avoiding them. Neither of which things should be done; but we should turn aside the head and look into the mirror of Pallas, that the onset may be rightly directed without either terror or fury.

From the conclusion of the war and victory follow two effects, first, the birth and springing up of Pegasus, which evidently enough signifies Fame that flies abroad and proclaims the victory, and so makes what remains of the war easy and satisfactory; secondly, the carrying of Medusa's head on the shield; to which for excellence no other kind of defence can be compared. For one great and memorable enterprise successfully carried out paralyses every movement of the enemy, and stupefies disaffection itself.

The third Example of Philosophy according to the Ancient Fables, in Moral Philosophy. Of Desire, according to the fable of Dionysus.[67]
They say that Semele, the mistress of Jupiter, having bound him by an inviolable oath to grant her a request whatever it might be, desired of him to come to her arms in the same form as he would to Juno; and so she was scorched to death in his embrace. The child which she bore in her womb was taken by his father and sewn up in his thigh, till the time of gestation was accomplished. And because the child, when in the thigh of Jupiter, pinched and galled him so as to make him limp, he received the name of Dionysus. After he was brought forth he was nursed for some years by Proserpine;[68] and when he grew up his face was so like a woman's that it seemed doubtful of which sex he was. He was likewise once dead and buried for a time, but came to life again not long after. In his early youth he was the first to invent and explain the culture of the vine, and the making of wine, and its use; whereby becoming renowned and illustrious, he subdued the whole world and advanced to the furthest parts of India. He rode in a chariot drawn by tigers, round which danced certain deformed demons called Cobali, Acratus and others.[69] The Muses also attended in his train. He took to wife Ariadne, whom Theseus had deserted and abandoned.[70] His sacred tree was the ivy. He was regarded likewise as the inventor and institutor of sacred rites and orgies; but such as were fanatical and full of corruption and moreover cruel. He had also the power of exciting phrensy. At least it was by women excited to phrensy in his orgies that two renowned men, Pentheus and Orpheus, are said to have been torn to pieces;[71] the one having climbed into a tree out of curiosity to see what they were doing; the other while playing sweetly and skilfully on the lyre. Moreover the actions of this god are often confounded with those of Jupiter.

The fable appears to relate to morals; and indeed there is scarcely anything better to be found in moral philosophy. Under the person of Bacchus is depicted the nature of Desire, or the passions and perturbations of the mind. First, therefore, with regard to the origin of Desire. The mother of all desire (though ever so hurtful) is nothing else than apparent good.[72] For as the mother of virtue is real good, so the mother of desire is apparent good. One the lawful wife of Jupiter (in whose person the human soul is represented), the other his mistress; who nevertheless aspires, like Semele, to the honours of Juno. Now the conception of Desire is always in some unlawful wish, rashly granted before it has been understood and weighed; and as the passion warms, its mother (which is the nature and species of good), not able to endure the heat of it, is destroyed and perishes in the flame. Then the progress of Desire from its first conception is of this kind. It is both nursed and concealed in the human mind (which is its father); especially in the lower part of it, as in the thigh; where it causes such prickings, pains and depressions, that the actions and resolutions of the mind labour and limp with it. And even when it has grown strong with indulgence and custom, and breaks forth into acts (as if it had now accomplished its time and were fairly born and delivered), yet at first it is brought up for a time by Proserpine; that is, it seeks hiding-places and keeps itself secret, and as it were underground; until throwing off all restraints of shame and fear, and growing bolder and bolder, it either assumes the mask of some virtue, or sets infamy itself at defiance. And it is most true that every passion[73] of the more violent kind is as it were of doubtful sex; for it has at once the force of a man and the weakness of a woman. It is well said likewise that Bacchus died and came to life again; for the passions seem sometimes lulled to sleep, and as it were dead; yet can they never be trusted, no not though they be buried. For give them matter and opportunity and they will rise again.

It is a wise allegory, too, that of the invention of the vine. For every passion is very ingenious and sagacious in discovering the things which nourish and foster itself. Now of all things known to man wine is the most powerful and efficacious in stimulating and inflaming every kind of excitement; serving as a common fuel to desires in general. Very elegantly too is passion or desire described as the subduer of provinces and the undertaker of an endless course of conquests. For it is never content with what it has got, but with infinite and insatiable appetite tries for something more, and ever craves for new triumphs. Tigers likewise are kept in the stables of the passions, and at times yoked to their chariot; for when passion ceases to go on foot and comes to ride in its chariot, as in celebration of its victory and triumph over reason, then is it cruel, savage, and pitiless towards all that withstand or oppose it. Again there is humour in making those ridiculous demons dance about the chariot of Bacchus.

For every passion of the more vehement kind produces motions in the eyes, and indeed in the whole countenance and gesture, which are uncomely, unsettled, skipping, and deformed; insomuch that when a man under the influence of any passion (as anger, scorn, love, or the like) seems most grand and imposing in his own eyes, to the lookers on he appears unseemly and ridiculous. It is true also that the Muses are seen in the train of passion; there being scarce any passion which has not some branch of learning to flatter it. For herein the majesty of the Muses suffers immensely from the licence and wantonness of men's wits, turning those that should be the guides and standard-bearers of men's life into mere followers in the train and ministers to the pleasures of the passions.

Especially noble again is that part of the allegory which represents Bacchus as lavishing his love upon one whom another man had cast off. For most certain it is that passion ever seeks and aspires after that which experience has long since repudiated. And let all men who in pursuit and indulgence of their passions care not what price they pay for the enjoyment of them, know this: that whatever be the object of their pursuit—be it honour or fortune or love or glory or knowledge, or what it may—they are paying court to things cast off—things which many men in all times have tried and upon trial rejected with disgust.[74]

Nor is the consecration of Ivy to Bacchus without its mystery. For this has a double propriety. First, because ivy flourishes in the winter; next because it has the property of creeping and spreading about so many things, as trees, walls, buildings, etc. For as to the first, every passion flourishes and acquires vigour by being resisted and forbidden, as by reaction or *antiperistasis*;[75] like the ivy by the cold of winter. As to the second, any predominant passion in the human spirit spreads itself like ivy[76] round all its actions and resolves, so that you cannot find anything free from the embrace of its tendrils. Neither is it to be wondered at if superstitious rites are attributed to Bacchus; for almost every insane passion grows rank in depraved religions, insomuch that the pollutions of heretics are worse than the Bacchanalian orgies of the heathen; whose superstitions likewise have been no less bloody than foul. Neither again is it wonderful that phrensies are thought to be inspired by Bacchus; since every passion, in the excess thereof, is like a short madness, and if it continue vehement and obstinate, commonly ends in insanity. And that circumstance of the tearing to pieces of Pentheus and Orpheus amid the orgies of Bacchus, has an evident allegorical meaning; for every ruling passion is extremely hostile and inveterate against two things; whereof the one is curious inquisition; the other, free and wholesome advice. Nor does it make any difference if that inquisition be merely for the sake of looking on, as from a tree, without any ill-feeling; nor again if the advice be tendered ever so sweetly and skilfully;

for the orgies cannot upon any conditions endure either Pentheus or Orpheus. Lastly, the confusion of the persons of Jupiter and Bacchus may well be taken in an allegorical sense. For noble and illustrious actions and glorious and distinguished services proceed sometimes from virtue, right reason, and magnanimity; and sometimes (however they are extolled and applauded without distinction) only from lurking passion and hidden desire; and thus the deeds of Bacchus are not easily distinguished from the deeds of Jupiter.

But we stay too long in the theatre; let us now pass to the palace of the mind, which we are to approach and enter with more reverence and attention.

The Great Instauration:
Part III—Natural History
Sylva Sylvarum

The last six years of his life Bacon spent in furthering his plans for the advancement of learning by collecting and publishing materials for the third part of his Great Instauration. This part was to contain 'the Phenomena of the Universe', to be a collection of Natural History, arranged so that the new method, as set forth in the *Novum Organum*, could be applied by other men. Bacon believed that his collection would be more useful in itself, even if he never lived to finish his exposition of the method. Most of his collections are in Latin—*The Alphabet of Nature, History of the Winds, History of Life and Death, History of Dense and Rare*—but the *Sylva Sylvarum* or 'Forest of Materials' was dictated in English to his chaplain Rawley, who published it in 1627. It is a series of numbered observations and experiments divided into ten 'centuries', that is, groups of a hundred. Centuries 2 and 3 deal with Music and Sound; Century 4 with means of accelerating natural processes, such as ripening fruit; Centuries 5, 6 and most of 7 with plants and gardening; Century 9 with prognostics of pestilence and weather; Century 10 with the 'force of imagination'; the remainder is miscellaneous, mostly maxims about health. In his Preface, Rawley suggests that there is a *hidden* order in the arrangement, though it will appear 'an indigested heap of particulars'. But he also suggests that in eschewing systematic order, Bacon is avoiding the too hasty embracing of 'deceiving notions and theories', which prevents men seeing the material of nature freshly. On Bacon's behalf Rawley defends the collection against accusations of triviality and vulgarity: 'As long as they be God's works, they are honourable enough.' Bacon's Natural History is 'fundamental to the building of a true philosophy'.

Much of the material Bacon has extracted from Porta's *Natural Magic*, Aristotle's *Problems*, Cardan's *De Subtilitate* and *De Rerum Varietate*, Pliny's *Natural History*, Sandys's *Travels* and Scaliger's

Adversus Cardanum. But he does not mention this, since he explained in the *Parasceve* (his general introduction to his Natural History collections) that he intended to abandon the irritating habit of always citing authors—'Never cite an author except in a matter of doubtful credit.' Bacon, however, frequently comments on the experiments as though he had tried them. Thus he refutes the old belief that a vessel full of ashes will receive an equal quantity of water (34), gives us his own tried cure for gout (60), wonders how children and birds ever learn to imitate speech (236), tells us how he learned that an echo will not return the letter 's', tries to ripen apples by immersing them in various substances—wax, straw, flour, lime, onions and ashes (316 f.)— and to preserve them by refrigeration (379). The work is full of characteristic comments: 'no instrument hath the sound so melting and prolonged as the Irish harp' (223); 'in frosty weather music within doors soundeth better' (231); 'women live longer than men because they stir less' (299); 'putrefaction is the work of the spirits of bodies, which ever are unquiet to get forth and congregate with the air, and to enjoy the sunbeams' (328); 'divers we see do stut. The cause may be, in most the refrigeration of the tongue; whereby it is less apt to move' (386); birds 'have not instruments for urine; and so all the excrementious moisture goeth into the feathers' (680); 'looking against the sun doth induce sneezing' (687). He notes that 'teeth are much hurt by sweetmeats' (756), that when it is going to rain corns hurt more and fleas bite more (828–9), that longevity would be assisted by such exercises as rowing or sawing (733), and that 'gentlewomen may do themselves much good by kneeling upon a cushion and weeding' (928).

Like the *Essays* and *The Wisdom of the Ancients*, the *Sylva Sylvarum* was a popular book, being reprinted 14 times in the following century. The extracts are chosen to give an idea of the range of Bacon's experimental interests. In them one can catch glimpses of Bacon engaged in curious experiments, and hear the sound of his voice as he dictated to Rawley.

I

Experiment solitary touching the secret nature of flame.[1]

31. Take a small wax candle, and put it in a socket of brass or iron; then set it upright in a porringer[2] full of spirit of wine heated: then set both the candle and spirit of wine on fire, and you shall see the flame of the candle open itself, and become four or five times bigger than otherwise it would have been; and appear in figure globular, and not in pyramis.[3] You shall see also, that the inward flame of the candle keepeth colour, and doth not wax[4] any whit blue towards the colour of the outward flame of the spirit of wine. This is a noble instance; wherein two things are most remarkable: the one, that one flame within another quencheth not, but is a fixed body, and continueth as air or water do. And therefore flame would still ascend upwards in one greatness, if it were not quenched on the sides: and the greater the flame is at the bottom, the higher is the rise. The other, that flame doth not mingle with flame, as air doth with air, or water with water, but only remaineth contiguous; as it cometh to pass betwixt consisting bodies. It appeareth also, that the form of a pyramis in flame, which we usually see, is merely by accident, and that the air about, by quenching the sides of the flame, crusheth it, and extenuateth it into that form; for of itself it would be round; and therefore smoke is in the figure of a pyramis reversed; for the air quencheth the flame, and receiveth the smoke. Note also, that the flame of the candle, within the flame of the spirit of wine, is troubled; and doth not only open and move upwards, but moveth waving, and to and fro; as if flame of its own nature, if it were not quenched, would roll and turn, as well as move upwards. By all which it should seem, that the celestial bodies, most of them, are true fires or flames, as the Stoics held; more fine, perhaps, and rarified than our flame is. For they are all globular and determinate; they have rotation; and they have the colour and splendour of flame; so that flame above is durable, and consistent, and in its natural place; but with us it is a stranger, and momentary, and impure: like Vulcan[5] that halted with his fall.

2

Experiments in consort touching the magnitude and exility and damps of sounds.[6]

155. ... let a man go into a bath, and take a pail, and turn the bottom upward, and carry the mouth of it, even, down to the level of the water, and so press it down under the water some handful and an half, still keeping it even that it may not tilt on either side, and so the air get out: then let him that is in the bath dive with his head so far under water, as he may put his head into the pail, and there will come as much air bubbling forth, as will make room for his head. Then let him speak, and any that shall stand without shall hear his voice plainly; but yet made extreme sharp and exile,[7] like the voice of puppets: but yet the articulate sounds of the words will not be confounded. Note, that it may be much more handsomely done, if the pail be put over the man's head above water, and then he cower down, and the pail be pressed down with him. Note, that a man must kneel or sit, that he may be lower than the water. A man would think that the Sicilian poet[8] had knowledge of this experiment; for he saith, that Hercules's page, Hylas, went with a water-pot to fill it at a pleasant fountain that was near the shore, and that the nymph of the fountain fell in love with the boy, and pulled him under water, keeping him alive; and that Hercules missing his page, called him by his name aloud, that all the shore rang of it; and that Hylas from within the water answered his master, but that which is to the present purpose, with so small and exile a voice, as Hercules thought he had been three miles off, when the fountain, indeed, was fast by.

3

Experiment solitary touching the making of gold.

327. Let there be a small furnace made of a temperate heat; let the heat be such as may keep the metal perpetually molten, and no more; for that above all importeth to the work. For the material, take silver, which is the metal that in nature symbolizeth most with gold; put in also with the silver, a tenth part of quicksilver,[9] and a twelfth part of nitre, by weight; both these to quicken and open the body of the metal; and so let the work be continued by the space of six months at the least. I wish also, that there be at sometimes an injection of some oiled substance, such as they use in the recovering of gold, which by vexing with separations hath been made churlish;[10] and this is to lay the parts more close and smooth, which is the main work. For gold, as we see, is the closest, and therefore the heaviest of metals; and is likewise the most flexible and tensible. Note, that to think to make gold of quicksilver, because it is the

heaviest, is a thing not to be hoped; for quicksilver will not indure the manage of the fire. Next to silver, I think copper were fittest to be the material.

4

328. . . . *Experiments in consort touching the inducing and accelerating of putrefaction.*

The inducing and accelerating of putrefaction, is a subject of a very universal inquiry: for corruption is a reciprocal to generation: and they two are as nature's two terms or boundaries; and the guides to life and death. Putrefaction is the work of the spirits[11] of bodies, which ever are unquiet to get forth and congregate in the air, and to enjoy the sunbeams. The getting forth, or spreading of the spirits, which is a degree of getting forth, hath five differing operations. If the spirits be detained within the body, and move more violently, there followeth colliquation,[12] as in metals, &c. If more mildly, there followeth digestion or maturation,[13] as in drinks and fruits. If the spirits be not merely detained, but protrude a little, and that motion be confused and inordinate, there followeth putrefaction; which ever dissolveth the consistence of the body into much inequality, as in flesh, rotten fruits, shining wood, &c., and also in the rust of metals. But if that motion be in a certain order, there followeth vivification and figuration; as both in living creatures bred of putrefaction, and in living creatures perfect. But if the spirits issue out of the body, there followeth desiccation, induration,[14] consumption,[15] &c., as in brick, evaporation of bodies liquid, &c.

5

354. . . . *Experiments in consort touching sulphur and mercury, two of Paracelsus's principles.*[16]

. . . There be two great families of things, you may term them by several names; sulphureous and mercurial, which are the chemists'[17] words, for as for their *sal*,[18] which is their third principle, it is a compound of the other two; inflammable and not inflammable; mature and crude, oily and watery. For we see that in subterranies[19] there are, as the fathers of their tribes,[20] brimstone and mercury; in vegetables and living creatures there is water and oil: in the inferior order of pneumaticals[21] there is air and flame, and in the superior there is the body of the star and the pure sky. And these pairs, though they be unlike in the primitive differences of matter, yet they seem to have many consents:[22] for mercury and sulphur are principal materials of metals; water and oil are principal materials of vegetables and animals, and seem to differ but in maturation or concoction:[23] flame, in vulgar opinion, is but air incensed;[24] and they both have quickness of motion, and facility of cession,[25] much alike: and the interstellar sky, though the opinion be vain, that the star is the denser part of his orb, hath notwithstanding so much affinity with the star, that there is a rotation of that, as well as of the star. Therefore it is one of the greatest *magnalia naturae*,[26] to turn water or watery juice into oil or oily juice: greater in nature, than to turn silver or quicksilver into gold.

6

Experiments in consort touching the acceleration of germination.

... 401. There were sown in a bed, turnip-seed, radish-seed, wheat, cucumber-seed, and peas. The bed we call a hot-bed, and the manner of it is this: there was taken horse-dung, old and well rotted; this was laid upon a bank half a foot high, and supported round about with planks; and upon the top was cast sifted earth, some two fingers deep, and then the seed sprinkled upon it, having been steeped all night in water mixed with cow-dung. The turnip-seed and the wheat came up half an inch above ground within two days after, without any watering. The rest the third day. The experiment was made in October; and, it may be, in the spring, the accelerating would have been the speedier. This is a noble experiment; for without this help they would have been four times as long in coming up. But there doth not occur to me, at this present, any use thereof for profit, except it should be for sowing of peas, which have their price very much increased by the early coming. It may be tried also with cherries, strawberries, and other fruit, which are dearest when they come early.

7

Experiments in consort touching the sympathy and antipathy of plants.

... 494. What a little moisture will do in vegetables, even though they be dead and severed from the earth, appeareth well in the experiment of jugglers. They take the beard of an oat, which if you mark it well, is wreathed at the bottom, and one smooth entire straw at the top. They take only the part that is wreathed, and cut off the other, leaving the beard half the breadth of a finger in length. Then they make a little cross of a quill, longways of that part of the quill which hath the pith; and cross-ways of that piece of the quill without pith; the whole cross being the breadth of a finger high. Then they prick the bottom where the pith is, and thereinto they put the oaten beard, leaving half of it sticking forth of the quill: then they take a little white box of wood, to deceive men, as if somewhat in the box did work the feat, in which, with a pin, they make a little hole, enough to take the beard, but not to let the cross sink down, but to stick. Then likewise, by way of imposture, they make a question; as, Who is the fairest woman in company? or, Who hath a glove or a card? and cause another to name divers persons; and upon every naming they stick the cross in the box, having first put it towards their mouth, as if they charmed it, and the cross stirreth not; but when they come to the person that they would take, as they hold the cross to their mouth, they touch the beard with the tip of their tongue and wet it, and so stick the cross in the box; and then you shall see it turn finely and softly three or four turns, which is caused by the untwining of the beard by the moisture. You may see it more evidently, if you stick the cross between your fingers instead of the box; and therefore you may see that this motion, which is effected by so little wet, is stronger than the closing or bending of the head of a marygold.

8

Experiments in consort touching the impression which the passions of the mind make upon the body.

713. The passions of the mind work upon the body the impressions following. Fear causeth paleness, trembling, the standing of the hair upright, starting and shrieking. The paleness is caused, for that the blood runneth inward to succour the heart. The trembling is caused, for that through the flight of the spirits inward, the outward parts are destituted, and not sustained. Standing upright of the hair is caused, for that by the shutting of the pores of the skin, the hair that lieth aslope must needs rise. Starting is both an apprehension of the thing feared, and in that kind it is a motion of shrinking, and likewise an inquisition in the beginning, what the matter should be, and in that kind it is a motion of erection, and therefore when a man would listen suddenly to any thing, he starteth; for the starting is an erection of the spirits to attend. Skreeching is an appetite of expelling that which suddenly striketh the spirits: for it must be noted, that many motions, though they be unprofitable to expel that which hurteth, yet they are offers of nature, and cause motions by consent, as in groaning, or crying upon pain.

714. Grief and pain cause sighing, sobbing, groaning, screaming, and roaring; tears, distorting of the face, grinding of the teeth, sweating. Sighing is caused by the drawing in of a greater quantity of breath to refresh the heart that laboureth; like a great draught when one is thirsty. Sobbing is the same thing stronger. Groaning, and screaming, and roaring, are caused by an appetite of expulsion, as hath been said: for when the spirits cannot expel the

thing that hurteth, in their strife to do it, by motion of consent, they expel the voice. And this is when the spirits yield, and give over to resist: for if one do constantly resist pain, he will not groan. Tears are caused by a contraction of the spirits of the brain: which contraction by consequence astringeth the moisture of the brain, and thereby sendeth tears into the eyes. And this contraction or compression causeth also wringing of the hands; for wringing is a gesture of expression of moisture. The distorting of the face is caused by a contention, first to bear and resist, and then to expel; which maketh the parts knit first, and afterwards open. Grinding of the teeth is caused likewise by a gathering and serring[27] of the spirits together to resist, which maketh the teeth also to sit hard one against another. Sweating is also a compound motion, by the labour of the spirits, first to resist, and then to expel.

715. Joy causeth a cheerfulness and vigour in the eyes, singing, leaping, dancing and sometimes tears. All these are the effects of the dilatation and coming forth of the spirits into the outward parts; which maketh them more lively and stirring. We know it hath been seen, that excessive sudden joy hath caused present death, while the spirits did spread so much as they could not retire again. As for tears, they are the effects of compression of the moisture of the brain, upon dilatation of the spirits. For compression of the spirits worketh an expression of the moisture of the brain by consent, as hath been said in grief. But then in joy, it worketh it diversly, viz, by propulsion of the moisture, when the spirits dilate, and occupy more room.

9

Experiment solitary, touching medicines that condense and relieve the spirits.[28]

738. They have in Turkey a drink called coffee, made of a berry of the same name, as black as soot, and of a strong scent, but not aromatical;[29] which they take, beaten into powder, in water, as hot as they can drink it: and they take it, and sit at it in their coffee-houses, which are like our taverns. This drink comforteth the brain and heart, and helpeth digestion. Certainly, this berry coffee, the root and leaf beetle,[30] the leaf tobacco, and the tear of poppy, opium, of which the Turks are great takers, supposing it expelleth all fear, do all condense the spirits, and make them strong and aleger.[31] But it seemeth they are taken after several manners; for coffee and opium are taken down, tobacco but in smoke, and beetle is but champed in the mouth with a little lime. It is like there are more of them, if they were well found out, and well corrected. Query, of henbane-seed; of mandrake;[32] of saffron,[33] root and flower; of folium indum;[34] of ambergrease;[35] of the Assyrian amomum,[36] if it may be had; and of the scarlet powder which they call kermes:[37] and, generally, of all

such things as do inebriate and provoke sleep. Note, that tobacco is not taken in root or seed, which are more forcible ever than leaves.

10

Experiment solitary touching the melioration of tobacco.

855. Tobacco is a thing of great price, if it be in request: for an acre of it will be worth, as is affirmed two hundred pounds by the year towards charge.[38] The charge of making the ground and otherwise is great, but nothing to the profit; but the English tobacco hath small credit, as being too dull and earthy: nay, the Virginian tobacco, though that be in a hotter climate, can get no credit for the same cause: so that a trial to make tobacco more aromatical, and better concocted, here in England, were a thing of great profit. Some have gone about to do it by drenching the English tobacco in a decoction or infusion of Indian tobacco; but those are but sophistications and toys; for nothing that is once perfect, and hath run his race, can receive much amendment. You must ever resort to the beginnings of things for melioration. The way of maturation of tobacco must, as in other plants, be from the heat either of the earth or of the sun: we see some leading of this in musk-melons, which are sown upon a hot-bed dunged below, upon a bank turned upon the south sun, to give heat by reflection; laid upon tiles, which increaseth the heat, and covered with straw to keep them from cold. They remove them also, which addeth some life: and by these helps they become as good in England, as in Italy or Provence. These, and the like means, may be tried in tobacco. Inquire also of the steeping of the roots in some such liquor as may give them vigour to put forth strong.

11

Experiment solitary touching the rise of water by means of flame.[39]

889. It is a common experiment, but the cause is mistaken. Take a pot, or better a glass, because therein you may see the motion, and set a candle lighted in the bottom of a bason of water, and turn the mouth of the pot or glass over the candle, and it will make the water rise. They ascribe it to the drawing of heat; which is not true: for it appeareth plainly to be but a motion of nexe,[40] which they call *ne detur vacuum*;[41] and it proceedeth thus. The flame of the candle, as soon as it is covered, being suffocated by the close air, lesseneth by little and little; during which time there is some little ascent of water, but not much; for the flame occupying less and less room, as it lesseneth, the water succeedeth. But upon the instant of the candle's going out, there is a sudden rise

of a great deal of water; for that the body of the flame filleth no more place, and so the air and the water succeed. It worketh the same effect, if instead of water you put flour or sand into the bason: which sheweth, that it is not the flame's drawing the liquor as nourishment, as it is supposed; for all bodies are alike unto it, as it is ever in motion of nexe; insomuch as I have seen the glass, being held by the hand, hath lifted up the bason and all; the motion of nexe did so clasp the bottom of the bason. That experiment, when the bason was lifted up, was made with oil, and not with water: nevertheless this is true, that at the very first setting of the mouth of the glass upon the bottom of the bason, it draweth up the water a little, and then standeth at a stay, almost till the candle's going out, as was said. This may shew some attraction at first: but of this we will speak more, when we handle attractions by heat.

12

Experiments in consort touching the emission of immateriate virtues from the minds and spirits of men, either by affections, or by imaginations, or by other impressions.

946. ... I related one time to a man that was curious and vain enough in these things, that I saw a kind of juggler, that had a pair of cards, and would tell a man what card he thought. This pretended learned man told me, it was a mistaking in me; 'for', said he, 'it was not the knowledge of the man's thought, for that is proper to God, but it was the enforcing of a thought upon him, and binding his imagination by a stronger, that he could think no other card.' And thereupon he asked me a question or two, which I thought he did but cunningly, knowing before what used to be the feats of the juggler. 'Sir', said he, 'do you remember whether he told the card the man thought, himself, or bade another to tell it?' I answered, as was true, that he bade another tell it. Whereunto he said, 'So I thought: for', said he, 'himself could not have put on so strong an imagination; but by telling the other the card, who believed that the juggler was some strange man, and could do strange things, that other man caught a strong imagination.' I hearkened unto him, thinking for a vanity he spoke prettily.[42] Then he asked me another question: saith he, 'Do you remember, whether he bade the man think the card first, and afterwards told the other man in his ear what he should think; or else that he did whisper first in the man's ear that should tell the card, telling that such a man should think such a card, and after bade the man think a card?' I told him, as was true; that he did first whisper the man in the ear, that such a man should think such a card: upon this the learned man did much exult and please himself, saying: 'Lo, you may see that my opinion is right: for if the man had thought first, his thought had been fixed; but the other imagining first, bound his thought.' Which though it did

somewhat sink with me, yet I made it lighter than I thought, and said; I thought it was confederacy between the juggler and the two servants: though indeed, I had no reason so to think, for they were both my father's servants,[43] and he had never played in the house before. The juggler also did cause a garter to be held up, and took upon him to know, that such an one should point in such a place of the garter, as it should be near so many inches to the longer end, and so many to the shorter; and still he did it, by first telling the imaginer, and after bidding the actor think.

Having told this relation, not for the weight thereof, but because it doth handsomely open the nature of the question, I return to that I said, that experiments of imagination must be practised by others, and not by a man's self. For there be three means to fortify belief: the first is experience; the second is reason; and the third is authority: and that of these which is far the most potent, is authority; for belief upon reason, or experience will stagger.

13

Experiments in consort touching the secret virtue of sympathy and antipathy.

985. It is a common experience, that dogs know the dog-killer; when, as in times of infection, some petty fellow is sent out to kill the dogs; and that though they have never seen him before, yet they will all come forth, and bark, and fly at him.

986. The relations touching the force of imagination, and the secret instincts of nature, are so uncertain, as they require a great deal of examination ere we conclude upon them. I would have it first thoroughly inquired, whether there be any secret passages of sympathy between persons of near blood, as parents, children, brothers, sisters, nurse-children,[44] husbands, wives, &c. There be many reports in history, that upon the death of persons of such nearness, men have had an inward feeling of it. I myself remember, that being in Paris, and my father dying in London, two or three days before my father's death,[45] I had a dream, which I told to divers English gentlemen, that my father's house in the country was plastered all over with black mortar. There is an opinion abroad, whether idle or no I cannot say, that loving and kind husbands have a sense of their wives breeding children, by some accident in their own body.

*   *   *

996. It is received, that it helpeth to continue love, if one wear a ring, or a bracelet, of the hair of the party beloved. But that may be by the exciting of the imagination: and perhaps a glove, or other like favour, may as well do it.

997. The sympathy of individuals, that have been entire, or have touched,[46] is of all others the most incredible; yet according unto our faithful manner of examination of nature, we will make some little mention of it. The taking away of warts, by rubbing them with somewhat that afterwards is put to waste and consume, is a common experiment; and I do apprehend it the rather because of my own experience. I had from my childhood a wart upon one of my fingers: afterwards, when I was about sixteen years old,[47] being then at Paris, there grew upon both my hands a number of warts, at the least an hundred, in a month's space. The English ambassador's lady, who was a woman far from superstition, told me one day, she would help me away with my warts: whereupon she got a piece of lard with the skin on, and rubbed the warts all over with fat side; and amongst the rest, that wart which I had had from my childhood: then she nailed the piece of lard, with the fat towards the sun, upon a post of her chamber window, which was to the south. The success was, that within five weeks' space all the warts went quite away: and that wart which I had so long endured, for company. But at the rest I did little marvel, because they came in a short time, and might go away in a short time again: but the going away of that which had stayed so long doth yet stick with me. They say the like is done by the rubbing of warts with a green elder stick, and then burying the stick to rot in muck. It would be tried with corns and wens, and other such excrescences. I would have it also tried with some parts of living creatures that are nearest the nature of excrescences; as the combs of cocks, the spurs of cocks, the horns of beasts, &c. And I would have it tried both ways; both by rubbing those parts with lard, or elder, as before, and by cutting off some piece of those parts, and laying it to consume: to see whether it will work any effect towards the consumption of that part which was once joined with it.

998. It is constantly received and avouched, that the anointing of the weapon that maketh the wound, will heal the wound itself. In this experiment, upon the relation of men of credit, though myself, as yet, am not fully inclined to believe it, you shall note the points following: first, the ointment wherewith this is done is made of divers ingredients; whereof the strangest and hardest to come by, are the moss upon the skull of a dead man unburied, and the fats of a boar and a bear killed in the act of generation. These two last I could easily suspect to be prescribed as a starting-hole:[48] that if the experiment proved not, it might be pretended that the beasts were not killed in the due time; for as for the moss, it is certain there is great quantity of it in Ireland, upon slain bodies, laid on heaps unburied. The other ingredients are, the blood-stone in powder,[49] and some other things, which seem to have a virtue to stanch blood; as also the moss hath. And the description of the whole ointment is to be found in the chemical dispensatory of Crollius.[50] Secondly, the same kind of ointment

applied to the hurt itself worketh not the effect; but only applied to the weapon. Thirdly, which I like well, they do not observe the confecting of the ointment under any certain constellation; which commonly is the excuse of magical medicines when they fail, that they were not made under a fit figure of heaven. Fourthly, it may be applied to the weapon, though the party hurt be at great distance. Fifthly, it seemeth the imagination of the party cured is not needful to concur; for it may be done without the knowledge of the party wounded: and thus much has been tried, that the ointment, for experiment's sake, hath been wiped off the weapon, without the knowledge of the party hurt, and presently the party hurt hath been in great rage of pain, till the weapon was re-anointed. Sixthly, it is affirmed, that if you cannot get the weapon, yet if you put an instrument of iron or wood, resembling the weapon, into the wound, whereby it bleedeth, the anointing of that instrument will serve and work the effect. This I doubt should be a device to keep this strange form of cure in request and use; because many times you cannot come by the weapon itself. Seventhly, the wound must be at first washed clean with white wine, or the party's own water; and then bound up close in fine linen, and no more dressing renewed till it be whole. Eighthly, the sword itself must be wrapped up close, as far as the ointment goeth, that it taketh no wind. Ninthly, the ointment, if you wipe it off from the sword and keep it, will serve again; and rather increase in virtue than diminish. Tenthly, it will cure in far shorter time than ointments of wounds commonly do. Lastly, it will cure a beast, as well as a man, which I like best of all the rest, because it subjecteth the matter to an easy trial.

New Atlantis

The fable of *New Atlantis* was printed in the volume containing the *Sylva Sylvarum* (1627), and this, Rawley tells us, was where it was intended to come. It embodies Bacon's vision of a Christian civilization which has mastered scientific knowledge. All his life Bacon had longed for associates in his scientific work. In an early draft of an introduction to what was later called *Novum Organum*, the *Redargutio Philosopharum*, written about 1608, he imagines a figure like the Father of Solomon's House portrayed in the *New Atlantis*. Like the Father, he was of an aspect 'mild and exceedingly placid, yet the comportment of his features was as of one that pitied men'. Bacon set him not in a dream world, but in Paris, talking to an assembly of statesmen, senators and ecclesiastics. '*I* have not even a person with whom I can converse without reserve on such subjects', Bacon lamented. 'Why I met not long ago a certain evil-eyed old fortune-telling woman who . . . prophesied that my offspring should die in the desert' (*Works, III,* 559). The King had been deaf to his request to 'set men on work for the collecting of a natural and experimental history', and it must have been clear that he failed completely to understand the *Novum Organum*. The *New Atlantis* attempts to persuade not by arguing what should be done, but by showing a society in which all has been accomplished.

The society practises a patriarchal religion, tolerant of all creeds and races. It is the chastest nation in the world, bound by the honour paid to family life. It is firm but charitable, its servants incorruptible. It is a serious-minded world, full of dignity and courtesy and gentleness, without passions or conflicts. This dream-world of the scholar supports and is supported by the College of the Six Days' Works, where teams of scientists investigate the Natural World. A list of the subjects investigated shows the same interests as Bacon has in the *Sylva*—refrigeration, gardening and agriculture, longevity, brewing and baking, furnaces, light, music and sound, perfumes, engines and motion, deceits of the senses—and some others, such as microscopes and telescopes, clocks and perpetual motions, submarines and flying and mathematics. The division of scientific labour into collectors of experiments, experimenters, abstracters and compilers, men who investigate the practical application of discoveries, men who direct new research, those who follow it out, and those who extract fundamental principles from all the work, follows Bacon's ideal of scientific organization. And in the last resort the Fathers of Solomon's House are supreme in deciding which discoveries are safe to be communicated to the State and used.

Bacon's vision is nowhere more persuasively and more succinctly expounded. Had he finished it, he would have added a legal framework such as he was constantly offering to draw up for James. The whole society envisaged is the smooth, gentle, dedicated world of the scholar, which to the outsider must seem dull. But Bacon's fable is not dull; it is fired with imagination and hope. 'He doth not only shew the way, but giveth so sweet a prospect into the way as will entice any man to enter into it.' Cowley wrote of Bacon that, like Moses, he led men from the wilderness and

> *Did on the very border stand*
> *Of the blest promis'd land;*
> *And from the mountain top of his exalted wit,*
> *Saw it himself, and shew'd us it.*

New Atlantis

We sailed from Peru (where we had continued by the space of one whole year) for China and Japan, by the South Sea, taking with us victuals for twelve months; and had good winds from the east, though soft and weak, for five months' space and more. But then the wind came about, and settled in the west for many days, so as we could make little or no way, and were sometimes in purpose to turn back. But then again there arose strong and great winds from the south, with a point east; which carried us up, for all that we could do, towards the north: by which time our victuals failed us, though we had made good spare of them. So that finding ourselves, in the midst of the greatest wilderness of waters in the world, without victual, we gave ourselves for lost men, and prepared for death. Yet we did lift up our hearts and voices to God above, who 'showeth His wonders in the deep'; beseeching Him of His mercy, that as in the beginning He discovered the face of the deep, and brought forth dry land, so He would now discover land to us, that we mought not perish.

And it came to pass, that the next day about evening we saw within a kenning[1] before us, towards the north, as it were thick clouds, which did put us in some hope of land; knowing how that part of the South Sea was utterly unknown; and might have islands or continents that hitherto were not come to light. Wherefore we bent our course thither, where we saw the appearance of land, all that night; and in the dawning of the next day, we might plainly discern that it was a land, flat to our sight, and full of boscage,[2] which made it show the more dark. And after an hour and a half's sailing, we entered into a good haven, being the port of a fair city: not great indeed, but well built, and that gave a pleasant view from the sea. And we thinking every minute long till we were on land, came close to the shore and offered to land. But straightways we saw divers of the people, with bastons[3] in their hands, as it were, forbidding us to land: yet without any cries or fierceness, but only as warning us off, by signs that they made. Whereupon being not a little discomforted, we were advising with ourselves what we should do.

During which time there made forth to us a small boat, with about eight persons in it, whereof one of them had in his hand a tipstaff of a yellow cane, tipped at both ends with blue, who came aboard our ship, without any show of distrust at all. And when he saw one of our number present himself somewhat afore the rest, he drew forth a little scroll of parchment (somewhat yellower than our parchment, and shining like the leaves of writing tables,[4] but otherwise soft and flexible), and delivered it to our foremost man. In which scroll were written in ancient Hebrew, and in ancient Greek, and in good Latin of the School, and in Spanish, these words: 'Land ye not, none of you, and provide to be gone from this coast within sixteen days, except you have further time given you. Meanwhile, if you want fresh water, or victual, or help for your sick, or that your ship needeth repair, write down your wants, and you shall have that which belongeth to mercy.' This scroll was signed with a stamp of cherubin's wings, not spread, but hanging downwards; and by them a cross. This being delivered, the officer returned, and left only a servant with us to receive our answer.

Consulting hereupon amongst ourselves, we were much perplexed. The denial of landing, and hasty warning us away, troubled us much: on the other side, to find that the people had languages, and were so full of humanity, did comfort us not a little. And above all, the sign of the Cross to that instrument was to us a great rejoicing, and as it were a certain presage of good. Our answer was in the Spanish tongue, 'That for our ship, it was well; for we had rather met with calms and contrary winds, than any tempests. For our sick, they were many, and in very ill case; so that if they were not permitted to land, they ran in danger of their lives.' Our other wants we set down in particular, adding, 'That we had some little store of merchandise, which if it pleased them to deal for, it might supply our wants, without being chargeable unto them.' We offered some reward in pistolets[5] unto the servant, and a piece of crimson velvet to be presented to the officer: but the servant took them not, nor would scarce look upon them; and so left us, and went back in another little boat which was sent for him.

About three hours after we had dispatched our answer there came towards us a person (as it seemed) of place. He had on him a gown with wide sleeves, of a kind of water chamolet,[6] of an excellent azure colour, far more glossy than ours: his under apparel was green, and so was his hat, being in the form of a turban, daintily made, and not so huge as the Turkish turbans; and the locks of his hair came down below the brims of it. A reverend man was he to behold. He came in a boat, gilt in some parts of it, with four persons more only in that boat; and was followed by another boat, wherein were some twenty. When he was come within a flight-shot of our ship, signs were made to us that we should send forth some to meet him upon the water, which we presently did in our ship-boat, sending the principal man amongst us save one, and four of our number with him.

When we were come within six yards of their boat, they called to us to stay, and not to approach farther, which we did. And thereupon the man, whom I before described, stood up, and with a loud voice, in Spanish, asked, 'Are ye Christians?' We answered, we were; fearing the less, because of the Cross we had seen in the subscription.[7] At which answer the said person lift up his right hand towards Heaven, and drew it softly to his mouth (which is the gesture they use, when they thank God,) and then said: 'If ye will swear, all of you, by the merits of the Saviour, that ye are no pirates, nor have shed blood, lawfully nor unlawfully, within forty days past, you may have licence to come on land.' We said, we were all ready to take that oath. Whereupon one of those that were with him, being (as it seemed) a notary, made an entry of this act. Which done, another of the attendants of the great person, which was with him in the same boat, after his lord had spoken a little to him, said aloud: 'My lord would have you know that it is not of pride, or greatness, that he cometh not aboard your ship: but for that, in your answer, you declare that you have many sick amongst you, he was warned by the Conservator of Health of the city that he should keep a distance.' We bowed ourselves towards him, and answered, we were his humble servants; and accounted for great honour and singular humanity towards us, that which was already done; but hoped well, that the nature of the sickness of our men was not infectious. So he returned; and a while after came the notary to us aboard our ship, holding in his hand a fruit of that country, like an orange, but of colour between orange-tawney and scarlet: which cast a most excellent odour. He used it (as it seemed) for a preservative against infection. He gave us our oath, 'By the name of Jesus, and His merits': and after told us, that the next day, by six of the clock in the morning, we should be sent to, and brought to the Strangers' House, (so he called it), where we should be accommodated of things, both for our whole[8] and for our sick. So he left us; and when we offered him some pistolets, he smiling, said, he must not be twice paid for one labour: meaning (as I take it) that he had salary sufficient of the State for his service. For (as I after learned) they call an officer that taketh rewards, twice-paid.

[They are conducted to the Strangers' House, to which they are to be confined for three days.]

The next day, after that our trouble of carriage and removing of our men and goods out of our ship was somewhat settled and quiet, I thought good to call our company together, and when they were assembled, said unto them, 'My dear friends, let us know ourselves, and how it standeth with us. We are men cast on land, as Jonas was out of the whale's belly, when we were as buried in the deep; and now we are on land, we are but between death and life, for we are beyond both the Old World and the New; and whether ever we shall see

Europe, God only knoweth. It is a kind of miracle hath brought us hither, and it must be little less that shall bring us hence. Therefore in regard of our deliverance past, and our danger present and to come, let us look up to God, and every man reform his own ways. Besides we are come here amongst a Christian people, full of piety and humanity: let us not bring that confusion of face upon ourselves, as to show our vices or unworthiness before them. Yet there is more, for they have by commandment (though in form of courtesy) cloistered us within these walls for three days: who knoweth whether it be not to take some taste of our manners and conditions? And if they find them bad, to banish us straightways; if good, to give us further time. For these men that they have given us for attendance, may withal have an eye upon us. Therefore, for God's love, and as we love the weal⁹ of our souls and bodies, let us so behave ourselves, as we may be at peace with God, and may find grace in the eyes of this people.' Our company with one voice thanked me for my good admonition, and promised me to live soberly and civilly, and without giving any the least occasion of offence. So we spent our three days joyfully, and without care, in expectation what would be done with us when they were expired. During which time, we had every hour joy of the amendment of our sick, who thought themselves cast into some divine pool of healing, they mended so kindly¹⁰ and so fast.

The morrow after our three days were past, there came to us a new man, that we had not seen before, clothed in blue as the former was, save that his turban was white with a small red cross on the top. He had also a tippet¹¹ of fine linen. At his coming in, he did bend to us a little, and put his arms abroad. We of our parts saluted him in a very lowly and submissive manner; as looking that from him we should receive sentence of life or death. He desired to speak with some few of us. Whereupon six of us only stayed, and the rest avoided the room. He said, 'I am by office Governor of this House of Strangers, and by vocation I am a Christian priest; and therefore am come to you to offer you my service, both as strangers, and chiefly as Christians. Some things I may tell you, which I think you will not be unwilling to hear. The State hath given you licence to stay on land for the space of six weeks: and let it not trouble you, if your occasions ask further time, for the law in this point is not precise; and I do not doubt but myself shall be able to obtain for you such further time as shall be convenient. Ye shall also understand, that the Strangers' House is at this time rich, and much aforehand; for it hath laid up revenue these thirty-seven years: for so long it is since any stranger arrived in this part: and therefore take ye no care; the State will defray you all the time you stay. Neither shall you stay one day the less for that. As for any merchandise ye have brought, ye shall be well used, and have your return, either in merchandise or in gold and silver:

for to us it is all one. And if you have any other request to make, hide it not; for ye shall find we will not make your countenance to fall by the answer ye shall receive. Only this I must tell you, that none of you must go above a karan (that is with them a mile and a half) from the walls of the city, without especial leave.'

We answered, after we had looked awhile one upon another, admiring this gracious and parent-like usage, that we could not tell what to say, for we wanted words to express our thanks; and his noble free offers left us nothing to ask. It seemed to us, that we had before us a picture of our salvation in Heaven; for we that were a while since in the jaws of death, were now brought into a place where we found nothing but consolations. For the commandment laid upon us, we would not fail to obey it, though it was impossible but our hearts should be inflamed to tread further upon this happy and holy ground.

[They ask the Governor how Bensalem was converted to Christianity. He replies.]

'About twenty years after the Ascension of our Saviour it came to pass, that there was seen by the people of Renfusa (a city upon the eastern coast of our island), within sight, (the night was cloudy and calm), as it might be some mile in the sea, a great pillar of light; not sharp, but in form of a column, or cylinder, rising from the sea, a great way up towards Heaven; and on the top of it was seen a large cross of light, more bright and resplendent than the body of the pillar. Upon which so strange a spectacle the people of the city gathered apace together upon the sands, to wonder; and so after put themselves into a number of small boats to go nearer to this marvellous sight. But when the boats were come within about sixty yards of the pillar they found themselves all bound, and could go no further, yet so as they might move to go about, but might not approach nearer: so as the boats stood all as in a theatre, beholding this light, as an heavenly sign. It so fell out, that there was in one of the boats one of our wise men, of the Society of Salomon's House; which house or college, my good brethren, is the very eye of this kingdom, who having awhile attentively and devoutly viewed and contemplated this pillar and cross, fell down upon his face; and then raised himself upon his knees, and lifting up his hands to Heaven, made his prayers in this manner:

"Lord God of Heaven and Earth; Thou hast vouchsafed of Thy Grace, to those of our order, to know Thy works of creation, and the secrets of them; and to discern (as far as appertaineth to the generations of men) between divine miracles, works of Nature, works of art, and impostures and illusions of all sorts. I do here acknowledge and testify before this people, that the thing which we now see before our eyes is Thy finger, and a true miracle. And forasmuch as we learn in our books that Thou never workest miracles, but to a divine and excellent end (for the laws of nature are Thine own laws, and Thou exceedest them not but upon great cause), we most humbly beseech thee to prosper this great sign and to give us the interpretation and use of it in mercy; which Thou dost in some part secretly promise, by sending it unto us."[12]

'When he had made his prayer, he presently found the boat he was in movable and unbound; whereas all the rest remained still fast; and taking that for an assurance of leave to approach, he caused the boat to be softly and with silence rowed towards the pillar. But ere he came near it, the pillar and cross of light broke up, and cast itself abroad, as it were, into a firmament of many stars, which also vanished soon after, and there was nothing left to be seen but a small ark, or chest of cedar, dry, and not wet at all with water, though it swam. And in the fore-end of it, which was towards him, grew a small green branch of palm; and when the wise man had taken it with all reverence into his boat, it opened of itself, and there were found in it a book and a letter, both written in fine parchment, and wrapped in sindons[13] of linen. The book contained all the canonical books of the Old and New Testament, according as you have them (for we know well what the churches with you receive), and the Apocalypse itself; and some other books of the New Testament, which were not at that time written, were nevertheless in the book. And for the letter, it was in these words:

"I Bartholomew, a servant of the Highest, and apostle of Jesus Christ, was warned by an angel that appeared to me in a vision of glory, that I should commit this ark to the floods of the sea. Therefore I do testify and declare unto that people where God shall ordain this ark to come to land, that in the same day is come unto them salvation and peace, and goodwill, from the Father, and from the Lord Jesus."

There was also in both these writings, as well the book as the letter, wrought a great miracle, conform to that of the apostles, in the original gift of tongues. For there being at that time, in this land, Hebrews, Persians and Indians, besides the natives, every one read upon the book and letter, as if they had been written in his own language. And thus was this land saved from infidelity (as the remain of the Old World was from water) by an ark, through the apostolical and miraculous evangelism of St. Bartholomew.'[14] And here he paused, and a messenger came, and called him forth from us. So this was all that passed in that conference.

The next day, the same Governor came again to us, immediately after dinner, and excused himself, saying, that the day before he was called from us somewhat abruptly, but now he would make us amends, and spend time with us, if we held his company and conference agreeable. We answered, that we held it so agreeable and pleasing to us, as we forgot both dangers past, and fears to come, for the time we heard him speak; and that we thought an hour spent with him was worth years of our former life. He bowed himself a little to us, and after we were set again, he said, 'Well, the questions are on your part.'

One of our number said, after a little pause, that there was a matter we were no less desirous to know than fearful to ask, lest we might presume too far. But encouraged by his rare humanity towards us (that could scarce think ourselves strangers, being his vowed and professed servants), we would take the hardness to propound it; humbly beseeching him, if he thought it not fit to be answered, that he would pardon it, though he rejected it. We said, we well observed those his words, which he formerly spake, that this happy island, where we now stood, was known to few, and yet knew most of the nations of the world, which we found to be true, considering they had the languages of Europe, and knew much of our state and business; and yet we in Europe (notwithstanding all the remote discoveries and navigations of this last age) never heard any of the least inkling or glimpse of this island. This we found wonderful strange; for that all nations have interknowledge one of another, either by voyage into foreign parts, or by strangers that come to them; and though the traveller into a foreign country doth commonly know more by the eye than he that stayeth at home can by relation of the traveller; yet both ways suffice to make a mutual knowledge, in some degree, on both parts. But for this island, we never heard tell of any ship of theirs that had been seen to arrive upon any shore of Europe; no, nor of either the East or West Indies, nor yet of any ship of any other part of the world, that had made return from them. And yet the marvel rested not in this; for the situation of it, (as his lordship said) in the secret conclave of such a vast sea mought cause it. But then that they should have knowledge of the languages, books, affairs, of those that lie such a distance from them, it was a thing we could not tell what to make of; for that it seemed to us a condition and propriety of divine powers and beings, to be hidden and unseen to others, and yet to have others open, and as in a light to them.

At this speech the Governor gave a gracious smile and said, that we did well to ask pardon for this question we now asked, for that it imported, as if we thought this land a land of magicians, that sent forth spirits of the air into all parts, to bring them news and intelligence of other countries. It was answered by us all, in all possible humbleness, but yet with a countenance taking knowledge,[15] that we knew he spake it but merrily; that we were apt enough to think there was somewhat supernatural in this island, but yet rather as angelical than magical. But to let his lordship know truly what it was that made us tender and doubtful to ask this question, it was not any such conceit, but because we remembered he had given a touch in his former speech that this land had laws of secrecy touching strangers. To this he said, 'You remember it aright; and therefore in that I shall say to you, I must reserve some particulars, which it is not lawful for me to reveal, but there will be enough left to give you satisfaction.

'You shall understand (that which perhaps you will scarce think credible) that about three thousand years ago, or somewhat more, the navigation of the world (especially for remote voyages) was greater than at this day. Do not think with yourselves, that I know not how much it is increased with you, within these six-score years;[16] I know it well, and yet I say, greater then than now; whether it was, that the example of the Ark, that saved the remnant of men from the universal deluge, gave men confidence to adventure upon the waters, or what it was; but such is the truth. The Phoenicians, and especially the Tyrians, had great fleets; so had the Carthaginians their colony, which is yet further west. Toward the east the shipping of Egypt, and of Palestine, was likewise great. China also, and the great Atlantis (that you call America) which have now but junks and canoes, abounded then in tall ships. This island (as appeareth by faithful registers of those times) had then fifteen hundred strong ships, of great content. Of all this there is with you sparing memory, or none; but we have large knowledge thereof.

'At that time, this land was known and frequented by the ships and vessels of all the nations before named. And (as it cometh to pass) they had many times men of other countries, that were no sailors, that came with them; as Persians, Chaldeans, Arabians, so as almost all nations of might and fame resorted hither; of whom we have some stirps[17] and little tribes with us at this day. And for our own ships, they went sundry voyages, as well to your straits, which you call the Pillars of Hercules,[18] as to other parts in the Atlantic and Mediterranean Seas; as to Paguin (which is the same with Cambaline) and Quinzy,[19] upon the Oriental Seas, as far as to the borders of the East Tartary.

'At the same time, and an age after or more, the inhabitants of the great Atlantis did flourish. For though the narration and description which is made by a great man[20] with you, that the descendants of Neptune planted there, and of the magnificent temple, palace, city, and hill; and the manifold streams of goodly navigable rivers (which as so many chains invironed the same site and temple); and the several degrees of ascent, whereby men did climb up to the same, as if it had been a Scala Caeli;[21] be all poetical and fabulous; yet so much is true, that the said country of Atlantis, as well that of Peru, then called Coya, as that of Mexico, then named Tyrambel, were mighty and proud kingdoms, in arms, shipping, and riches: so mighty as at one time (or at least within the space of ten years), they both made two great expeditions; they of Tyrambel through the Atlantic to the Mediterranean Sea; and they of Coya, through the South Sea upon this our island; and for the former of these, which was into Europe, the same author amongst you (as it seemeth) had some relation from the Egyptian priest, whom he citeth. For assuredly such a thing there was. But whether it were the ancient Athenians that had the glory of the repulse and resistance of those forces, I can say nothing; but certain it is there never came back either ship or man from that voyage. Neither had the other voyage of those of Coya upon us had better fortune, if they had not met with enemies of greater clemency. For the king of this island, by name Altabin, a wise man and a great warrior, knowing well both his own strength and that of his enemies, handled the matter so, as he cut off their land forces from their ships, and entoiled²² both their navy and their camp, with a greater power than theirs, both by sea and land, and compelled them to render themselves without striking stroke; and after they were at his mercy, contenting himself only with their oath, that they should no more bear arms against him, dismissed them all in safety.

'But the divine revenge overtook not long after those proud enterprises. For within less than the space of one hundred years the Great Atlantis was utterly lost and destroyed; not by a great earthquake, as your man saith (for that whole tract is little subject to earthquakes), but by a particular deluge or inundation, those countries having at this day far greater rivers and far higher mountains to pour down waters, than any part of the Old World. But it is true that the same inundation was not deep, not past forty foot in most places from the ground, so that although it destroyed man and beast generally, yet some few wild inhabitants of the wood escaped. Birds also were saved by flying to the high trees and woods. For as for men, although they had buildings in many places higher than the depth of the water, yet that inundation though it were shallow, had a long continuance, whereby they of the vale that were not drowned perished for want of food, and other things necessary.

'So as marvel you not at the thin population of America, nor at the rudeness and ignorance of the people; for you must account your inhabitants of America as a young people, younger a thousand years at the least than the rest of the world, for that there was so much time between the universal flood and their particular inundation. For the poor remnant of human seed which remained in their mountains peopled the country again slowly, by little and little, and being simple and savage people (not like Noah and his sons, which was the chief family of the earth) they were not able to leave letters, arts, and civility to their posterity; and having likewise in their mountainous habitations been used (in respect of the extreme cold of those regions) to clothe themselves with the skins of tigers, bears, and great hairy goats, that they have in those parts; when after they came down into the valley, and found the intolerable heats which are there, and knew no means of lighter apparel, they were forced to begin the custom of going naked which continueth at this day. Only they take great pride and delight in the feathers of birds, and this also they took from those their ancestors of the mountains, who were invited unto it, by the infinite flight of birds that came up to the high grounds, while the waters stood below. So you see by this main accident of time, we lost our traffic with the Americans, with whom of all others, in regard they lay nearest to us, we had most commerce. As for the other parts of the world, it is most manifest that in the ages following (whether it were in respect of wars, or by a natural revolution of time) navigation did everywhere greatly decay, and specially far voyages (the rather by the use of galleys, and such vessels as could hardly brook the ocean) were altogether left and omitted. So then, that part of intercourse which could be from other nations, to sail to us, you see how it hath long since ceased; except it were by some rare accident, as this of yours.[23] But now of the cessation of that other part of intercourse, which mought be by our sailing to other nations, I must yield you some other cause. For I cannot say, if I shall say truly, but our shipping, for number, strength, mariners, pilots, and all things that appertain to navigation, is as great as ever; and therefore why we should sit at home, I shall now give you an account by itself; and it will draw nearer, to give you satisfaction, to your principal question.

'There reigned in this island, about 1,900 years ago, a king, whose memory of all others we most adore; not superstitiously, but as a divine instrument, though a mortal man: his name was Solamona; and we esteem him as the law-giver[24] of our nation. This king had a large heart, inscrutable for good, and was wholly bent to make his kingdom and people happy. He therefore taking into consideration how sufficient and substantive[25] this land was, to maintain itself without any aid at all of the foreigner; being 5,600 miles in circuit, and of rare fertility of soil, in the greatest part thereof; and finding also the shipping of this country mought be plentifully set on work, both by fishing and by transportations from port to port, and likewise by sailing unto some small islands that are not far from us, and are under the crown and laws of this state; and recalling into his memory the happy and flourishing estate wherein this land then was, so as it mought be a thousand ways altered to the worse, but scarce any one way to the better; though nothing wanted to his noble and heroical intentions, but only (as far as human foresight mought reach) to give perpetuity to that which was in his time so happily established. Therefore amongst his other fundamental laws of this kingdom he did ordain the inter-dicts and prohibitions which we have touching entrance of strangers; which at that time (though it was after the calamity of America) was frequent; doubting novelties[26] and commixture of manners. It is true, the like law against the admission of strangers without licence is an ancient law in the kingdom of China, and yet continued in use. But there it is a poor thing; and hath made them a curious,[27] ignorant, fearful, foolish nation. But our lawgiver made his law of another temper. For first, he hath preserved all points of humanity, in taking order and making provision for the relief of strangers distressed; whereof you have tasted.'

At which speech (as reason was) we all rose up, and bowed ourselves. He went on:

'That king also still desiring to join humanity and policy together; and thinking it against humanity, to detain strangers here against their wills; and against policy, that they should return, and discover their knowledge of this estate, he took this course: he did ordain, that of the strangers that should be permitted to land, as many (at all times) mought depart as would; but as many as would stay, should have very good conditions, and means to live from the State. Wherein he saw so far, that now in so many ages since the prohibition, we have memory not of one ship that ever returned, and but of thirteen persons only, at several times, that chose to return in our bottoms. What those few that returned may have reported abroad I know not. But you must think, whatsoever they have said, could be taken where they came but for a dream. Now for our travelling from hence into parts abroad, our lawgiver thought fit altogether to restrain it. So is it not in China. For the Chinese sail where they will, or can; which showeth, that their law of keeping out strangers is a law of pusillanimity and fear. But this restraint of ours hath one only exception, which is admirable; preserving the good which cometh by communicating with strangers, and avoiding the hurt: and I will now open it to you. And here I shall seem a little to digress, but you will by and by find it pertinent.

'Ye shall understand, my dear friends, that amongst the excellent acts of that king, one above all hath the pre-eminence. It was the erection and institution of an order, or society, which we call Salomon's House;[28] the noblest foundation, as we think, that ever was upon the earth, and the lantern of this kingdom. It is dedicated to the study of the works and creatures of God. Some think it beareth the founder's name a little corrupted, as if it should be Solamona's House. But the records write it as it is spoken. So as I take it to be denominate of the king of the Hebrews, which is famous with you, and no stranger to us; for we have some parts of his works which with you are lost; namely, that Natural History[29] which he wrote of all plants, from the cedar of Libanus to the moss that groweth out of the wall; and of all things that have life and motion. This maketh me think that our king finding himself to symbolize, in many things, with that king of the Hebrews (which lived many years before him) honoured him with the title of this foundation. And I am the rather induced to be of this opinion, for that I find in ancient records, this order or society is sometimes called Salomon's House, and sometimes the College of the Six Days' Works;[30] whereby I am satisfied that our excellent king had learned from the Hebrews that God had created the world, and all that therein is, within six days: and therefore he instituting that house, for the finding out of the true nature of all things (whereby God mought have the more glory in the workmanship of them, and men the more fruit in the use of them), did give it also that second name.

'But now to come to our present purpose. When the king had forbidden to all his people navigation into any part that was not under his crown, he made nevertheless this ordinance: that every twelve years there should be set forth out of this kingdom two ships, appointed to several voyages; that in either of these ships there should be a mission of three of the fellows or brethren of Salomon's House, whose errand was only to give us knowledge of the affairs and state of those countries to which they were designed; and especially of the sciences, arts, manufactures, and inventions of all the world; and withal to bring unto us books, instruments, and patterns in every kind: that the ships, after they had landed the brethren, should return; and that the brethren should stay abroad till the new mission. These ships are not otherwise fraught than with store of victuals, and good quantity of treasure to remain with the brethren, for the buying of such things, and rewarding of such persons, as they should think fit. Now for me to tell you how the vulgar sort of mariners are contained from being discovered at land, and how they that must be put on shore for any time, colour themselves under the names of other nations, and to what places these voyages have been designed, and what places of rendezvous are appointed for the new missions, and the like circumstances of the practice, I may not do it, neither is it much to your desire. But thus you see we maintain a trade, not for gold, silver, or jewels, nor for silks, nor for spices, nor any other commodity of matter; but only for God's first creature,[31] which was light: to have light, I say, of the growth of all parts of the world.'

And when he had said this, he was silent, and so were we all; for indeed we were all astonished to hear so strange things so probably told. And he perceiving that we were willing to say somewhat, but had it not ready, in great courtesy took us off,[32] and descended to ask us questions of our voyage and fortunes, and in the end concluded that we mought do well to think with ourselves, what time of stay we would demand of the State, and bade us not to scant ourselves; for he would procure such time as we desired. Whereupon we all rose up and presented ourselves to kiss the skirt of his tippet, but he would not suffer us, and so took his leave. But when it came once amongst our people, that the State used to offer conditions to strangers that would stay, we had work enough to get any of our men to look to our ship, and to keep them from going presently to the Governor, to crave conditions; but with much ado we restrained them, till we mought agree what course to take.

[Two of the visitors are invited to a 'feast of the family', a feast given by the State to any man who has thirty living descendants. The ritual of it is described. The narrator talks to a Jewish merchant and learns his attitude to Christianity, and of the nation's marriage laws. One of the fathers of the House of Salomon arrives at the city.]

The day being come he made his entry. He was a man of middle stature and age, comely of person, and had an aspect as if he pitied men. He was clothed in a robe of fine black cloth, with wide sleeves, and a cape: his under garment was of excellent white linen down to the foot, girt with a girdle of the same; and a sindon or tippet of the same about his neck. He had gloves that were curious, and set with stone; and shoes of peach-coloured velvet. His neck was bare to the shoulders. His hat was like a helmet, or Spanish montero;[33] and his locks curled below it decently: they were of colour brown. His beard was cut round and of the same colour with his hair, somewhat lighter. He was carried in a rich chariot, without wheels, litter-wise, with two horses at either end, richly trapped in blue velvet embroidered; and two footmen on each side in the like attire. The chariot was all of cedar, gilt, and adorned with crystal; save that the fore-end had panels of sapphires, set in borders of gold, and the hinder-end the like of emeralds of the Peru colour. There was also a sun of gold, radiant upon the top, in the midst; and on the top before, a small cherub of gold, with wings displayed. The chariot was covered with cloth of gold tissued upon blue. He had before him fifty attendants, young men all, in white satin loose coats to the midleg; and stockings of white silk, and shoes of blue velvet; and hats of blue velvet, with fine plumes of divers colours, set round like hat-bands. Next before the chariot went two men, bare-headed, in linen garments down to the foot, girt,[34] and shoes of blue velvet, who carried the one a crosier, the other a pastoral staff like a sheep-hook: neither of them of metal, but the crosier of balmwood, the pastoral staff of cedar. Horsemen he had none, neither before nor behind his chariot: as it seemeth, to avoid all tumult and trouble. Behind his chariot went all the officers and principals of the companies of the city. He sat alone, upon cushions, of a kind of excellent plush, blue; and under his foot curious carpets of silk of divers colours, like the Persian, but far finer. He held up his bare hand, as he went, as blessing the people, but in silence. The street was wonderfully well kept; so that there was never any army had their men stand in better battle-array than the people stood. The windows likewise were not crowded, but every one stood in them, as if they had been placed.

When the show was passed, the Jew said to me, 'I shall not be able to attend you as I would, in regard of some charge the city hath laid upon me for the entertaining of this great person.' Three days after the Jew came to me again, and said, 'Ye are happy men; for the father of Salomon's House taketh knowledge of your being here, and commanded me to tell you, that he will admit all your company to his presence, and have private conference with one of you, that ye shall choose; and for this hath appointed the next day after tomorrow. And because he meaneth to give you his blessing, he hath appointed it in the forenoon.'

We came at our day and hour, and I was chosen by my fellows for the private access. We found him in a fair chamber, richly hanged, and carpeted under foot, without any degrees to the state.[35] He was set upon a low throne richly adorned, and a rich cloth of state over his head, of blue satin embroidered. He was alone, save that he had two pages of honour, on either hand one, finely attired in white. His under garments were the like that we saw him wear in the chariot; but instead of his gown, he had on him a mantle with a cape, of the same fine black, fastened about him. When we came in, as we were taught, we bowed low at our first entrance; and when we were come near his chair, he stood up, holding forth his hand ungloved, and in posture of blessing; and we every one of us stooped down, and kissed the hem of his tippet. That done, the rest departed and I remained. Then he warned the pages forth of the room, and caused me to sit down beside him, and spake to me thus in the Spanish tongue:

'God bless thee, my son; I will give thee the greatest jewel I have. For I will impart unto thee, for the love of God and men, a relation of the true state of Salomon's House. Son, to make you know the true state of Salomon's House, I will keep this order. First, I will set forth unto you the end of our foundation. Secondly, the preparations and instruments we have for our works. Thirdly, the several employments and functions whereto our fellows are assigned. And fourthly, the ordinances and rites which we observe.

'The end of our foundation is the knowledge of causes, and secret motions of things; and the enlarging of the bounds of human empire, to the effecting of all things possible.

'The preparations and instruments are these. We have large and deep caves[36] of several depths: the deepest are sunk six hundred fathoms; and some of them are digged and made under great hills and mountains; so that if you reckon together the depth of the hill and the depth of the cave, they are, some of them, above three miles deep. For we find that the depth of a hill, and the depth of a cave from the flat, is the same thing; both remote alike from the sun and heaven's beams, and from the open air. These caves we call the lower region, and we use them, for all coagulations, indurations,[37] refrigerations, and conservations of bodies. We use them likewise for the imitation of natural mines, and the producing also of new artificial metals, by compositions and materials which we use, and lay there for many years. We use them also sometimes (which may seem strange) for curing of some diseases, and for prolongation of life, in some hermits that choose to live there, well accommodated of all things necessary, and indeed live very long; by whom also we learn many things.

'We have burials in several earths, where we put divers cements, as the Chinese do their porcelain. But we have them in greater variety, and some of them more fine. We also have great variety of composts and soils, for the making of the earth fruitful.

'We have high towers, the highest about half a mile in height, and some of them likewise set upon high mountains, so that the vantage of the hill, with the tower, is in the highest of them three miles at least. And these places we call the upper region, accounting the air between the high places and the low as a middle region. We use these towers, according to their several heights and situations, for insulation, refrigeration, conservation, and for the view of divers meteors[38]—as winds, rain, snow, hail; and some of the fiery meteors also. And upon them, in some places, are dwelling of hermits, whom we visit sometimes, and instruct what to observe.

'We have great lakes, both salt and fresh, whereof we have use for the fish and fowl. We use them also for burials of some natural bodies, for we find a difference in things buried in earth, or in air below the earth, and things buried in water. We have also pools, of which some do strain fresh water out of salt,[39] and others by art do turn fresh water into salt. We have also some rocks in the midst of the sea, and some bays upon the shore for some works, wherein is required the air and vapour of the sea. We have likewise violent streams and cataracts, which serve us for many motions; and likewise engines for multiplying and enforcing of winds to set also on divers motions.

'We have also a number of artificial wells and fountains, made in imitation of the natural sources and baths, as tincted upon[40] vitriol, sulphur, steel, brass, lead, nitre, and other minerals; and again, we have little wells for infusions of many things, where the waters take the virtue quicker and better than in vessels or basins. And amongst them we have a water, which we call Water of Paradise, being by that we do to it made very sovereign for health and prolongation of life.[41]

'We have also great and spacious houses, where we imitate and demonstrate meteors—as snow, hail, rain, some artificial rains of bodies, and not of water, thunders, lightnings; also generations of bodies in air—as frogs, flies, and divers others.

'We have also certain chambers, which we call chambers of health, where we qualify the air as we think good and proper for the cure of divers diseases, and preservation of health.

'We have also fair and large baths, of several mixtures, for the cure of diseases, and the restoring of man's body from arefaction;[42] and others for the confirming of it in strength of sinews, vital parts, and the very juice and substance of the body.

'We have also large and various orchards and gardens, wherein we do not so much respect beauty as variety of ground and soil, proper for divers trees and herbs, and some very spacious, where trees and berries are set, whereof we make divers kinds of drinks, besides the vineyards. In these we practise likewise all conclusions of grafting and inoculating,[43] as well of wild-trees as fruit-trees, which produceth many effects. And we make by art, in the same orchards and gardens, trees and flowers, to come earlier or later than their seasons, and to come up and bear more speedily than by their natural course they do. We make them also by art greater much than their nature: and their fruit greater and sweeter, and of differing taste, smell, colour, and figure, from their nature. And many of them we so order as they become of medicinal use.

'We have also means to make divers plants rise by mixtures of earths without seeds, and likewise to make divers new plants, differing from the vulgar, and to make one tree or plant turn into another.

'We have also parks, and enclosures of all sorts, of beasts and birds; which we use not only for view or rareness, but likewise for dissections and trials,[44] that thereby we make take light what may be wrought upon the body of man. Wherein we find many strange effects: as continuing life in them, though divers parts, which you account vital, be perished and taken forth; resuscitating of some that seem dead in appearance, and the like. We try also all poisons, and other medicines upon them, as well of chirurgery[45] as physic. By art likewise we make them greater or taller than their kind is, and contrariwise dwarf them and stay their growth; we make them more fruitful and bearing than their kind is, and contrariwise barren and not generative. Also we make them differ in colour, shape, activity, many ways. We find means to make commixtures and copulations of divers kinds, which have produced many new kinds, and them not barren, as the general opinion is. We make a number of kinds, of serpents, worms, flies, fishes, of putrefaction, whereof some are advanced (in effect) to be perfect creatures, like beasts or birds, and have sexes, and do propagate. Neither do we this by chance, but we know beforehand of what matter and commixture, what kind of those creatures will arise.

'We have also particular pools where we make trials upon fishes, as we have said before of beasts and birds.

'We have also places for breed and generation of those kinds of worms and flies which are of special use; such as are with you your silkworms and bees.

'I will not hold you long with recounting of our brew-houses, bake-houses and kitchens, where are made divers drinks, breads, and meats, rare and of special effects. Wines we have of grapes, and drinks of other juice, of fruits, of grains, and of roots, and of mixtures with honey, sugar, manna, and fruits dried and decocted;[46] also of the tears or woundings of trees, and of the pulp of canes. And these drinks are of several ages, some to the age or last of forty years. We have drinks also brewed with several herbs, and roots and spices; yea, with several fleshes and white-meats; whereof some of the drinks are such as they are in effect meat and drink both, so that divers, especially in age, do desire to live with them with little or no meat or bread. And above all we strive to have drinks of extreme thin parts, to insinuate into the body, and yet without all biting, sharpness, or fretting; insomuch as some of them, put upon the back of your hand, will with a little stay pass through to the palm, and taste yet mild to the mouth. We have also waters, which we ripen in that fashion, as they become nourishing, so that they are indeed excellent drinks, and many will use no other. Bread we have of several grains, roots, and kernels; yea, and some of flesh, and fish, dried; with divers kinds of leavenings and seasonings; so that some do extremely move[47] appetites, some do nourish so, as divers do live of them, without any other meat, who live very long. So for meats, we have some of them so beaten, and made tender, and mortified, yet without all corrupting, as a weak heat of the stomach will turn them into good chilus,[48] as well as a strong heat would meat otherwise prepared. We have some meats also, and breads, and drinks, which taken by men, enable them to fast long after; and some other, that used make the very flesh of men's bodies sensibly more hard and tough, and their strength far greater than otherwise it would be.

'We have dispensatories or shops of medicines; wherein you may easily think, if we have such variety of plants, and living creatures, more than you have in Europe (for we know what you have), the simples, drugs and ingredients of medicines, must likewise be in so much the greater variety. We have them likewise of divers ages, and long fermentations. And for their preparations, we have not only all manner of exquisite distillations and separations, and especially by gentle heats, and percolations through divers strainers, yea, and substances; but also exact forms of composition, whereby they incorporate almost as they were natural simples.[49]

'We have also divers mechanical arts, which you have not; and stuffs made by them, as papers, linen, silks, tissues, dainty works of feathers of wonderful lustre, excellent dyes, and many others: and shops likewise, as well for such as are not brought into vulgar use amongst us, as for those that are. For you must know, that of the things before recited, many of them are grown into use throughout the kingdom, but yet, if they did flow from our invention, we have of them also for patterns and principles.

'We have also furnaces of great diversities, and that keep great diversity of heats:[50] fierce and quick, strong and constant, soft and mild; blown, quiet, dry, moist, and the like. But above all we have heats, in imitation of the sun's and heavenly bodies' heats, that pass divers inequalities, and (as it were) orbs, progresses, and returns, whereby we produce admirable effects. Besides, we have heats of dungs, and of bellies and maws of living creatures and of their bloods and bodies, and of hays and herbs laid up moist, of lime unquenched, and such like. Instruments also which generate heat only by motion. And, farther, places for strong insulations; and again, places under the earth, which by nature or art yield heat. These divers heats we use as the nature of the operation which we intend requireth.

'We have also perspective houses,[51] where we make demonstrations of all lights and radiations, and of all colours; and out of things uncoloured and transparent, we can represent unto you all several colours, not in rainbows (as it is in gems and prisms), but of themselves single. We represent also all multiplications of light, which we carry to great distance, and make so sharp, as to discern small points and lines. Also all colourations of light; all delusions and deceits of the sight, in figures, magnitudes, motions, colours; all demonstrations of shadows. We find also divers means yet unknown to you, of producing of light originally from divers bodies. We procure means of seeing objects afar off, as in the heaven and remote places; and represent things near as afar off, and things afar off as near; making feigned distances. We have also helps for the sight, far above spectacles and glasses in use. We have also glasses and means to see small and minute bodies, perfectly and distinctly; as the shapes and colours of small flies and worms, grains, and flaws in gems which cannot otherwise be seen, observations in urine and blood not otherwise to be seen. We make artificial rainbows, halos, and circles about light. We represent also all manner of reflections, refractions, and multiplications of visual beams of objects.

'We have also precious stones of all kinds, many of them of great beauty and to you unknown; crystals likewise, and glasses of divers kinds; and amongst them some of metals vitrificated, and other materials, besides those of which you make glass. Also a number of fossils[52] and imperfect minerals, which you have not. Likewise loadstones of prodigious virtue: and other rare stones, both natural and artificial.

'We have also sound-houses, where we practise and demonstrate all sounds and their generation. We have harmonies which you have not, of quarter-sounds and lesser slides[53] of sounds. Divers instruments of music likewise to you unknown, some sweeter than any you have; together with bells and rings that are dainty and sweet. We represent small sounds as great and deep; likewise great sounds, extenuate and sharp; we make divers tremblings and warblings of sounds, which in their original are entire. We represent and imitate all articulate sounds and letters, and the voices and notes of beasts and birds. We have certain helps, which set to the ear do further the hearing greatly. We have also divers strange and artificial echoes, reflecting the voice many times, and as it were tossing it; and some that give back the voice louder than it came, some shriller and some deeper; yea, some rendering the voice, differing in the letters or articulate sound from that they receive. We have also means to convey sounds in trunks and pipes, in strange lines and distances.

'We have also perfume-houses, wherewith we join also practices of taste. We multiply smells, which may seem strange: we imitate smells, making all smells to breathe out of other mixtures than those that give them. We make divers imitations of taste likewise, so that they will deceive any man's taste. And in this house we contain also a confiture-house, where we make all sweetmeats, dry and moist, and divers pleasant wines, milks, broths, and salads, far in greater variety than you have.

'We have also engine-houses, where are prepared engines and instruments for all sorts of motions. There we imitate and practise to make swifter motions than any you have, either out of your muskets or any engine that you have; and to make them and multiply them more easily and with small force, by wheels and other means, and to make them stronger and more violent than yours are, exceeding your greatest cannons and basilisks.[54] We represent also ordnance and instruments of war and engines of all kinds; and likewise new mixtures and compositions of gunpowder, wild-fires burning in water and unquenchable, also fire-works of all variety, both for pleasure and use. We imitate also flights of birds; we have some degrees of flying in the air. We have ships and boats for going under water and brooking of seas, also swimming-girdles and supporters. We have divers curious clocks, and other like motions of return,[55] and some perpetual motions. We imitate also motions of living creatures by images of men, beasts, birds, fishes, and serpents; we have also a great number of other various motions, strange for equality,[56] fineness, and subtilty.

'We have also a mathematical-house,[57] where are represented all instruments, as well of geometry as astronomy, exquisitely made.

'We have also houses of deceits of the senses, where we represent all manner of feats of juggling, false apparitions, impostures and illusions, and their fallacies. And surely you will easily believe that we, that have so many things truly natural which induce admiration, could in a world of particulars deceive the senses if we would disguise those things, and labour to make them seem more miraculous. But we do hate all impostures and lies, insomuch as we have severely forbidden it to all our fellows, under pain of ignominy and fines, that they do not show any natural work or thing adorned or swelling,[58] but only pure as it is, and without all affectation of strangeness.

'These are, my son, the riches of Salomon's House.

'For the several employments and offices of our fellows, we have twelve that sail into foreign countries under the names of other nations (for our own we conceal), who bring us the books and abstracts, and patterns of experiments of all other parts. These we call Merchants of Light.

'We have three that collect the experiments which are in all books. These we call Depredators.

'We have three that collect the experiments of all mechanical arts, and also of liberal sciences, and also of practices which are not brought into arts. These we call Mystery-men.[59]

'We have three that try new experiments, such as themselves think good. These we call Pioneers or Miners.

'We have three that draw the experiments of the former four into titles and tables, to give the better light for the drawing of observations and axioms out of them. These we call Compilers.[60]

'We have three that bend themselves, looking into the experiments of their fellows, and cast about how to draw out of them things of use and practice for man's life and knowledge, as well for works as for plain demonstration of causes, means of natural divinations,[61] and the easy and clear discovery of the virtues and parts of bodies. These we call dowry-men or Benefactors.[62]

'Then after divers meetings and consults of our whole number, to consider of the former labours and collections, we have three that take care out of them to direct new experiments, of a higher light, more penetrating into Nature than the former. These we call Lamps.

'We have three others that do execute the experiments so directed, and report them. These we call Inoculators.

'Lastly, we have three that raise the former discoveries by experiments into greater observations, axioms, and aphorisms. These we call Interpreters of Nature.

'We have also, as you must think, novices and apprentices, that the succession of the former employed men do not fail; besides a great number of servants and attendants, men and women. And this we do also: we have consultations, which of the inventions and experiences which we have discovered shall be published, and which not: and take all an oath of secrecy for the concealing of those which we think fit to keep secret: though some of those we do reveal sometimes to the State, and some not.

'For our ordinances and rites, we have two very long and fair galleries; in one of these we place patterns and samples of all manner of the more rare and excellent inventions: in the other we place the statues of all principal inventors.[63] There we have the statue of your Columbus, that discovered the West Indies: also the inventor of ships: your Monk that was the inventor of ordnance and of gunpowder: the inventor of music: the inventor of letters: the inventor of printing: the inventor of observations of astronomy: the inventor of works in metal: the inventor of glass: the inventor of silk of the worm: the inventor of wine: the inventor of corn and bread: the inventor of sugars: and all these by more certain tradition than you have. Then we have divers inventors of our own, of excellent works, which since you have not seen, it were too long to make descriptions of them; and besides, in the right understanding of those descriptions you might easily err. For upon every invention of value we erect a statue to the inventor, and give him a liberal and honourable reward. These statues are some of brass, some of marble and touchstone, some of cedar and other special woods gilt and adorned; some of iron, some of silver, some of gold.

'We have certain hymns and services, which we say daily, of laud and thanks to God for His marvellous works. And forms of prayer,[64] imploring His aid and blessing for the illumination of our labours, and the turning of them into good and holy uses.

'Lastly, we have circuits or visits, of divers principal cities of the kingdom; where, as it cometh to pass, we do publish such new profitable inventions as we think good. And we do also declare natural divinations of diseases, plagues, swarms of hurtful creatures, scarcity, tempests, earthquakes, great inundations, comets, temperature of the year, and divers other things; and we give counsel thereupon, what the people shall do for the prevention and remedy of them.'

And when he had said this he stood up; and I, as I had been taught, knelt down; and he laid his right hand upon my head, and said ,'God bless thee, my son, and God bless this relation which I have made. I give thee leave to publish it, for the good of other nations; for we here are in God's bosom, a land unknown.' And so he left me; having assigned a value of about two thousand ducats for a bounty to me and my fellows. For they give great largesses, where they come, upon all occasions.

The rest was not perfected.

The History of Henry VII

Between his sentence by the House of Lords on 3 May 1621 and the sealing of his pardon by James in the following November Bacon wrote his *History of Henry VII*. The King read the manuscript in October, and made some trifling alterations. By March 1622 it was published and dedicated to Charles, Prince of Wales. During the period of rapid composition, Bacon was forbidden to enter London, and was forced to rely for information on the published accounts of Henry's reign, by Polydore Vergil, Fabyan, Hall, Holinshed, Stowe and Speed. But he also used at least one document—Perkin Warbeck's proclamation of 1497—in the possession of the great collector Sir Robert Cotton. The inaccuracies in the *History* are those of his sources; the clear and substantially correct interpretation of the reign and character of Henry is Bacon's own.

In the *Advancement of Learning* (II. ii), and in a letter to the Lord Chancellor Ellesmere written at the same time, Bacon discusses various types of histories and the inadequacy of existing histories of England, and hopes that the Chancellor will encourage a history 'from the uniting of the Roses to the uniting of the kingdoms'. And where Bacon was conscious, in his survey of human learning, that there was deficiency, he was equally anxious to describe the ideal to be aimed at, and the method to be used, and to provide a model himself to show that he was not asking for the impossible. Thus he very early made a draft of his characterization of Henry, and fragments of accounts of English sixteenth-century history survive to show that he might have completed the whole work himself.

The reader of Bacon is often conscious that Bacon is addressing himself to the king or to his most powerful servants. The historian honours his country by preserving its annals, but he also serves his prince. For history is a storehouse of practical psychology from which a ruler can learn 'how affections are kindled and incited; and how pacified and refrained' (*Advancement*, II. xxii. 6). From history a prince can learn what to avoid and what to pursue in policy and action and can set himself exemplars to imitate. Bacon draws Henry as true to life as he can, including as much detail of the reign as possible and commenting on motive, situation and character frequently. The detailed narrative, especially of the affairs of Lambert Simnel and Perkin Warbeck, is rapid and vivid. The two extracts dealing with Henry's statutes printed below illustrate Bacon's enlightened interest in good laws as one of the chief foundations of states, and are a reminder that all his professional life was spent in the company of lawyers.

The *History* ends with the characterization of Henry, printed here as the third extract. Here Bacon the historian rises from details to principles, from narrative to sustained interpretation and assessment. The character which emerges is that of a living person, and it is the portrait of Henry that has formed the basis for all later portraits. Bacon valued biographies of important historical figures because they were more useful than chronicles or narratives of particular actions. By 'useful' he meant that they 'give a more genuine, native, and lively representation, and such as is fitter for imitation', and this they do, if written 'with care and judgment', because they intermingle actions great and small, public and private. The *History* comes under Bacon's own category of 'Lives'. It is not praise or dispraise, panegyric or satire, but an honest account of actions and inferred characteristics, in reading which a prince might exercise his intellect.

'The soil is fruitful and the men are bold'[1]

Another statute was made, of singular policy, for the population, apparently, and, if it be thoroughly considered, for the soldiery and military forces of the realm.

Inclosures at that time began to be more frequent, whereby arable land, which could not be manured without people and families, was turned into pasture, which was easily rid by a few herdsmen; and tenances for years, lives, and at will, whereupon much of the yeomanry lived, were turned into demesnes.[2] This bred a decay of people, and, by consequence, a decay of towns, churches, tithes, and the like. The king likewise knew full well, and in no wise forgot, that there ensued withal upon this a decay and diminution of subsidies, and taxes; for the more gentlemen, ever the lower books of subsidies.[3] In remedying of this inconvenience the king's wisdom was admirable, and the parliament's at that time. Inclosures they would not forbid, for that had been to forbid the improvement of the patrimony of the kingdom; nor tillage they would not compell, for that was to strive with nature and utility: but they took a course to take away depopulating inclosures and depopulating pasturage, and yet not that by name, or by any imperious express prohibition, but by consequence. The ordinance was, 'That all houses of husbandry, that were used with twenty acres of ground and upwards, should be maintained and kept up for ever; together with a competent proportion of land to be used and occupied with them;' and in no wise to be severed from them, as by another statute, made afterwards in his Successor's time, was more fully declared: this upon forfeiture to be taken, not by way of popular action, but by seizure of the land itself by the king and lords of the fee,[4] as to half the profits, till the houses and lands were restored. By this means the houses being kept up, did of necessity enforce a dweller; and the proportion of land for occupation being kept up, did of necessity enforce that dweller not to be a beggar or cottager, but a man of some substance, that might keep hinds[5] and servants, and set the plough on going. This did wonderfully concern the might and mannerhood[6] of the kingdom, to have farms as it were of a standard, sufficient to maintain an able body out of penury, and did in effect amortise[7] a great part of the lands of the kingdom unto the hold and occupation of the yeomanry or middle people, of a condition between gentlemen and cottagers or peasants. Now, how much this did advance the military power of the kingdom is apparent by the true principles of war and the examples of other kingdoms. For it hath been held by the general opinion of men of best judgement in the wars, howsoever some few have varied, and that it may receive some distinction of case, that the principal strength of an army consisteth in the infantry or foot. And to make good infantry, it requireth men bred, not in a servile or indigent fashion, but in some free and plentiful manner. Therefore if a state run most to noblemen and gentlemen, and that the husbandmen and ploughmen be but as their workfolk or labourers, or else mere cottagers, which are but housed beggars, you may have a good cavalry but never good stable bands of foot; like to coppice woods, that if you leave in them staddles[8] too thick, they will run to bushes and briars, and have little clean underwood. And this is to be seen in France and Italy, and some other parts abroad, where in effect all is noblesse or peasantry (I speak of people out of towns), and no middle people; and therefore no good forces of foot; insomuch as they are enforced to employ mercenary bands of Switzers, and the like, for their battalions of foot. Whereby also it comes to pass, that those nations have much people and few soldiers. Whereas the king saw, that contrariwise it would follow, that England, though much less in territory, yet should have infinitely more soldiers of their native forces than those other nations have. Thus did the king secretly sow Hydra's teeth; whereupon, according to the poet's fiction, should rise up armed men for the service of this kingdom.[9] . . . And here I do desire those into whose hands this work shall fall, that they do take in good part my long insisting upon the laws that were made in this king's reign. Whereof I have these reasons: both because it was the pre-eminent virtue and merit of this king, to whose memory I do honour; and because it hath some correspondence to my person; but chiefly because, in my judgement, it is some defect even in the best writers of history, that they do not often enough summarily deliver and set down the most memorable laws that passed in the times whereof they write, being indeed the principal acts of peace. For though they may be had in original books of law themselves; yet that informeth not the judgement of kings and counsellors, and persons of estate, so well as to see them described, and entered in the table[10] and portrait of the times.

A law: that the subject should not suffer for his obedience[11]

The principal law that was made this parliament, was a law of a strange nature; rather just than legal; and more magnanimous than provident.[12] This law did ordain, That no person that did assist in arms, or otherwise, the king for the time being, should after be impeached therefore, or attainted,[13] either by the course of law, or by act of parliament. But if any such act of attainder did happen to be made, it should be void and of none effect; for that it was agreeable to reason of estate,[14] that the subject should not inquire of the justness of the king's title or quarrel; and it was agreeable to good conscience, that, whatsoever the fortunes of the war were, the subject should not suffer for his obedience. The spirit of this law was wonderful pious and noble, being like, in matter of war, unto the spirit of David in matter of plague; who said, *If I have sinned strike me: but what have these sheep done?*[15] Neither wanted this law parts of prudent and deep foresight; for it did the better take away occasion for the people to busy themselves to pry into the king's title; for that howsoever it fell, their safety was already provided for. Besides, it could not but greatly draw unto him the love and hearts of the people, because he seemed more careful for them than for himself. But yet nevertheless it did take off from his party that great tie and spur of necessity, to fight and go victors out of the field; considering their lives and fortunes were put in safety and protected, whether they stood to it or ran away. But the force and obligation of this law was in itself illusory, as to the latter part of it, by a precedent act of parliament to bind or frustrate a future. For a supreme and absolute power cannot conclude itself,[16] neither can that which is in nature revocable be made fixed, no more than if a man should appoint or declare by his will, that if he made any latter will it should be void. And for the case of the act of parliament, there is a notable precedent of it in King Henry the Eighth's time; who doubting he might die in the minority of his son, procured an act to pass, That no statute made during the minority of a king, should bind him or his successors, except it were confirmed by the king under his great seal at his full age. But the first act that passed in King Edward the Sixth's time, was an act of repeal of that former act; at which time nevertheless the king was minor. But things that do not bind, may satisfy for the time.

3

The character of Henry VII

This king, to speak of him in terms equal to his deserving, was one of the best sort of wonders; a wonder for wise men. He had parts, both in his virtues and his fortune, not so fit for a common-place, as for observation.[17] Certainly he was religious, both in his affection and observance. But as he could see clear, for those times, through superstition, so he would be blinded, now and then, by human policy. He advanced church-men: he was tender[18] in the privilege of sanctuaries, though they wrought him much mischief. He built and endowed many religious foundations, besides his memorable hospital of the Savoy:[19] and yet was he a great alms-giver in secret; which shewed, that his works in public were dedicated rather to God's glory than his own. He professed always to love and seek peace; and it was his usual preface in his treaties, that when Christ came into the world, peace was sung; and when he went out of the world, peace was bequeathed. And this virtue could not proceed out of fear or softness; for he was valiant and active, and therefore, no doubt, it was truly Christian and moral. Yet he knew the way to peace was not to seem to be desirous to avoid wars: therefore would he make offers and fames of wars,[20] till he had mended the conditions of peace. It was also much, that one that was so great a lover of peace, should be so happy in war. For his arms, either in foreign or civil wars, were never unfortunate; neither did he know what a disaster meant. The war of his coming in, and the rebellions of the Earl of Lincoln, and the Lord Audley, were ended by victory.[21] The wars of France and Scotland, by peaces sought at his hands.[22] That of Britain, by accident of the duke's death.[23] The insurrection of the Lord Lovel, and that of Perkin at Exeter, and in Kent, by flight of the rebels before they came to blows.[24] So that his fortune of arms was still inviolate; the rather sure, for that in the quanching[25] of the commotions of his subjects, he ever went in person: sometimes reserving himself to back and second his lieutenants, but ever in action; and yet that was not merely forwardness,[26] but partly distrust of others.

He did much maintain and countenance[27] his laws; which, nevertheless, was no impediment to him to work his will: for it was so handled, that neither prerogative nor profit went to diminution.[28] And yet as he would sometimes strain up his laws[29] to his prerogative, so would he also let down his prerogative[30] to his parliament. For mint,[31] and wars, and martial discipline, things of absolute power, he would nevertheless bring to parliament. Justice was well administered in his time, save where the king was party: save also, that the council-table[32] intermeddled too much with *meum* and *tuum*. For it was a very court of justice during his time, especially in the beginning; but in that part both of justice and policy, which is the durable part, and cut, as it were, in brass or marble, which is the making of good laws, he did excel. And with his justice, he was also a merciful prince: as in whose time, there were but three of the nobility that suffered: the Earl of Warwick, the Lord Chamberlain, and the Lord Audley;[33] though the first two were instead of numbers, in the dislike and obloquy of the people. But there were never so great rebellions, expiated with so little blood, drawn by the hand of justice, as the two rebellions of Blackheath and Exeter. As for the severity used upon those which were taken in Kent, it was but upon a scum of people. His pardons went ever both before and after his sword. But then he had withal a strange kind of interchanging of large and unexpected pardons, with severe executions; which, his wisdom considered, could not be imputed to any inconstancy or inequality; but either to some reason which we do not now know, or to a principle he had set unto himself, that he would vary, and try both ways in turn. But the less blood he drew, the more he took of treasure. And, as some construed it, he was the more sparing in the one, that he might be the more pressing in the other; for both would have been intolerable. Of nature assuredly he coveted to accumulate treasure, and was a little poor in admiring riches. The people, into whom there is infused, for the preservation of monarchies, a natural desire to discharge their princes,[34] though it be with the unjust charge of their counsellors and ministers, did impute this unto Cardinal Morton and Sir Reginald Bray, who, as it after appeared, as counsellors of ancient authority[35] with him, did so second his humours, as nevertheless they did temper them. Whereas Empson and Dudley that followed, being persons that had no reputation with him, otherwise than by the servile following of his bent, did not give way only, as the first did, but shape him way to those extremities, for which himself was touched with remorse at his death, and which his successor renounced, and sought to purge.[36] This excess of his had at that time many glosses and interpretations. Some thought the continual rebellions wherewith he had been vexed, had made him grow to hate his people: some thought it was done to pull down their stomachs, and to keep them low: some, for that he would leave his son a golden fleece: some suspected he had some high design upon foreign parts: but those perhaps shall come nearest the truth, that fetch not their reasons so far off: but rather impute it to nature, age, peace, and a mind fixed upon other ambition or pursuit. Whereunto I should add, that having every day occasion to take notice of the necessities and shifts for money of other great princes abroad, it did the better, by comparison, set off to him the felicity of full coffers. As to his expending of treasure, he never spared charge which his affairs required: and in his buildings was magnificent, but his rewards were very limited: so that his liberality was rather upon his own state and memory than upon the deserts of others.

He was of an high mind,[37] and loved his own will, and his own way: as one that revered himself, and would reign indeed. Had he been a private man, he would have been termed proud. But in a wise prince, it was but keeping of distance, which indeed he did towards all; not admitting any near or full approach, either to his power, or to his secrets, for he was governed by none. His queen, notwithstanding she had presented him with divers children, and with a crown also, though he would not acknowledge it, could do nothing with him. His mother he reverenced much, heard little. For any person agreeable to him for society, such as was Hastings to King Edward the Fourth, or Charles Brandon after to King Henry the Eighth, he had none: except we should account for such persons, Fox and Bray, and Empson, because they were so much with him: but it was but as the instrument is much with the workman. He had nothing in him of vain glory, but yet kept state and majesty to the height; being sensible, that majesty maketh the people bow, but vain glory boweth to them.

To his confederates[38] abroad he was constant and just, but not open. But rather such was his inquiry, and such his closeness, as they stood in the light towards him, and he stood in the dark to them. Yet without strangeness,[39] but with a semblance of mutual communication of affairs. As for little envies,[40] or emulations upon foreign princes, which are frequent with many kings, he had never any: but went substantially to his own business. Certain it is, that though his reputation was great at home, yet it was greater abroad. For foreigners that could not see the passages of affairs, but made their judgments upon the issues of them, noted that he was ever in strife, and ever aloft. It grew also from the airs[41] which the princes and states abroad received from their ambassadors and agents here; which were attending the court in great number: whom he did not only content with courtesy, reward, and privateness: but, upon such conferences as passed with them, put them in admiration to find his universal insight into the affairs of the world: which though he did suck chiefly from themselves, yet that which he had gathered from them all, seemed admirable to every one. So that they did write ever to their superiors in high terms, concerning his wisdom and art of rule; nay, when they were returned, they did commonly maintain intelligence with him. Such a dexterity he had to impropriate[42] to himself all foreign instruments.

He was careful and liberal to obtain good intelligence from all parts abroad: wherein he did not only use his interest in the liegers[43] here, and his pensioner,[44] which he had both in the court of Rome, and other the courts of Christendom; but the industry and vigilancy of his own ambassadors in foreign parts. For which purpose his instructions were ever extreme curious, and articulate:[45] and in them more articles touching inquisition, than touching negotiation: requiring likewise from his ambassadors an answer, in particular distinct articles respectively to his questions.

As for his secret spials,[46] which he did employ both at home and abroad, by them to discover what practices and conspiracies were against him, surely his case required it: he had such moles perpetually working and casting to undermine him. Neither can it be reprehended: for if spials be lawful against lawful enemies, much more against conspirators and traitors. But indeed to give them credence by oaths or curses, that cannot be well maintained: for those are too holy vestments for a disguise. Yet surely there was this further good in his employing of these flies[47] and familiars; that as the use of them was cause that many conspiracies were revealed, so the fame and suspicion of them kept, no doubt, many conspiracies from being attempted.

Towards his queen he was nothing uxorious, nor scarce indulgent: but companiable [sic] and respective,[48] and without jealousy. Towards his children he was full of paternal affection, careful of their education, aspiring to their high advancement, regular to see that they should not want of any due honour and respect, but not greatly willing to cast any popular lustre upon them.

To his council he did refer much, and sat oft in person: knowing it to be the way to assist his power, and inform his judgement. In which respect also he was fairly patient of liberty, both of advice, and of vote, till himself were declared.[49] He kept a strait hand on his nobility, and chose rather to advance clergymen and lawyers, which were more obsequious to him, but had less interest in the people; which made for his absoluteness, but not for his safety. Insomuch as, I am persuaded, it was one of the causes of his troublesome reign; for that his nobles, though they were loyal and obedient, yet did not co-operate with him, but let every man go his own way. He was not afraid of an able man, as Lewis the Eleventh was; but contrariwise, he was served by the ablest men that were to be found; without which his affairs could not have prospered as they did. For war, Bedford, Oxford, Surrey, D'Aubigny, Brooke, Poynings: for other affairs, Morton, Fox, Bray, the Prior of Lanthony, Warham, Urswick, Hussey, Frowick, and others. Neither did he care how cunning they were that he did employ: for he thought himself to have the master-reach. And as he chose well, so he held them up well; for it is a strange thing, that though he were a dark prince,[50] and infinitely suspicious, and his times full of secret conspiracies and troubles: yet in twenty-four years' reign, he never put down, or discomposed counsellor, or near servant, save only Stanley, the lord chamberlain. As for the disposition of his subjects in general towards him, it stood thus with him; that of the three affections, which naturally tie the hearts of the subjects to their sovereigns, love, fear, and reverence; he had the last in height, the second in good measure, and so little of the first, as he was beholden to the other two.

He was a prince, sad,[51] serious, and full of thoughts, and secret observations, and full of notes and memorials of his own hand, especially touching persons. As, whom to employ, whom to reward, whom to enquire of, whom to beware of, what were the dependencies, what were the factions, and the like; keeping, as it were, a journal of his thoughts. There is to this day a merry tale; that his monkey, set on as it was thought by one of his chamber, tore his principal notebook all to pieces, when by chance it lay forth: whereat the court, which liked not those pensive accounts, was almost tickled with sport.

He was indeed full of apprehensions and suspicions; but as he did easily take them, so he did easily check them and master them; whereby they were not dangerous, but troubled himself more than others. It is true, his thoughts were so many, as they could not well always stand together; but that which did good one way, did hurt another. Neither did he at sometimes weigh them aright in their proportions. Certainly, that rumour which did him so much mischief, that the Duke of York should be saved and alive, was, at the first, of his own nourishing; because he would have more reason not to reign in the right of his wife. He was affable, and both well and fair-spoken; and would use strange sweetness and blandishments of words, where he desired to effect or persuade any thing that he took to heart. He was rather studious than learned; reading most books that were of any worth, in the French tongue, yet he understood the Latin, as appeareth in that Cardinal Hadrian and others, who could very well have written French, did use to write to him in Latin.

For his pleasures, there is no news of them; and yet by his instructions to Marsin and Stile, touching the Queen of Naples,[52] it seemeth he could interrogate well touching beauty. He did by pleasures, as great princes do by banquets, come and look a little upon them, and turn away. For never prince was more wholly given to his affairs, nor in them more of himself: insomuch as in triumphs of justs and tourneys, and balls, and masks, which they then called disguises, he was rather a princely and gentle spectator, than seemed much to be delighted.

No doubt, in him, as in all men, and most of all in kings, his fortune wrought upon his nature and his nature upon his fortune. He attained to the crown, not only from a private fortune, which might endow him with moderation, but also from the fortune of an exiled man, which had quickened in him all seeds of observation and industry. And his times being rather prosperous than calm, had raised his confidence by success, but almost marred his nature by troubles. His wisdom, by often evading from perils, was turned rather into a dexterity to deliver himself from dangers, when they pressed him, than into a providence to prevent and remove them afar off. And even in nature, the sight of his mind was like some sights of eyes; rather strong at hand, than to carry afar off. For his wit[53] increased upon the occasion: and so much the more, if the occasion were sharpened by danger. Again, whether it were the shortness of his foresight, or the strength of his will, or the dazzling of his suspicions, or what it was, certain it is, that the perpetual troubles of his fortunes, there being no more matter out of which they grew, could not have been without some great defects and main errors in his nature, customs, and proceedings, which he had enough to do to save and help with a thousand little industries and watches.[54] But those do best appear in the story itself. Yet take him with all his defects, if a man should compare him with the kings his concurrents in France and Spain, he shall find him more politic[55] than Lewis the Twelfth of France, and more entire and sincere[56] than Ferdinando of Spain. But if you shall change Lewis the Twelfth for Lewis the Eleventh, who lived a little before, then the consort[57] is more perfect. For that Lewis the Eleventh, Ferdinando, and Henry, may be esteemed for the *tres magi* of kings of those ages. To conclude, if this king did no greater matters, it was long of himself: for he minded what he compassed.[58]

He was a comely personage, a little above just stature, well and straight limbed, but slender. His countenance was reverend, and a little like a church-man: and as it was not strange or dark,[59] so neither was it winning or pleasing, but as the face of one well disposed. But it was to the disadvantage of the painter, for it was best when he spake.

His worth may bear a tale or two, that may put upon him somewhat that may seem divine. When the Lady Margaret his mother had divers great suitors for marriage, she dreamed one night, that one in the likeness of a bishop in pontifical habit did tender her Edmund, Earl of Richmond, the king's father, for her husband, neither had she ever any child but the king, though she had three husbands. One day when King Henry the Sixth, whose innocency gave him holiness, was washing his hands at a great feast, and cast his eye upon King Henry, then a young youth, he said, 'This is the lad that shall possess quietly that, that we now strive for.' But that, that was truly divine in him, was that he had the fortune of a true Christian, as well as of a great king in living exercised,[60] and dying repentant: so as he had an happy warfare in both conflicts, both of sin and the cross.

He was born at Pembroke castle, and lieth buried at Westminster, in one of the stateliest and daintiest monuments of Europe, both for the chapel and for the sepulchre. So that he dwelleth more richly dead, in the monument of his tomb,[61] than he did alive in Richmond, or any of his palaces. I could wish he did the like in this monument of his fame.

The Trial of the Earl of Somerset

In the opinion of Ben Jonson, Bacon was the greatest orator of his time. Applying to Bacon what Seneca had said of Severus Cassius, Jonson wrote, 'No man ever spoke more neatly, more presly [concisely], more weightily, or suffered less emptiness, less idleness, in what he uttered . . . His hearers could not cough, or look aside from him, without loss . . . The fear of every man that heard him was lest he should make an end.' As a lawyer, a Judge, and a Member of Parliament throughout his life, Bacon must have made numerous speeches. He spoke from notes, afterwards, at leisure, writing out a full text of any important speech, as he remembered it. The manuscripts of such speeches he left, at his death, to his successor as Lord Keeper, John Williams, Bishop of Lincoln, to be published.

The speech reprinted here was made when Bacon was Attorney-General. It is the main speech of the prosecutor at the trial of Robert Carr, Earl of Somerset, for complicity in the murder of Sir Thomas Overbury, Carr's secretary. Overbury is remembered now as the author of some imitations of the 'characters' of Theophrastus. His death, while a close prisoner in the Tower of London, on 15 September 1613, was attributed to poison, administered by agents instigated by Frances Howard, Countess of Essex. The Countess had been married, when only 13 to the Earl of Essex, then aged 14. They had then separated, the Earl to continue his education abroad. During his absence his wife had flirted with Henry, the Prince of Wales, and then with Robert Carr, the young and handsome favourite of James I. Prince Henry died on 6 November 1612, and though his death was due to typhoid, it was rumoured that he had been poisoned. The Countess of Essex was determined not to consummate her marriage with Essex, but to seek a divorce or annulment and marry Robert Carr. Overbury, whose services to the favourite included advice on matters of State (it was said that 'Overbury governed Carr and Carr governed the king'), opposed the match, and thereby earned the hatred of the Countess. He seems to have feared that the marriage would weaken his position with the favourite, for Frances' family, the Howards, would themselves seek to influence the King through the favourite. Carr, encouraged by Frances, decided to be rid of Overbury, at least until after the divorce, and so trapped Overbury into refusing the post of Ambassador to the Low Countries or to France. The refusal was represented to James as an insult and Overbury was sent to the Tower on 21 April 1613. The Earl of Northampton, a Howard, intrigued to replace the Lieutenant of the Tower by his own nominee, Elwes; Overbury was denied all visitors, and many attempts were made to poison him before he was finally dispatched by the administration of a clyster by an apothecary's boy.

Meanwhile James used all his influence to secure the divorce and on 4 November 1613 Carr was created Earl of Somerset and on 29 December married to Frances Howard. For this marriage Donne provided an Epithalamium and Bacon a Masque of Flowers which cost him £2,000. It was not until after James had begun to fall under the spell of a new favourite, George Villiers, later Marquis of Buckingham, that Somerset's enemies were able to bring about his downfall by the investigation of Overbury's death. Sir Ralph Winwood and Sir Edward Coke assembled the evidence and in November 1615 the lesser figures in the conspiracy—Elwes, Weston, Mrs. Turner and Franklin— were found guilty and hanged. Frances Howard, now Countess of Somerset, was induced to plead guilty to being an accessory, at her trial on 24 May 1616. But Somerset, in spite of all the inducements offered by James, stubbornly refused to confess that he had known that Overbury was being poisoned. Bacon's speech at the opening of the trial shows how flimsy was the evidence against Somerset, but he was found guilty. James, however, pardoned both and in 1621 released them from the Tower.

The surviving texts of Bacon's speech show many variants, and the reports of the speech as delivered suggest that it was not in exactly the form that Bacon afterwards wrote down. See Spedding, *Life, &c.*, V.307 f. A detailed account of the trial is to be found in W. McElwee, *The Murder of Sir Thomas Overbury* (1952). Chapman's play *The*

Tragedy of Chabot has been thought to be based on the trials of Somerset and Bacon, but on this see Irving Ribner's article in *Modern Language Review* for 1960.

The Charge of Sir Francis Bacon, his Majesty's Attorney-General, by way of Evidence, before the Lord High Steward, and the Peers, against Robert, Earl of Somerset, concerning the poisoning of Overbury.

It may please your Grace, my lord High Steward of England,[1]
and you my lords the Peers;

You have here before you Robert Earl of Somerset, to be tried for his life, concerning the procuring and consenting to the impoisonment of Sir Thomas Overbury, then the king's prisoner in the Tower of London, as an accessary before the fact.

I know your lordships cannot behold this nobleman, but you must remember his great favour with the king, and the great place that he hath had and borne, and must be sensible that he is yet of your number and body, a peer as you are; so as you cannot cut him off from your body but with grief; and therefore that you will expect from us, that give in the king's evidence, sound and sufficient matter of proof, to satisfy your honours and consciences.

And for the manner of the evidence also the king our master (who among his other virtues excelleth in that virtue of the imperial throne, which is justice) hath given us commandment that we should not expatiate, nor make invectives, but materially pursue the evidence, as it conduceth to the point in question;[2] a matter that (tho' we are glad of so good a warrant) yet we should have done of ourselves; for far be it from us, by any strains of wit or art to seek to play prizes,[3] or to blazon our names in blood, or to carry the day otherwise than upon just grounds. We shall carry the lanthorn of justice (which is the evidence) before your eyes upright, and be able to save it from being put out with any winds of evasions, or vain defences, that is our part; and within that we shall contain ourselves, not doubting at all, but that this evidence in itself will carry that force, as it shall little need vantages or aggravations.

My lords, the course which I shall hold in delivering that which I shall say (for I love order) is this,

First, I will speak somewhat of the nature and greatness of the offence which is now to be tried; not to weigh down my lord with the greatness of it, but rather contrariwise to shew that a great offence needs a great proof, and that the king, however he might use this gentleman heretofore, as the signet upon his finger,[4] to use the Scripture-phrase, yet in this case could not but put him off, and deliver him into the hands of justice.

Secondly, I will use some few words touching the nature of the proofs, which in such a case are competent.[5]

Thirdly, I will state the proofs.

And lastly, I will produce the proofs, either out of examinations and matters in writing, or witnesses, *viva voce*.

For the offence itself, it is of crimes, next unto high treason, the greatest; it is the foulest of felonies. And take this offence with the circumstances, it hath three degrees or stages; that it is murder; that it is murder by impoisonment; that it is murder committed upon the king's prisoner in the Tower: I might say, that it is murder under the colour of friendship; but that is a circumstance moral; I leave that to the evidence itself.

For murder, my lords, the first record of justice which was in the world was a judgment upon murder in the person of Adam's firstborn, Cain;[6] and though it were not punished by death, but with banishment and mark of ignominy, in respect of the primogeniture, or of the population of the world, or other points of God's secret will, yet it was adjudged, and was (as I said) the first record of justice. So it appeareth likewise in Scripture, that the murder of Abner by Joab,[7] though it were by David respited in respect of great services past, or reason of state, yet it was not forgotten. But of this I will say no more, because I will not discourse. It was ever admitted, and so ranked in God's own tables,[8] that murder is of offences between man and man (next to treason and disobedience of authority, which some divines have referred to the first table, because of the lieutenancy of God in princes[9] and fathers) the greatest.

For impoisonment, I am sorry it should be heard of in this kingdom: it is not *nostri generis nec sanguinis*:[10] it is an Italian crime, fit for the court of Rome, where that person[11] that intoxicateth the kings of the earth with his cup of poison in heretical doctrine, is many times really and materially intoxicated and impoisoned himself.

But it hath three circumstances, which make it grievous beyond other murders: whereof the first is, that it takes a man in full peace, in God's and the king's peace; he thinks no harm, but is comforting nature with refection and food; so that, as the Scripture saith, *his table is made a snare.*[12]

The second is, that it is easily committed, and easily concealed; and on the other side, hardly prevented, and hardly discovered: for murder by violence, princes have guards, and private men have houses, attendants, and arms: neither can such murders be committed but *cum sonitu*[13], and with some overt and apparent act that may discover and trace the offender. But as for poison, the cup itself of princes will scarce serve, in regard of many poisons that neither discolour nor distaste; and so passeth without noise or observation.

And the last is, because it concerneth not only the destruction of the maliced man, but of any other; *Quis modo tutus erit?*[14] for many times the poison is prepared for one, and is taken by another: so that men die other men's deaths; *concidit infelix alieno vulnere:*[15] and it is, as the Psalm calleth it *sagitta nocte volans; the arrow that flieth by night,*[16] it hath no aim or certainty.

And therefore if any man shall say to himself here is great talk of empoisonment but I am sure I am safe, for I have no enemies, neither have I anything that another man should long for, why that is all one: he may sit next him at the table that is meant to be poisoned and pledge him of his cup; as we may see by an example in the 21st year of King Henry the eighth, that where the purpose was to poison one man there was poison put into barm or yeast, and with that barm pottage or gruel was made, whereby sixteen of the Bishop of Rochester's servants were empoisoned; nay it went into the alms basket likewise, and the poor at the gate were poisoned. And therefore with great judgment did the statute made that year touching this accident make this empoisoning high treason, because it tendeth to the dissolution of human society; for whatsoever offence doeth so, is in the nature thereof of high treason.

Now for the third degree of this particular offence, which is, that it was committed upon the king's prisoner, who was out of his own defence, and merely in the king's protection, and for whom the king and state was a kind of respondent;[17] it is a thing that aggravates the fault much. For certainly, my lord of Somerset, let me tell you this, that Sir Thomas Overbury is the first man that was murdered in the Tower of London, since the murder of the two young princes. Thus much of the offence, now to the proofs.

For the nature of the proofs, your lordships must consider, that impoisonment, of all offences is the most secret; so secret, as if in all cases of impoisonment you should require testimony, you were as good proclaim impunity. I will put book-examples.

Who could have impeached Livia, by testimony, of the impoisoning of the figs upon the tree, which her husband was wont for his pleasure to gather with his own hands?[18]

Who could have impeached Parisatis[19] for the poisoning of one side of the knife that she carved with, and keeping the other side clean; so that herself did eat of the same piece of meat that the lady did that she did impoison? The cases are infinite, and indeed not fit to be spoken of, of the secrecy of impoisonments; but wise triers[20] must take upon them, in these secret cases, Salomon's spirit, that, where there could be no witnesses, collected the act by the affection[21].

But yet we are not at our case: for that which your lordships are to try is not the act of impoisonment, for that is done to your hand; all the world by law is concluded to say, that Overbury was impoisoned by Weston.[22]

But the question before you is of the procurement only, and of the abetting, as the law termeth it, as accessary before the fact: which abetting is no more but to do or use any act or means, which may aid or conduce unto the impoisonment.

So that it is not the buying or making of the poison, or the preparing, or confecting, or commixing of it, or the giving or sending or laying the poison, that are the only acts that do amount unto abetment. But if there be any other act or means done or used to give the opportunity of impoisonment, or to facilitate the execution of it, or to stop or divert any impediments that might hinder it, and this be with an intention to accomplish and achieve the impoisonment; all these are abetments, and accessories before the fact, I will put you a familiar example. Allow there be a conspiracy to murder a man as he journeys by the way, and it be one man's part to draw him forth to that journey by invitation, or by colour of some business; and another takes upon him to dissuade some friend of his, whom he had a purpose to take in his company, that he be not too strong to make his defence; and another hath the part to go along with him, and to hold him in talk till the first blow be given; all these, my lords, without scruple are abettors to this murder, though none of them give the blow, nor assist to give the blow.

My lords, he is not the hunter alone that lets slip the dog upon the deer, but he that lodges the deer, or raises him, or puts him out, or he that sets a toil[23] that he cannot escape, or the like.

But this, my lords, little needeth in this present case, where there is such a chain of acts of impoisonment as hath been seldom seen, and could hardly have been expected, but that greatness of fortune maketh commonly grossness in offending.

To descend to the proofs themselves, I shall keep this course.

First, I will make a narrative or declaration of the fact itself.

Secondly, I will break and distribute the proofs as they concern the prisoner.

And thirdly, according to that distribution, I will produce them, and read them, or use them.

So there is nothing that I shall say, but your lordship, my lord of Somerset, shall have three thoughts or cogitations to answer it: First, when I open it, you may take your aim. Secondly, when I distribute it, you may prepare your answers without confusion. And lastly, when I produce the witnesses or examinations themselves, you may again ruminate and re-advise how to make your defence. And this I do the rather, because your memory or understanding may not be oppressed or overladen with the length of evidence, or with confusion of order. Nay more, when your lordship shall make your answers in your time, I will put you in mind, when cause shall be, of your omissions.

First, therefore, for the simple narrative of the fact. Sir Thomas Overbury for a time was known to have had great interest and great friendship with my lord of Somerset, both in his meaner fortunes, and after; insomuch as he was a kind of oracle of direction unto him; and, if you will believe his own vaunts, being of an insolent Thrasonical[24] disposition, he took upon him, that the fortune, reputation, and understanding of this gentleman, who is well known to have had a better teacher,[25] proceeded from his company and counsel.

And this friendship rested not only in conversation[26] and business of court, but likewise in communication of secrets of estate. For my lord of Somerset, at that time exercising, by his majesty's special favour and trust, the office of the Secretary[27] provisionally, did not forbear to acquaint Overbury with the king's packets of dispatches from all parts, Spain, France, the Low Countries, &c. And this not by glimpses, or now and then rounding in the ear[28] for a favour, but in a settled manner: packets were sent, sometimes opened by my lord, sometimes unbroken, unto Overbury, who perused them, copied, registered them, made tables[29] of them as he thought good: so that, I will undertake, the time was when Overbury knew more of the secrets of state than the council-table[30] did. Nay, they were grown to such an inwardness,[31] as they made a play of all the world besides themselves: so as they had ciphers and jargons[32] for the king, the queen, and all the great men; things seldom used, but either by princes and their ambassadors and ministers or by such as work and practise against, or at least upon, princes.

But understand me, my Lord, I shall not charge you this day with any disloyalty; only I lay this for a foundation, that there was a great communication of secrets between you and Overbury, and that it had relation to matters of estate, and the greatest causes of this kingdom.

But, my lords, as it is a principle in nature, that the best things are in their corruption the worst, and the sweetest wine makes the sharpest vinegar; so fell it out with them, that this excess, as I may term it, of friendship ended in mortal hatred on my Lord of Somerset's part.

For it fell out, some twelve months before Overbury's imprisonment in the Tower, that my lord of Somerset was entered into an unlawful love towards his unfortunate lady, then countess of Essex: which went so far, as it was then secretly projected, chiefly between my Lord Privy Seal[33] and my lord of Somerset, to effect a nullity in the marriage with my lord of Essex, and so to proceed to a marriage with Somerset.

This marriage and purpose did Overbury mainly oppugn, under pretence to do the true part of a friend, for that he counted her an unworthy woman; but the truth was, that Overbury, who, to speak plainly, had little that was solid for religion or moral virtue, but was a man possessed with ambition and vain-glory, was loth to have any partners in the favour of my lord of Somerset, and especially not the house of the Howards, against whom he had always professed hatred and opposition: so all was but miserable bargains of ambition.

And, my lords, that this is no sinister construction, will well appear unto you, when you shall hear that Overbury makes his brags to my Lord of Somerset, that he had won him the love of the lady by his letters and industry:[34] so far was he from cases of conscience in this matter. And certainly, my lords, howsoever the tragical misery of that poor gentleman Overbury ought somewhat to obliterate his faults; yet because we are not now upon point of civility, but to discover the face of truth to the face of justice; and that it is material to the true understanding of the state of this cause; Overbury was naught[35] and corrupt, the ballads[36] must be amended for that point.

But to proceed; when Overbury saw that he was like to be dispossessed of my lord here, whom he had possessed so long, and by whose greatness he had promised himself to do wonders; and being a man of an unbounded and impetuous spirit, he began not only to dissuade, but to deter him from that love and marriage; and finding him fixed, thought to try stronger remedies, supposing that he had my lord's head under his girdle, in respect of communication of secrets of estate, or, as he calls them himself in his letters, secrets of all natures; and therefore dealt violently with him, to make him desist, with menaces of discovery of secrets, and the like.

Hereupon grew two streams of hatred upon Overbury; the one, from the lady, in respect that he crossed her love, and abused her name, which are furies to women; the other, of a deeper and more mineral[37] nature, from my Lord of Somerset himself; who was afraid of Overbury's nature, and that if he did break from him and fly out, he would mine into him and trouble his whole fortunes.

I might add a third stream from the earl of Northampton's ambition, who desires to be first in favour with my lord of Somerset; and knowing Overbury's malice to himself and his house, thought that man must be removed and cut off. So it was amongst them resolved and decreed that Overbury must die.

Hereupon they had variety of devices. To send him beyond sea, upon occasion of employment, that was too weak; and they were so far from giving way to it, as they crossed it. There rested but two ways, quarrel or assault, and poison. For that of assault, after some proposition and attempt, they passed from it; it was a thing too open, and subject to more variety of chances. That of poison likewise was a hazardous thing, and subject to many preventions and cautions; especially to such a jealous and working brain as Overbury had, except he were first fast in their hand.

Therefore the way was first to get him into a trap, and lay him up, and then they could not miss the mark. Therefore in execution of this plot it was devised, that Overbury should be designed to some honourable employment in foreign parts, and should under-hand by the lord of Somerset be encouraged to refuse it; and so upon that contempt he should be laid prisoner in the Tower, and then they would look he should be close enough and death should be his bail. Yet were they not at their end. For they considered that if there was not a fit lieutenant of the Tower for their purpose, and likewise a fit under-keeper of Overbury; first, they should meet with many impediments in the giving and exhibiting the poison. Secondly, they should be exposed to note and observation that might discover them. And thirdly, Overbury in the meantime might write clamorous and furious letters to other his friends, and so all might be disappointed. And therefore the next link of the chain was to displace the then lieutenant Waade,[38] and to place Helwisse, a principal abettor in the impoisonment: again, to displace Cary, that was the under-keeper in Waade's time, and to place Weston,[39] who was the principal actor in the impoisonment: and this was done in such a while, that it may appear to be done, as it were, with one breath, as there were but fifteen days between the commitment of Overbury, the displacing of Waade, the placing of Helwisse, the displacing of Cary the under-keeper, the placing of Weston, and the first poison given two days after.[40]

Then when they had this poor gentleman in the Tower close prisoner, where he could not escape nor stir, where he could not feed but by their hands, where he could not speak nor write but through their trunks;[41] then was the time to execute the last act of this tragedy.

Then must Franklin[42] be purveyor of the poisons, and procure five, six, seven several potions, to be sure to hit his complexion. Then must Mrs. Turner be the say-mistress[43] of the poisons to try upon poor beasts, what is present, and what works at distance of time. Then must Weston be the tormentor, and chase him with poison after poison; poison in salts, poison in meats, poison in sweetmeats, poison in medicines and vomits, until at last his body was almost come, by use of poisons, to the state that Mithridates's body was by the use of treacle[44] and preservatives, that the force of the poisons, were blunted upon him: Weston confessing, when he was chid for not dispatching him, that he had given him enough to poison twenty men. Lastly, because all this asked time, courses were taken by Somerset, both to divert all means of Overbury's delivery, and to entertain Overbury by continual letters, partly of hopes and projects for his delivery, and partly of other fables and negotiations; somewhat like some kind of persons, which I will not name, which keep men in talk of fortune-telling, when they have a felonious meaning.

And this is the true narrative of this act of impoisonment, which I have summarily recited.

Now for the distribution of the proofs, there are four heads of proofs to prove you guilty, my Lord of Somerset, of this impoisonment; whereof two are precedent to the impoisonment, the third is present, and the fourth is following or subsequent. For it is in proofs as it is in lights, there is a direct light, and there is a reflexion of light, or back-light.

The first head or proof thereof is, That there was a root of bitterness, a mortal malice or hatred, mixed with deep and bottomless fears, that you had towards Sir Thomas Overbury.

The second is, That you were the principal actor, and had your hand in all those acts, which did conduce to the impoisonment, and which gave opportunity and means to effect it; and without which the impoisonment could never have been, and which could serve or tend to no other end but to the impoisonment.

The third is, That your hand was in the very impoisonment itself, which is more than needs to be proved; that you did direct poison; that you did deliver poison; that you did continually hearken to the success of the impoisonment; and that you spurred it on, and called for dispatch when you thought it lingered.

And lastly, That you did all the things after the impoisonment, which may detect a guilty conscience, for the smothering of it, and avoiding punishment for it: which can be but of three kinds; That you suppressed, as much as in you was, testimony: That you did deface, and destroy, and clip[45] and misdate all writings that might give light to the impoisonment; and that you did fly to the altar of guiltiness, which is a pardon, and a pardon of murder, and a pardon for yourself,[46] and not for your lady.

In this, my lord, I convert[47] my speech to you, because I would have you attend the points of your charge, and so of your defence the better. And two of these heads I have taken to myself, and left the other two to the King's two Sergeants.

For the first main part, which is, the mortal hatred, coupled with fear, that was in my lord of Somerset towards Overbury, although he did palliate it with a great deal of hypocrisy and dissimulation even to the end; I shall prove it, my lord Steward, and you my lords and peers, manifestly, by matter both of oath and writing. The root of this hatred was that that hath cost many a man's life, that is, fear of discovering secrets: secrets I say, of a high and dangerous nature: Wherein the course that I will hold, shall be this:

First, I will shew that such a breach and malice was between my lord and Overbury, and that it burst forth into violent menaces and threats on both sides.

Secondly, That these secrets were not light, but of a high nature; for I will give you the elevation of the pole.[48] They were such as my lord of Somerset for his part had made a vow, that Overbury should neither live in court nor country. That he had likewise opened himself and his own fears so far, that if Overbury ever came forth of the Tower, either Overbury or himself must die for it. And of Overbury's part, he had threatened my lord, that whether he did live or die, my lord's shame should never die, but he would leave him the most odious man of the world. And farther, that my lord was like enough to repent it, in the place where Overbury wrote, which was the Tower of London. He was a true prophet in that: so here is the height of the secrets.

Thirdly, I will shew you, that all the king's business was by my lord put into Overbury's hands: so as there is work enough for secrets, whatsoever they were: and like Princes' confederates, they had their ciphers and jargons.

And lastly, I will shew you that it is but a toy[49] to say that the malice was only in respect he spake dishonourably of the lady; or for doubt of breaking the marriage: for that Overbury was a coadjutor to that love, and the lord of Somerset was as deep in speaking ill of the lady as Overbury. And again, it was too late for that matter, for the bargain of the match was then made and past. And if it had been no more but to remove Overbury from disturbing of the match, it had been an easy matter to have banded over Overbury beyond seas, for which they had a fair way; but that would not serve their turn.

And lastly, *periculum periculo vincitur*,[50] to go so far as an impoisonment, must have a deeper malice than flashes:[51] for the cause must bear a proportion to the effect.

For the next general head of proofs, which consists in acts preparatory to the middle acts, they are in eight several points of the compass, as I may term it.

First, That there were devices and projects to dispatch Overbury, or to overthrow him, plotted between the countess of Somerset, the earl of Somerset, and the earl of Northampton, before they fell upon the impoisonment: for always before men fix upon a course of mischief, there be some rejections: but die he must one way or other.

Secondly, That my lord of Somerset was a principal practiser, I must speak it, in a most perfidious manner, to set a train or trap for Overbury to get him into the Tower; without which they never durst have attempted the impoisonment.

Thirdly, That the placing of the Lieutenant Helwisse, one of the impoisoners, and the displacing of Waade, was by the means of my lord of Somerset.

Fourthly, That the placing of Weston the underkeeper, who was the principal impoisoner, and the displacing of Cary, and the doing of all this within fifteen days after Overbury's commitment, was by the means and countenance of my lord of Somerset. And these two were the active instruments of the impoisonment: and this was a business that the lady's power could not reach unto.

Fifthly, That because there must be a time for the tragedy to be acted, and chiefly because they would not have the poisons work upon the sudden; and for that the strength of Overbury's nature, or the very custom of receiving poison into his body, did overcome the poisons, that they wrought not so fast; therefore Overbury must be held in the Tower. And as my lord of Somerset got him into the trap, so he kept him in, and abused him with continual hopes of liberty; and diverted all the true and effectual means of his liberty, and made light of his sickness and extremities.

Sixthly, That not only the plot of getting Overbury into the Tower, and the devices to hold him and keep him there; but the strange manner of his close keeping, being in but for a contempt, was by the device and means of my lord of Somerset, who denied his father to see him, denied his servants that offered to be shut up close prisoners with him; and in effect handled it so, that he was close prisoner to all his friends, and open and exposed to all his enemies.

Seventhly, That the advertisements which my lady received from time to time from the Lieutenant or Weston, touching Overbury's state of body or health, were ever sent up to the court, though it were in progress,[52] and that from my lady: such a thirst and listening this lord had to hear that he was dispatched.

Lastly, There was a continual negotiation to set Overbury's head on work, that he should make some recognition to clear the honour of the lady; and that he should become a good instrument towards her and her friends: all which was but entertainment; for your lordships shall plainly see divers of my lord of Northampton's letters, whose hand was deep in this business, written, I must say it, in dark words[53] and clauses; that there was one thing pretended, another intended; that there was a real charge, and there was somewhat not real; a main drift, and a dissimulation. Nay farther, there are some passages which the peers in their wisdom will discern to point directly at the impoisonment.

Letters &c.

Many of Bacon's letter have survived, but they are mainly on professional, day-to-day affairs, legal and political. It should be possible to construct a man's biography from his letters. In the following extracts Bacon is writing of himself, his hopes and ambitions, his works, his fears, his misery, his consolation, and finally, of his last illness.

1. Letter to Burghley, 1592. Burghley was Bacon's uncle and Lord Treasurer, but was not inclined to help his nephew to preferment. Here Bacon outlines his life's plan.

2. Preface to a tract 'Of the Interpretation of Nature', written c. 1603, translated by Spedding. A statement of Bacon's assessment of his own personality, and his scientific hopes.

3. Letter to Sir Thomas Bodley, with a copy of The Advancement of Learning, 1605. His pleasure in writing and his preference for a scholar's life.

4. Letter to James I, 25 March 1621. Written when the first charges of bribery were made, two days before Parliament adjourned for Easter. Bacon is clearly perplexed by the attack, and knows that the King can save him if he would.

5. Letter to Lancelot Andrewes, prefixed to An Advertisement Touching an Holy War, 1623. The consolation he found in writing, with an account of his works.

6. Letter to the Earl of Arundel and Surrey, c. 3 April 1626. Bacon's last letter; he died on 9 April, at the Earl's house in Highgate. He was buried in his mother's grave in the Church of St Michael, St Albans.

Sir Francis Bacon to the
Lord Treasurer Burghley (1592)

My Lord,

With as much confidence as mine own honest and faithful devotion unto
your service, and your honourable correspondence[1] unto me and my poor
estate can breed in a man, do I commend myself unto your lordship. I wax now
somewhat ancient; one and thirty years is a great deal of sand in the hour-glass.
My health, I thank God, I find confirmed;[2] and I do not fear that action shall
impair it: because I account my ordinary course of study and meditation to be
more painful[3] than most parts of action are. I ever bear a mind, in some middle
place that I could discharge, to serve her majesty; not as a man born under Sol,
that loveth honour; nor under Jupiter, that loveth business, for the contemplative planet[4] carrieth me away wholly: but as a man born under an excellent
sovereign, that deserveth the dedication of all men's abilities. Besides I do not
find in myself so much self-love, but that the greater parts of my thoughts are to
deserve well, if I were able, of my friends, and namely of your lordship; who
being the Atlas of this commonwealth, the honour of my house, and the second
founder[5] of my poor estate, I am tied by all duties, both of a good patriot, and of
an unworthy kinsman, and of an obliged servant, to employ whatsoever I am,
to do you service. Again, the meanness of my estate doth somewhat move me:
for though I cannot accuse myself, that I am either prodigal or slothful, yet my
health is not to spend, nor my course to get.[6] Lastly, I confess that I have as
vast contemplative ends, as I have moderate civil ends: for I have taken all
knowledge to be my province;[7] and if I could purge it of two sorts of rovers,
whereof the one with frivolous disputations, confutations, and verbosities:
the other with blind experiments and auricular traditions and impostures, hath
committed so many spoils; I hope I should bring in industrious observations,
grounded conclusions, and profitable inventions and discoveries; the best state
of that province. This, whether it be curiosity, or vain glory, or nature, or,
if one take it favourably, philanthropia, is so fixed in my mind, as it cannot be
removed. And I do easily see, that place of any reasonable countenance[8] doth
bring commandment of more wits than of a man's own, which is the thing I
greatly affect. And for your lordship, perhaps you shall not find more strength
and less encounter[9] in any other. And if your lordship shall find now or at any

time, that I do seek or affect any place, whereunto any that is nearer unto your lordship shall be concurrent, say then that I am a most dishonest man. And if your lordship will not carry me on, I will not do as Anaxagoras[10] did, who reduced himself with contemplation unto voluntary poverty: but this I will do, I will sell the inheritance that I have, and purchase some lease of quick revenue, or some office of gain, that shall be executed by deputy, and so give over all care of service, and become some sorry[11] book-maker, or a true pioneer in that mine of truth, which, he said, lay so deep. This which I have writ unto your lordship, is rather thoughts than words, being set down without all art, disguising, or reservation: wherein I have done honour both to your lordship's wisdom, in judging that that will be best believed of your lordship which is truest; and to your lordship's good nature, in retaining nothing from you. And even so, I wish your lordship all happiness, and to myself means and occasion to be added to my faithful desire to do you service.

From my lodging at Gray's Inn.

2

Preface to 'Of the Interpretation of Nature' (c. 1603, translated)

Believing that I was born for the service of mankind, and regarding the care of the Commonwealth as a kind of common property which, like the air and water, belongs to everybody, I set myself to consider in what way mankind might be best served, and what service I was myself best fitted by nature to perform.

Now among all the benefits that could be conferred upon mankind, I found none so great as the discovery of new arts, endowments, and commodities for the bettering of man's life. . . . But if a man could succeed, not in striking out some particular invention, however useful, but in kindling a light in nature—a light that should in its very rising touch and illuminate all the border regions that confine upon the circle of our present knowledge; and so spreading further and further should presently disclose and bring into sight all that is most hidden and secret in the world—that man (I thought) would be the benefactor indeed of the human race, the propagator of man's empire over the universe, the champion of liberty, the conqueror and subduer of necessities.

For myself, I found that I was fitted for nothing so well as for the study of

Truth; as having a mind nimble and versatile enough to catch the resemblances of things (which is the chief point), and at the same time steady enough to fix and distinguish their subtler differences; as being gifted by nature with desire to seek, patience to doubt, fondness to meditate, slowness to assert, readiness to reconsider, carefulness to dispose and set in order; and as being a man that neither affects what is new nor admires what is old, and that hates every kind of imposture. So I thought my nature had a kind of familiarity and relationship with Truth.

Nevertheless, because my birth and education had seasoned me in business of State; and because opinions (so young as I was) would sometimes stagger me; and because I thought that a man's own country has some special claims upon him more than the rest of the world; and because I hoped that, if I rose to any place of honour in the State, I should have a larger command of industry and ability to help me in my work; for these reasons I both applied myself to acquire the arts of civil life, and commended my service, so far as in modesty and honesty I might, to the favour of such friends as had any influence. In which also I had another motive: for I felt that those things I have spoken of—be they great or small—reach no further than the condition and culture of this mortal life; and I was not without hope (the condition of religion being at that time not very prosperous) that if I came to hold office in the State, I might get something done too for the good of men's souls. When I found, however, that my zeal was mistaken for ambition, and my life had already reached the turning-point, and my breaking health reminded me how ill I could afford to be so slow, and I reflected moreover that in leaving undone the good that I could do by myself alone, and applying myself to that which could not be done without the help and consent of others, I was by no means discharging the duty that lay upon me, I put all those thoughts aside, and (in pursuance of my old determination) betook myself wholly to this work. Nor am I discouraged from it because I see signs in the times of the decline and overthrow of that knowledge and erudition which is now in use. Not that I apprehend any more barbarian invasions (unless possibly the Spanish empire should recover its strength, and having crushed other nations by arms should itself sink under its own weight): but the civil wars[12] which may be expected, I think (judging from certain fashions which have come in of late), to spread through many countries—together with the malignity of sects, and those compendious artifices and devices which have crept into the place of solid erudition—seem to portend for literature and the sciences a tempest not less fatal, and one against which the Printing office will be no effectual security. And no doubt but that fair-weather learning which is nursed by leisure, blossoms under reward and praise, which cannot withstand the shock of opinion, and is liable to be abused by tricks and quackery, will sink under such impediments as these. Far otherwise is it with that knowledge, whose dignity is maintained by works of utility and power. For the injuries, therefore, which should proceed from the times, I am not afraid of them; and for the injuries which proceed from men, I am not concerned. For if any one charge me with seeking to be wise over-much, I answer simply that modesty and civil respect are fit for civil matters; in contemplations nothing is to be respected but Truth. If any one call on me for *works*, and that presently: I tell him frankly, without any imposture at all, that for me—a man not old, of weak health, my hands full of civil business, entering without guide or light upon an argument of all others the most obscure—I hold it enough to have constructed the machine, though I may not succeed in setting it on work. . . . If, again, any one ask me, not indeed for actual works, yet for definite promises and forecasts of the works that are to be, I would have him know that the knowledge which we now possess will not teach a man even what to *wish*. Lastly—though this is a matter of less moment—if any of our politicians, who use to make their calculations and conjectures according to persons and precedents, must needs interpose his judgment in a thing of this nature, I would but remind him how (according to the ancient fable) the lame man keeping the course won the race of the swift man who left it; and that there is no thought to be taken about precedents, for the thing is without precedent.

For myself, my heart is not set upon any of those things which depend upon external accidents. I am not hunting for fame: I have no desire to found a sect, after the fashion of heresiarchs; and to look for any private gain from such an undertaking as this, I count both ridiculous and base. Enough for me the consciousness of well-deserving, and those real and effectual results with which Fortune itself cannot interfere.

3
Sir Francis Bacon to Sir Thomas Bodley, upon sending him his Book of the Advancement of Learning (1605)

Sir,

I think no man may more truly say with the psalm, *multum incola fuit anima mea*.[13] For I do confess, since I was of any understanding, my mind hath in effect, been absent from that I have done, and in absence errors are committed, which I do willingly acknowledge; and amongst the rest, this great one that led the rest; that knowing myself by inward calling to be fitter to hold a book, than to play a part, I have led my life in civil causes, for which I was not very fit by nature, and more unfit by the preoccupation of my mind. Therefore, calling myself home, I have now for a time enjoyed myself, where likewise I desire to make the world partaker; my labours (if so I may term that which was the comfort of my other labours) I have dedicated to the king, desirous if there be any good in them, it may be as fat of a sacrifice incensed to his honour; and the second copy I have sent unto you, not only in good affection, but in a kind of congruity,[14] in regard of your great and rare desert of learning: for books are the shrines where the saint is, or is believed to be. And you having built an ark,[15] to save learning from deluge, deserve, in propriety, any new instrument or engine, whereby learning should be improved or advanced. So, etc.

4

The Lord Chancellor Bacon to the King (1621)

It may please your most excellent Majesty,

Time hath been, when I have brought unto you *Gemitum Columbae*[16] from others, now I bring it from myself. I fly unto your majesty with the wings of a dove, which, once within these seven days, I thought would have carried me a higher flight.[17] When I enter into myself, I find not the materials of such a tempest as is come upon me. I have been, (as your majesty knoweth best) never author of any immoderate counsel, but always desired to have things carried *suavibus modis*.[18] I have been no avaricious oppressor of the people. I have been no haughty, or intolerable, or hateful man, in my conversation or carriage: I have inherited no hatred from my father,[19] but am a good patriot born. Whence should this be; for these are the things that use to raise dislikes abroad.

For the House of Commons, I began my credit there, and now it must be the place of the sepulture thereof. And yet this parliament, upon the message touching religion, the old love revived, and they said, I was the same man still, only honesty was turned into honour.

For the upper-house, even within these days, before these troubles, they seemed as to take me into their arms, finding in me ingenuity, which they took to be the true straight line of nobleness, without crooks or angles.

And for the briberies and gifts wherewith I am charged, when the books of hearts shall be opened, I hope I shall not be found to have the troubled fountain of a corrupt heart, in a depraved habit of taking rewards to pervert justice; howsoever I may be frail, and partake of the abuses of the times.

And therefore I am resolved, when I come to my answer, not to trick[20] my innocency, (as I writ to the lords) by cavillations or voidances; but to speak to them the language that my heart speaketh to me, in excusing, extenuating, or ingenuous confessing; praying God to give me the grace to see to the bottom of my faults, and that no hardness of heart do steal upon me, under shew of more neatness of conscience,[21] than is cause.

But not to trouble your majesty any longer, craving pardon for this long mourning letter; that which I thirst after, as the hart after the streams, is, that I may know, by my matchless friend[22] that presenteth to you this letter, your majesty's heart (which is an abyssus of goodness, as I am an abyssus of misery) towards me. I have been ever your man, and counted myself but an usufructuary[23] of myself, the property being yours. And now making myself an oblation,[24] to do with me as may best conduce to the honour of your justice, the honour of your mercy, and the use of your service, resting as

clay in your majesty's gracious hands,
FR. ST. ALBAN. CAN.

Mar. 25, 1621

5

An Advertisement Touching an Holy War. To the Right Reverend Father in God, Lancelot Andrewes, Lord Bishop of Winchester, and Counsellor of Estate to His Majesty (1622)

MY LORD,

Amongst consolations, it is not the least to represent to a man's self like examples of calamity in others. For examples give a quicker impression than arguments; and besides, they certify us, that which the Scripture also tendereth for satisfaction: *that no new thing is happened unto us.*[25] This they do the better, by how much the examples are liker in circumstances to our own case; and more especially if they fall upon persons that are greater and worthier than ourselves. For as it savoureth of vanity, to match ourselves highly in our own conceit; so on the other side it is a good sound conclusion, that if our betters have sustained the like events, we have the less cause to be grieved.

In this kind of consolation I have not been wanting to myself, though as a Christian, I have tasted, through God's great goodness, of higher remedies. Having therefore, through the variety of my reading, set before me many examples both of ancient and later times, my thoughts, I confess, have chiefly stayed upon three particulars, as the most eminent and the most resembling. All three persons that had held chief place of authority in their countries; all three ruined, not by war, or by any other disaster, but by justice and sentence as delinquents and criminals; all three famous writers, insomuch as the remembrance of their calamity is now as to posterity but as a little picture of nightwork, remaining amongst the fair and excellent tables of their acts and works; and all three, if that were any thing to the matter, fit examples to quench any man's ambition of rising again; for that they were every one of them restored with great glory, but to their farther ruin and destruction, ending in a violent death. The men were, Demosthenes, Cicero, and Seneca;[26] persons that I durst not claim affinity with, except the similitude of our fortunes had contracted it. When I had cast mine eyes upon these examples, I was carried on farther to observe, how they did bear their fortunes, and principally, how they did employ their times, being banished, and disabled for public business: to the end that I might learn by them; and that they might be as well my counsellors as my comforters. Whereupon I happened to note, how diversly their fortunes wrought upon them; especially in that point at which I did most aim, which was the employing of their times and pens. In Cicero, I saw that during his banishment, which was almost two years, he was so softened and dejected, as he wrote nothing but a few womanish epistles. And yet, in mine opinion, he had least reason of the three to be discouraged: for although it was judged, and judged by the highest kind of judgment, in form of a statute or law, that he should be banished, and his whole estate confiscated and seized, and his houses pulled down, and that it should be highly penal for any man to propound a repeal; yet his case even then had no great blot of ignominy; for it was thought but a tempest of popularity which overthrew him. Demosthenes contrariwise, though his case was foul, being condemned for bribery, and not simple bribery, but bribery in the nature of treason and disloyalty, yet nevertheless took so little knowledge of his fortune, as during his banishment he did much busy himself, and intermeddle with matters of state; and took upon him to counsel the state, as if he had been still at the helm, by letters; as appears by some epistles of his which are extant. Seneca indeed, who was condemned for many corruptions and crimes, and banished into a solitary island, kept a mean; and though his pen did not freeze, yet he abstained from intruding into matters of business; but spent his time in writing books of excellent argument and use for all ages though he might have made better choice, sometimes, of his dedications.

These examples confirmed me much in a resolution, whereunto I was otherwise inclined, to spend my time wholly in writing; and to put forth that poor talent, or half talent, or what it is, that God hath given me, not as heretofore to particular exchanges, but to banks, or mounts[27] of perpetuity, which will not break. Therefore having not long since set forth a part of my Instauration; which is the work, that in mine own judgement, *si nunquam fallit imago*,[28] I do most esteem; I think to proceed in some new parts thereof. And although I have received from many parts beyond the seas, testimonies touching that work, such as beyond which I could not expect at the first in so abstruse an argument; yet nevertheless I have just cause to doubt, that it flies too high over men's heads: I have a purpose therefore, though I break the order of time, to draw it down to the sense, by some patterns of a Natural Story and Inquisition.[29] And again, for that my book of Advancement of Learning may be some preparative, or key, for the better opening of the Instauration; because it exhibits a mixture of new conceits and old; whereas the Instauration gives the new unmixed, otherwise than with some little aspersion of the old for taste's sake; I have thought good to procure a translation of that book into the general language, not without great and ample additions, and enrichment thereof, especially in the second book, which handleth the partition of sciences; in such sort, as I hold it may serve in lieu of the first part of the Instauration, and acquit my promise in that part. Again, because I cannot altogether desert the civil person that I have borne; which if I should forget, enough would remember; I have also entered into a work touching Laws, propounding a character of justice in a middle term, between the speculative and reverend discourses of philosophers, and the writings of lawyers, which are tied and obnoxious to their particular laws.[30] And although it be true, that I had a purpose to make a particular digest,[31] or recompilement of the laws of mine own nation; yet because it is a work of assistance, and that which I cannot master by mine own forces and pen, I have laid it aside. Now having in the work of my Instauration had in contemplation the general good of men in their very being, and the dowries of nature; and in my work of laws, the general good of men likewise in society, and the dowries of government; I thought in duty I owed somewhat unto my own country, which I ever loved; insomuch as although my place hath been far above my desert, yet my thoughts and cares concerning the good thereof were beyond, and over, and above my place: so now being, as I am, no more able to do my country service, it remained unto me to do it honour: which I have endeavoured to do in my work of the reign of King Henry the seventh. As for my Essays, and some other particulars of that nature, I count them but as the recreations of my other studies, and in that sort purpose to continue them; though I am not ignorant that those kind of writings would, with less pains and embracement,[32] perhaps, yield more lustre and reputation to my name than those other which I have in hand. But I account the use that a man should seek of the publishing of his own writings before his death, to be but an untimely anticipation of that which is proper to follow a man, and not to go along with him.

But revolving with myself my writings, as well those which I have published, as those which I had in hand, methought they went all into the city, and none into the temple; where, because I have found so great consolation, I desire likewise to make some poor oblation. Therefore I have chosen an argument, mixt of religious and civil considerations; and likewise mixt between contemplative and active. For who can tell whether there may not be an *exoriere aliquis*?[33] Great matters, especially if they be religious, have, many times, small beginnings: and the platform[34] may draw on the building. This work, because I was ever an enemy to flattering dedications, I have dedicated to your lordship, in respect of our ancient and private acquaintance; and because amongst the men of our times I hold you in special reverence.

Your lordship's loving friend,

FR. ST. ALBAN.

6

To the Earl of Arundel and Surrey
(c. 3 April 1626)

My very good Lord,

I was likely to have had the fortune of Cajus Plinius the elder, who lost his life by trying an experiment about the burning of the Mountain Vesuvius. For I was also desirous to try an experiment[35] or two, touching the conservation and induration of bodies. As for the experiment itself, it succeeded excellently well; but in the journey (between London and Highgate) I was taken with such a fit of casting,[36] as I knew not whether it were the stone, or some surfeit, or cold, or indeed a touch of them all three. But when I came to your lordship's house, I was not able to go back, and therefore was forced to take up my lodging here, where your housekeeper is very careful and diligent about me, which I assure myself your lordship will not only pardon towards him, but think the better of him for it. For indeed your lordship's house was happy to me; and I kiss your noble hands for the welcome which I am sure you give me to it, &c.

I know how unfit it is for me to write to your lordship with any other hand than my own; but by my troth, my fingers are so disjointed with this fit of sickness, that I cannot steadily hold a pen.

Notes

'A second thing belonging to criticism is the explanation and illustration of authors, comments, notes, collections, &c. But here an ill custom has prevailed among the critics of skipping over the obscure passages, and expatiating upon such as are sufficiently clear, as if their design were not so much to illustrate their author, as to take all occasions of showing their own learning and reading.'

(*De Augmentis*, VI.4)

A Conference of Pleasure: In Praise of Knowledge.

1   *The mind is the man*   cf. Cardan, 'A man is nothing but his mind; if that be out of order, all is amiss, and if that be well, all the rest is at ease'. (Quoted in O. Ore, *Cardano the Gambling Scholar* (Princeton, 1953), p. 46.)

2   *accident*   the mind is not an essential accompaniment of knowledge.

3   *knowledge is a double of that which is*   cf. Job, 11:5, 6, 'the secrets of wisdom ... are double to that which is'; *Novum Organum*, I.120, 'knowledge is the image of existence', and *Advancement*, I.iv.8.

4   cf. *Advancement*, I.viii.5.

5   cf. Lucretius, *De Rerum Natura*, II.1–10, which is quoted in *Advancement*, I.viii.5 and in essay 'Of Truth'.

6   cf. *Novum Organum*, I.85.

7   cf. *Novum Organum*, I.63, 71.
    Auditories   schools of philosophy.
    You Grecians ...   cf. p. 46 below.

8   Perhaps the best comment here is Ben Jonson's *The Alchemist*.

9   Man inhabits the 'waste ground' between the invariableness of heaven and of the bowels of the earth. In this middle region, which is inhabited by beings, creatures and things made of body impregnated by spirit, all the possibilities of change and transmutation exist. These possibilities fascinated Bacon. See Section X of *Cogitationes de Natura Rerum*.

10   The new 'carmen' are those who follow Copernicus and believe that the earth rotates round the sun. Bacon, while accepting the earth as the centre of the universe, laughs at those who believe that the planets rotate from

west to east at decreasing speeds according to their distance from the earth, and who therefore have to invent a 'contrary motion', of the Primum Mobile, from east to west, in order to explain irregularities. His own explanation is as amusing. See it in more detail in the *Thema Coeli*.

11 cf. *Novum Organum*, I.90.

12 *assever* assert.

13 cf. *Novum Organum*, I.85, 108–114, 119, 120, 129, and *Advancement*, I.iv.12. Printing by movable types began in Europe in the mid-fifteenth century; gunpowder was used in firearms from the fourteenth century; the combination of the wind-rose with the magnetic needle was developed in the fourteenth century. These are the three main inventions of the late Middle Ages. By 'a gross invention' Bacon probably means either that printing was a clumsy piece of technology, or that it was a combination of many different inventions—paper, suitable ink, type-casting, and the mechanical press. These are the inventions often pointed to, e.g. by Cardan in his autobiography, *De Vita propria*, ch. 41 (written *c.* 1544), and Jean Fernal in the Preface to Book I of his *Dialogi* (Paris, 1548).

14 *spials* spies.

Advancement of Learning, *Book I*

[I have not translated Latin quotations where Bacon has done so himself, nor glossed such doublets as 'depravation and calumny', where one word explains the other]

1 *the law* under Jewish law, as described in Exodus, 29:38, Leviticus, 22:18, and Numbers, 28:2, 3; 29:39.

2 *politiques* politicians.

3 *contristation* sadness. The quotations, here and below, attributed to Solomon, are from Ecclesiastes.
   caveat warning; Colossians, 2:8. For the remainder of the *Advancement* I shall not normally annotate Biblical references.

4 *second causes* Aristotle and the Schoolmen distinguish between four causes—the Material, Formal, Final and Efficient. By 'first cause' Bacon means God, by 'second cause' he means Nature, the means whereby God operates in the world.

5 *universality* general principles. Aquinas also says that the naming of the creatures in Paradise shows that Adam pursued natural knowledge.

6 *Ephemerides* the passage in Ecclesiastes 3, beginning 'To everything there is a season'.

7 *ill tradition* the imperfect transmitting of knowledge from age to age.

8 *coarctation* restriction.

9 *their particular* their own individual needs. *carefulness* anxiety.

10 *Lumen siccum* dry light, cf. note on *Novum Organum*, I.49. *madidum, maceratum* 'steeped and infused'.

11 *broken knowledge* wonder is fragmentary or disjointed knowledge. *One of Plato's school* Philo Judaeus in *De Somniis*.

12 *nature's chain* see n. 33 on p. 247 below.

13 *Tu regere* . . . *Aeneid*, VI.852 f.

> Let others better mould the running mass,
> Of metals, and inform the breathing brass,
> And soften into flesh a marble face; . . .
> But, Rome! 'tis thine alone, with awful sway,
> To rule mankind, and make the world obey. (Dryden)

14 *Socrates* in Plato's *Apology*.

15 *sequence in times* cf. Essay 58. According to Aristotle the body is strongest from 30 to 35, the mind at 40. The Renaissance ideal of a gentleman, *he durst and knew*.

16 *empiric physicians* practitioners without scientific knowledge, who confidently and rashly rely on a small number of agreeable medicines. *complexions* here probably 'habits'.
peril of accidents the dangerousness of symptoms.

17 *pedantes* teachers. Seneca was Nero's tutor. Gordianus III was only thirteen when he succeeded his father in A.D. 238; he was well served by the learned Timesitheus or Misitheus, his Praetorian Prefect, whose daughter he later married. Alexander Severus succeeded at seventeen, and the government was in the hands of his mother and grandmother. Pope Pius V (1565–72) was Pope when the battle of Lepanto was won. Pope Sixtus V (1585–90) made the roads safe for travellers, restored the finances, and built extensively in Rome.

18 *to seek* at a loss.
ragioni di stato reasons of state.

19 *hold way with* one man's income cannot keep pace with the Exchequer.

20 *positive and regular* confident and constant in behaviour.

21 *errors* Clement VII (1523–34); F. Guicciardini's *History of Italy, 1490–1532*, trans. A. P. Goddard, 1735.
Phocion see Plutarch's *Life* of Phocion.
Ixion in Book II, viii,3 Bacon interprets Ixion as 'a figure who designed

to enjoy Juno, the goddess of power; and instead of her had copulation with a cloud, of which mixture were begotten centaurs and chimeras'. *Cato* i.e. Uticensis, 95–46 B.C. See Cicero's *Epistle to Atticus*, II.1.

22 *Seneca Epistles*, I.3, 'There are some who live so remote from the world that they think that whatever is done in the public eye must be full of confusion.'

23 *Demosthenes* in Plutarch's *Life* of Demosthenes, though told of Pytheas, not Aeschines.

24 *doubt* fear.

25 *maniable* easy to handle.
thwart stubborn, perverse.

26 *Cato* he opposed the introduction of Greek learning into Rome, because he thought it would destroy the valour and simplicity of the Romans. Plutarch wrote a *Life* of Cato.
Virgil's verses see note 13 above.

27 *Socrates* Socrates was tried for impiety and corrupting the young men of Athens, in 399 B.C. The committee of thirty ruled Athens for eight months in 404–403 B.C.

28 *redargution* refutation.

29 *lucida sidera* shining stars, Horace, *Odes*, I.3,2.

30 *Titus Livius* 'There never was a republic greater, more venerable, and more abounding in good examples than the Roman, nor one that so long withstood avarice and luxury, or so much honoured poverty and parsimony.'

31 *verum haec* 'When the esteem paid to riches comes to an end, these and all other evils cease at the same time; if neither the magistracy, nor those other things that are desired by the common people, can be bought for money.'

32 *Rubor est . . .* 'Red [i.e. blushing] is the colour of virtue', so 'Poverty is the reward of virtue.'

33 *Salomon* Proverbs, 28:22 'He who makes haste to get riches shall not be guiltless.'

34 *Tacitus Annals*, III,76, 'They outshone the rest, because not seen.'

35 *traduced to contempt* transferred contemptuously to them.

36 *corroborate* grown strong.

37 *theatres* as Holofernes in *Love's Labour's Lost*.

38 *Jesuits* Founded by Ignatius Loyola in 1534.
Quo . . . 'the better the worse'.
Talis . . . 'since thou art such a one, would thou wert one of us.'

39 *Abeunt . . .* 'One's studies pass into one's character', Ovid, *Epistles*, XV, 83.

40 *indifferent* impartial.

41 *Non ad vetera ...* 'not referring to the old modes of life, which are held in contempt now that manners have been corrupt for such a long time.'

42 *Cato optime ...* 'Cato had the noblest sentiments, but sometimes he harmed the state, for he spoke as if in Plato's republic, not among the dregs of Romulus.'

43 *excuse and expound* offer an excuse for by explaining in detail.

44 *Isti ipsi ...* 'Those teachers and masters of virtue themselves seem to have prolonged their terms of office a little longer than nature requires, for when we have stretched our minds to the limit, that is the point at which we ought to call a halt' (Cicero, *Pro Murena*).

45 *Monitis ...* 'I am unequal to my teaching', Ovid, *Ars Amandi*, II, 548.

46 *Quinquennium Neronis* i.e. the five years of Nero's minority.

47 *Ecce ...* 'Behold, I have acquired this for thee' and not 'Behold, I have acquired this for myself.'

48 *stand* stand firm, keep their position, when the government is in a state of upheaval.

49 *Satis magnum ...* see n. 4, p. 239 below.

50 *Socrates* referring to the ugliness of Socrates. Plato, in the *Symposium*, says that Socrates' external form is 'like one of the sculptured Sileni' but within is 'temperance and wisdom'. What Bacon says is a summary of the first paragraph of the prologue to *Gargantua and Pantagruel*.

51 *Lucian* the story is in the essay 'Upon Hired Companions', which is about the humiliations to which a scholar is subjected in the family of a wealthy Roman. 'Cynic' is derived from the Greek for 'dog'.

52 *Du Bartas* in his *Second Jour de la Semaine*. Hecuba and Lucrece were renowned for their chastity.

53 *morigeration* obsequiousness.

54 *the state* its original condition.

55 *blemish and taint* stigmatise and sully.

56 *curious* scrupulous, fastidious, or, perhaps, as in IV.8 below, inquisitive.

57 *discourse of reason* a logical term, meaning the process or faculty of reasoning; cf. *Hamlet*, I.ii.150.

58 *pressing* urging. Bacon is explaining the revival of interest in 'pure' Latin as opposed to the Latin used by the Schoolmen.

59 *Execrabilis ...* 'But this people who knoweth not the law are cursed', John, 7:49.

60 *copie of speech* *copia verborum*, richness, fullness, copiousness of speech (achieved by imitating or 'copying' Cicero).

61 *more after words than matter* Ascham, a Ciceronian, had said, 'Ye know not what hurt ye do to learning than care not for words but for matter.'

62 *Osorius* Bishop of Sives, died 1580, a friend of Ascham.
   Sturmius Joannes Sturmius, 1507–89, the German Cicero; Bacon lists some of his works.
   Car Nicholas Carr, 1523–68, Regius Professor of Greek in 1547.
   Ascham Roger Ascham, 1515–68. Latin Secretary to Edward VI, Mary and Elizabeth. *The Scholemaster* (1570) contains his praise of Cicero.
   Erasmus 'I have spent ten years in reading Cicero', to which the echo replied 'thou burro' (*Colloquies*).

63 *weight* seriousness of content.

64 *secundum majus et minus* to a greater or less degree.

65 *a patent, or limned book* the first, decorated, letter in a document issued by the king or in an illuminated book.

66 *sensible and plausible elocution* easily understood or striking, and pleasing eloquence.

67 *a just period* a reasonable conclusion.
   satisfactory for Bacon this word means 'plausible', quickly satisfying the inquirer.

68 *Nil sacri es* 'there is no divinity in thee.'

69 In the *De Augmentis* (1623) the following paragraph was added here: 'The luxuriant style was succeeded by another, which, though more chaste, has still its vanity, as turning wholly upon pointed expressions and short periods, so as to appear concise and round rather than diffusive; by which contrivance the whole looks more ingenious than it is.' He adds that it is found in Seneca, and to a less extent in Tacitus and Pliny, and has 'been very pleasing unto the ears of our time'. He dismisses it as 'no more than a jingle, or peculiar quaint affectation of words'.

70 *Devita profanas . . .* 1 Timothy, 6:20, 'Turn a deaf ear to empty and worldly chatter, and the contradictions of so-called "knowledge".'

71 *strictness of positions* rigidity of logical propositions; see § 6 below.

72 *vermiculate* a word invented by Bacon, from the Latin word for a small worm.

73 *Aristotle* the Schoolmen, the most important of whom is Thomas Aquinas (*c.* 1225–74), based their Christian philosophy on the system of Aristotle.

74 *Verborum minutiis . . .* 'He breaks up matters of weight with verbal quibbles'; cf. essay 'Of Seeming Wise'.
   Quaestionum . . . 'They break up the solid worth of knowledge with the intricate detail of their questions.'

75 *Candida* . . . 'round the snowy waist begirt with barking monsters', Virgil, *Eclogues*, VI,75.

76 *digladiation* quarrelling.

77 *Verba ista* . . . 'It is old men's idle talk.'

78 *fierce with dark keeping* they undertake to occupy large areas of knowledge, and are as intractable as animals are who have been kept in the dark, and for the same reason.

79 *God's works* i.e. the natural, created world; *God's word* is the Bible.

80 *Percontatorem* . . . Horace, *Epistles*, I.18:69.

81 *Fingunt* . . . Tacitus, *Histories*, I.51. 'Invention and belief go hand in hand.'

82 *Plinius* Pliny the Elder, Governor of Spain, died 79 A.D. His *Natural History* is his only surviving work. Bacon used it for his *Sylva Sylvarum*. In his combination of an active life in politics and an intense literary life devoted largely to natural history, and in his death (see p. 216) Pliny's life is remarkably similar to Bacon's.

    Cardanus Geronimo Cardano (1501-76), a mathematician, physicist and physician. Bacon used some of his work for the *Sylva*.

    Albertus Albertus Magnus (c.1198-c.1280), besides divinity and philosophy, also made collections in natural history.

    Arabians probably Averroes, Avicenna, etc.

83 *into one book* Bacon refers first to Aristotle's collection *Historia Animalium*, and then to a spurious work attributed to Aristotle, 'De Mirabilibus Auscultationibus'.

84 *derivations and prosecutions* i.e. the subsidiary channels leading to these ends and the modes in which they have been followed (Wright).

85 *the use of man's life* see, for example, E. J. Holmyard, *Alchemy* (1957).

86 *leeseth and corrupteth* technology develops, while pure science has deteriorated with the passage of time. Technologists co-operate to improve the invention; so-called scientists, instead of following the method of investigation of Aristotle, do no more than write commentaries on his works.

87 *Oportet* . . . 'It is necessary for a scholar to believe', but 'a man well instructed must judge for himself.'

88 *peccant* morbid, unhealthy.

89 *he devoureth* alluding to the fable of Kronos, who swallowed his children at birth.

90 *State super* . . . Jeremiah, 6:16, 'That we make a stand upon the ancient way, and then look about us, and discover what is the straight and right way, and so walk in it.'

91 *Antiquitas saeculi juventus mundi* what we call antiquity is the youth of the world; cf. *Novum Organum*, I.84. The idea that 'the present time is the real antiquity' is to be found also in Gilbert, Galileo, and Giordano Bruno. In 2 Esdras, 14:10 we read 'For the world hath lost his youth, and the times begin to wax old.' For a discussion of the idea see W. von Leyden, 'Antiquity and Authority', *Journal of the History of Ideas*, XIX (1958), 473–92.

92 *Lucian* not Lucian but Seneca in Lactantius, *De Falsa Religione*, i.16. The Lex Papia regulated marriage among the Romans.

93 *generation* Men fear that perhaps Time can no longer bear children and be fruitful.

94 *Livy* 'It was but bravely venturing to despise vain opinions.' Book 9, ch. 17. cf. *Novum Organum*, I.97.

95 *time* an image used in *Novum Organum*, I.71 and the essay 'Of Fame'.

96 *arts and methods* though this observation comes in incidentally it is one of Bacon's most important comments, and is taken up again in Book II, xvii. By 'method' Bacon means the arrangement of knowledge according to some system—as the *Advancement* itself; by 'Aphorisms', the brief expression of ideas and observations, without linkage, as in the 1597 *Essays*. The *Novum Organum* is written in numbered Aphorisms, though in fact the book is systematically arranged in 'method'.

97 *philosophia prima* defined in II.v.2 as 'primitive or summary philosophy' and in II.vii.3 as 'the common principles and axioms which are promiscuous and indifferent to several sciences'.

98 *Plato . . .* cf. *Novum Organum* I.54, 63, 64, 96. For Gilbertus see n. 22 on p. 234 below.

99 *Cicero* 'This man has not gone outside his art.'
Aristotle 'Those who take in but a few considerations easily decide.'

100 *magistral* Defined in II.xvii, 'authoritative, dogmatic', related to 'methods'.

101 *Nil tam metuens* 'who feared nothing so much as the non-appearance of doubting.' Cicero, *De Natura Deorum*, I.8.18.

102 *Declinat cursus . . .* 'she ran out of her course and picked up the golden ball.' Ovid, *Metamorphoses*, X.667.

103 *fidelia vulnera . . .* 'Faithful are the wounds of a friend, but the kisses of an enemy are deceitful.' Proverbs, 27:6. Here Bacon begins his section on the Dignity of Learning.

104 *platform* plan.

105 *Dionysius* *The Celestial Hierarchy*, of which Colet made a close study, was for long attributed to a disciple of St. Paul's, Dionysius the Areopagite.

106   *the two estates* Bacon is interpreting the story of Cain and Abel, maintaining that while it is literally true it is also capable of allegorical interpretation. See n. 13 on p. 246.

107   *You Grecians . . .* *Timaeus* III.22; cf. p. 14 above.

108   *Salomon* His petition (1 Kings, 3:5 f.) was to be able to discern between good and bad. God's gift is described in 1 Kings, 4:29-34. The quotation from Proverbs, 25:2, 'The glory of God . . .' is a favourite one with Bacon.

109   *only learned* St Paul was the only learned Apostle.

110   *Julianus* Julian the Apostate, Emperor, A.D. 361-3, returned to the old religion.

111   *Gregory the first* the Pope (590-604) who sent Augustine to convert the English in 597. Supposed to have tried to extinguish all heathen antiquities. The reference to the invasions is to that of the Tartars in the fourth and of the Saracens in the seventh centuries.

112   *aura leni* with a gentle breeze.

113   *Then should people . . .* Plato, *Republic*, V.473.

114   *six princes* Domitian, Nerva, Trajan, Hadrian, Antoninus and Marcus Aurelius, whose reigns covered a century, A.D. 81-180. With Commodus began the decline. Marcus Aurelius was the author of a famous set of meditations.

115   *infolded* involved, intricate. In the *De Augmentis* he abridged the following section—it was indeed the wrong material for an intricate work; it holds up the argument by too much example.

116   *Neque semper . . .* 'Apollo does not always bend his bow', Horace, *Odes*, II.x:19.

117   *Postquam divus . . .* 'In the first dawn of this blessed age, Nerva Caesar harmonized the old discord of autocracy and freedom', *Agricola*, 3.

118   *Telis, Phoebe . . .* 'Phoebus, with thy darts revenge our tears', *Iliad*, i.42. Nerva adopted the young Trajan as his successor shortly before his death in A.D. 98. His actual message was 'May the Danubians expiate my tears under the stroke of thy darts.'

119   *Trajan's moral virtues* see n. 111 above. The story of Gregory's intercession for Trajan and its answer is discussed by Aquinas. See Dante, *Purgatorio*, x.73; *Paradiso*, xx.

120   *curious* Hadrian was eager to know everything.

121   *Apollonius* it was not Hadrian but Alexander Severus who placed figures of Christ, Apollonius, Abraham, Orpheus and others in one shrine. Apollonius of Tyana, almost contemporary with Christ, was a Neo-Pythagorean philosopher who pretended to miraculous powers.

122 *Quomodo Augustus* ... In the same way as you are styled 'Augustus' so also you shall be called 'Antoninus'.

123 *Queen Elizabeth* Bacon spoke of Elizabeth in similar terms in his letter to the Lord Chancellor, concerning the history of Britain. His 'Praise of Elizabeth' in the 1592 *Conference of Pleasure*, and the posthumously published 'Felicities of Queen Elizabeth' show Bacon's fine historical sense.

124 *temperature* here means 'the moderate maintenance of peace'.

125 *Callisthenes* only fragments of his writings survive. Bacon omits to mention that Alexander kept him in chains for seven months, at the end of which time he died.

126 *Venus' hand* in *Iliad*, v.340.

127 *tropes of rhetoric* figures of speech.
    translation metaphor, from Latin *translatio*. Puttenham calls metaphor 'the figure of transport'.

128 *Henry Duke of Guise* a story Bacon heard in France in 1576 when Henry, third Duke of Guise (1550–88), was head of the Catholic League.

129 *De Analogia* this does not survive, but fragments are quoted by Cicero and Aulus Gellius. According to Bacon, Caesar tried to provide rules for the use of Latin, so that men spoke and wrote according to the rules, not according to custom and usage.
    And took ... the pictures is an image from painting, and seems to mean that words were made to accord with what reason suggested as being real.

130 *the year* the reference is to the Julian Calendar.

131 *Anti-Cato* again it does not survive. Presumably it opposed Cicero's praise of Cato.

132 *Apophthegms* these were suppressed by Augustus. Bacon collected a number of anecdotes embodying pointed sayings, in 1625. Many of them he had already used in his works, e.g. No. 172 is the one about Alexander, 'Sir, what keep you for yourself?' He answered, 'Hope.'

133 *Verba sapientum* ... 'The words of the wise are as goads, and as nails fastened by the noble.' Ecclesiastes, 12:11.

134 *Quirites* the name used by Romans in their civil capacity.

135 *Non Rex sum* ... 'I am not King, but Caesar.' This is Bacon's Apophthegm 186.

136 *Xenophon* the story is told in Xenophon's *Persian Expedition*, where it is Theopompus who says this. Agesilaus invaded Persia in 396–394 B.C. Jason planned his expedition just before his murder in 370 B.C.

137 *Scilicet ingenuas* 'Certainly a faithful study of the liberal arts humanizes

227

character and permits it not to be cruel', Ovid, *Epistulae ex Ponto*, II. ix. 48–9.

138 *Nil novi super terram* 'There is no new thing under the sun', Ecclesiastes, 1:9.

139 *Heri vidi fragilem frangi . . .* 'Yesterday I saw a brittle thing broken, and today a mortal die.'

140 *Virgil*   Happy the man who, studying nature's laws,
           Through known effects can trace the secret cause,
           His mind possessing in a fearless state,
           Fearless of Fortune, and resigned to Fate. (Dryden)
    cf. *Georgics*, II.490–3.

141 *rationem totius* the reason of the whole, the conclusion of the whole matter.

142 *suavissima vita . . .* 'that most happy of lives, to feel himself daily get better and better.' A sentence that Bacon had jotted down in his *Promus* in 1595.

143 *Veritas and Bonitas* the man who knows the Truth will be Good.

144 *Victorque volentes . . .* 'victoriously dispensing laws among the willing nations, and pursuing the way to heaven.' *Georgics*, IV.561–2.

145 *Suave mari magno* see n.5, p. 218 above.

146 *the philosophers* the Epicureans, who denied the immortality of the soul and the interest of the Gods in human affairs.

147 *occidat matrem . . .* 'Let him kill his mother, as long as he can reign.' Tacitus, *Annals*, xiv.9. This is said of Nero, who had his mother assassinated in A.D. 59. Agrippina committed many crimes, including incest, for the sake of power.

148 *Ulysses* who preferred his aged wife to immortality. See n. 4, p. 239, to essay 'Of Marriage and Single Life'.

149 *Justificata est . . .* 'Wisdom is justified by her sons.' Matthew, 11:19.

Advancement of Learning, *Book II, Introduction*

1 *dearest pledges* cf. essay 'Of Parents and Children'.

2 *Hercules' columns* the name given by the ancients to the two rocks, Calpe (Gibraltar) and Abyla (Jebel el Mina) on either side of the Straits of Gibraltar. They were supposed to mark the western limits of Hercules' wanderings, and of geographical knowledge in that direction.

3 *overcommen* achieved, accomplished.

4 *claudus in via. . .* from St Augustine's Sermon 169, quoted also in

Novum Organum I.61 below, 'the lame man who keeps the right road outstrips the runner who takes a wrong one'. Bacon is concerned that men should make the right choice of Method.

5 *Principio sedes...* *Georgics*, IV.8-9:

> First, for thy bees a quiet station find,
> And lodge them under covert of the wind. (Dryden)

6 *Difficile non ...* 'It would be difficult not to omit someone, yet iniquitous to omit anyone' (Cicero).

7 *the ancient fable* see *Coriolanus*, I.i.99 f. The story is told by Livy and by Plutarch.

8 *Et patrum...* *Georgics*, III.128,

> He will be copied in his famished race. (Dryden)

9 *physic* medicine.

10 *Alexander* in Pliny, *Natural History*, viii.17. By *arts of nature*, Bacon means the experimental sciences.

11 *logic and rhetoric* the first two years of the course of study at Elizabethan Oxford and Cambridge were spent on logic and rhetoric. The students were very young, Bacon going up at the age of twelve. He stayed only two years. For Bacon on logic and rhetoric see pp. 69 ff. above.

12 *Cicero* in *De Oratore*, III.26.

13 *Caesar's letter* 'How this can be done, several things occur to me, and many others can be found out: I ask you to think about these matters.' Cicero, *Letters to Atticus*, IX.7.

14 *orders and foundations* Bacon must be thinking of the Jesuits, who had founded schools in many countries of Europe by this time.

15 *the Father* in James, 1:17 God is called 'the Father of lights'.

16 *opinion of plenty* one of the reasons for the scarcity is that people have believed there was plenty.

17 *Moses* Exodus, 7:12. It was Aaron's rod, not Moses', that turned into a serpent and swallowed the others.

18 *opera basilica* works for a king.

19 *inducing* introductory.

Advancement of Learning, *Book II, xvii.1-xviii.5*. On the Method and Illustration of Tradition.

1 *method of tradition* Bacon is dealing with 'intellectual arts'—'art of enquiry or invention: art of examination or judgement: art of custody or memory: and art of elocution or tradition' (II.xii.3). By 'tradition' he means communication, and considers it in terms of (1) speech and writing,

(2) the method, (3) the illustration. The controversy was that relating to Ramus's reform of dialectic and rhetoric. See W. S. Howell, *Logic and Rhetoric in England, 1500–1700* (Princeton, 1956), ch. 4. The most important work to come from the controversy about Method was Descartes' *Discours de la Méthode* (1637).

2   *a part of judgement*   Bacon had so placed Method or arrangement. Ramus also places Invention and Arrangement in Logic. Bacon's discussion of Judgment is in fact devoted to Logic—induction, syllogism, fallacies, leading to the Idols (II.xiv).

3   *invention*   In section xiii Bacon accepts this term in its normal meaning in logic and rhetoric of the recalling and assembling of relevant information when preparing a discourse. But he also urges that Invention means also the discovery of new knowledge, for which a new Method (the *Novum Organum*) is required.

4   *magistral*   the magistral method is dogmatic or doctrinal. It is used when a teacher wishes to convey information which is to be believed, and not questioned. The method of probation is that used when the matter delivered is to be questioned and examined. The magistral method is for use when existing knowledge is to be applied; the probational method is for use when the bounds of knowledge are to be expanded; the former for the ordinary audience, the latter for the learned audience.

5   *via deserta et interclusa*   a phrase of Cicero's meaning 'a way deserted and shut off'; cf. I.iv.4 above.

6   *knowledge induced*   knowledge derived by induction.

7   *anticipated and prevented*   knowledge which we already possess, *a priori* knowledge.

8   *secundum majus*   see n. 64, p. 223 above.

9   *slips*   shoots or cuttings. This method of delivery or communication is to be a retracing of the steps whereby the knowledge was discovered. This is a method for communication to the learned.

10   *enigmatical and disclosed*   the concealed or secretive method and the open method. The former, used by the alchemists, with their peculiar vocabulary, is what Bacon's remarks refer to.

11   *aphorisms or methods*   the aphorism as Bacon used it in the 1597 *Essays* is a brief statement of fact or observation, without illustration, examples, argumentative links with other aphorisms, etc. The aphorisms of the *Novum Organum* begin like this but soon cease to be either brief or without examples and links. Delivery in 'methods' here means the organization of a discourse, as for example the *Advancement* itself is organized. This is not really different from the magistral method.

12   *Tantum series* . . .   Horace, *Ars Poetica*, 242–3;
        Such grace can order and connexion give;
        Such beauties common subjects may receive. (Francis)

13   *particulars being dispersed*   actual things are not arranged in any pattern therefore observations on things are best left separate and unconnected.

14   *knowledge broken*   fragmentary; but cf. n. 11 on p. 220 above. Knowledge carefully arranged suggests that it is complete and inhibits further inquiry. cf. I.v above.

15   *piece*   cf. I.iv.6 above for the general idea. Bacon dislikes disputatious learning. A 'piece' is a stronghold. A general should not leave a strongly held enemy fort in his rear, while he goes ahead to subdue lightly held places—so a teacher will not use the question and answer method for anything but important prejudices held by a learner.

16   *immersed*   mathematics is the most abstracted from things and persons, politics the most involved. Here Bacon argues for different methods of communicating for each subject. Later he argues for different presentations according to the audience.

17   *judgement*   one would expect 'method' here, but 'method' is a part of 'judgement'. In the *De Augmentis* he says 'diversity of method to be used with judgement'.

18   *similitudes*   similes and allusions are necessary when doctrine quite new is to be imparted. Hence Bacon's use of figurative language.

19   *diversities of methods*   the terms *analysis*, *systasis* or synthesis, and *cryptic* are used in Ramistic rhetorical theory.

20   *Ramus*   Petrus Ramus or Pierre de la Ramée, French humanist philosopher (1515–1572), who provoked the hostility of the Aristotelians by his attempts to reform the science of logic. The ancient rules of 'method' developed by commentators on Aristotle's Logic were 'relation to the first principle, relation to all, and relation to itself'. Bacon is here referring to Ramus's Law of Wisdom, which demands that generalities be treated as generalities, and particularities as particularities. This was the basis of Ramus's definition of Method as arrangement, whereby subject matter is arranged in a descending order of generality, the most general being placed first, the least general last. See § 13 below.

21   *canker of epitomes*   the passion for abridgements of books was attributed to the influence of Ramus and Lipsius. Bacon calls epitomes 'the corruptions and moths of history'.

22   *non-promovent*   failing to advance, not making progress. *To make axioms convertible* is to transpose subject and predicate of a proposition, e.g. 'all

metals are elements' to 'all elements are metals'. One of the dangers here is of arguing on a circle, i.e. of taking the conclusion itself as one of the premises, or of using in a definition a word that is a synonym of the name defined.

23 Καθαυτό see note 20. This is the Law of Wisdom, the separating of statements according to their degree of generality and particularity.

24 *Ortelius* a sixteenth-century geographer. Bacon refers to his map of the world.

25 *Lullius* Raymond Lully (1235-1315). His method was a mechanical one, of listing all possible concepts and arranging them in all possible combinations. It is similar to the satirical invention of Swift in ch. 5 of the *Voyage to Laputa*.

typocosmy a method or system, intended as an aid to learning, in which words or terms are grouped according to types or classes (OED). A 'fripper's' shop is an old clothes shop.

26 *Sapiens corde* . . . 'The wise in heart shall be called prudent, but the charm of eloquence shall be found greater', Proverbs, 16:21.

27 *to apply reason to imagination* for Bacon, Rhetoric is to the imagination what Logic is to the understanding. His theory of persuasion is adopted from Plato in the *Phaedrus*. Control of the Will is fought for by Reason and Passion, each of which strives to enlist the aid of Imagination. Rhetoric is the diplomat that enlists the aid of Imagination on the side of Reason, so that man may lead a Rational life. Johnson defines Poetry as 'the art of uniting pleasure with truth, by calling imagination to the help of reason' (*Life of Milton*). This paragraph is the most obviously balanced piece of writing in Bacon's works.

28 *Plato* in the *Gorgias*, i.462.

29 *That virtue* . . . *Phaedrus*, iii. 250. For the opposite, see Pope, *Essay on Man*, ii.217,

> Vice is a monster of so frightful mien,
> As, to be hated, needs but to be seen.

Bacon, clearly, does not see Rhetoric as being limited to popular discourses. All men, learned and unlearned, tend towards unreason, prejudice and emotion, and cannot be won by mere proofs.

30 *Video meliora* . . . 'I see the better and approve it, but I follow the worse', Ovid, *Metamorphoses*, vii.20.

31 *the fist from the palm* an image borrowed from Zeno, via Cicero and Quintilian, to explain the preoccupation of Logic with the discourse of philosophy, and of Rhetoric with the discourses of orators. The complete theory of communication, it is implied, is made up of Logic and

Rhetoric. See Karl R. Wallace, *Francis Bacon on Communication and Rhetoric* (Chapel Hill, 1943), and W. S. Howell, pp. 364–75.

32 *Orpheus in silvis* . . . 'An Orpheus in the woods, an Arion among the dolphins', Virgil, *Eclogues*, viii.56.

Novum Organum: The Doctrine of the Idols

Full annotation is to be found in Thomas Fowler ed., *Novum Organum*, second edition, 1889.

1 *magician* e.g. Baptista Porta, whose *Magia Naturalis* was published in 1589. In *Advancement of Learning*, II.viii.3, Bacon condemns the 'credulous and superstitious conceits and observations of sympathies and antipathies, and hidden properties' of 'natural magic'. See also *De Augmentis*, III.v; *Novum Organum* I.85, 87. Bacon was not correct in thinking there was scanty success. Technology was advancing rapidly, see A. Wolf, *A History of Science, Technology and Philosophy in the 16th and 17th Centuries* (1935) and Lynn Thorndyke, *A History of Magic and Experimental Science*, vols. v–viii (New York, 1941, 1958). Kepler and Galileo in mathematics, Harvey and Gilbert in medicine, were successful.

2 *axioms* here, general principles or universal laws.

3 *experiment* here means 'mere experience', as distinct from scientific observation and experiment.

4 *logic* i.e. syllogistic logic, which depends on the truth of its major premises.

5 *a true induction* this Bacon describes in Book II.

6 *common induction* cf. Aphorism 105, 'induction by simple enumeration'.

7 on this see J. S. Mill, *A System of Logic*, VI.v.5.

8 *useless generalities* such as 'Nature abhors a vacuum', 'Nature does nothing in vain.'

9 *Idols* Bacon uses the word to mean 'illusions', 'false appearances', i.e. the false notions which have taken possession of men's minds.

10 Sir Thomas Bodley, having read this in *Cogitata et Visa*, replied that to begin from the foundations again 'would instantly bring us to barbarism' (Letter to Bacon of 19 February, 1607). But see Aphorism 128.

11 *wits* intellects.

12 One of Bacon's favourite illustrations. Borgia, Pope Alexander VI. Charles VIII of France overran Italy in five months in 1494.

13 cf. *Novum Organum* I.67, 75, 126. The sect of Greek Philosophers who believed that the only certain truth was that certainty could not be attained. The chief were Arcesilaus and Carneades.

14 *refutation of Sophisms* detection of fallacies.

15 Idols of the Tribe, Aphorisms 41, 45-52; of the Cave, 42, 53-8; of the Market-Place, 43, 59-60; of the Theatre, 44, 61-7.

16 *measure of things* attributed to Pythagoras. See Plato's *Theaetetus*.

17 (*according as it is meted out to different individuals*) Spedding disagrees with this translation of 'prout disponitur in hominibus singulis', since it suggests the doctrine of one intellect, of which each man has an undivided share. He would probably have preferred to read '(according to its several dispositions)'.

18 Bacon ignores, or did not know, Kepler's three laws concerning the elliptical paths of the planets. He suggests spiral and serpentine movements as a possibility. The four elements, earth, water, air, fire, were each assigned an orbit, that of fire being the outermost. That earth was ten times heavier than water, which was ten times heavier than air, etc., was assumed in medieval physics.

19 *dry light* the term is that of Heraclitus, who believed that the soul was a mixture of fire (the noble part) and water (the ignoble). The soul that has most fire he calls 'dry'.

20 *spirits enclosed in tangible bodies* see *Novum Organum*, II.7, 40, and cf. pp. 150, 250.

21 *chemists* alchemists.

22 *Gilbert* William Gilbert's *De Magnete* (1600) included acceptance of the Copernican theory, magnetic explanations of planetary motions and the earth's rotation, and a Neoplatonic discussion of magnetism and electricity. These may have been the object of Bacon's scorn. His philosophical views were printed posthumously (1651) in *De mundo mostro, sublunari Philosophia nova*.

23 Bacon's own 'weakness' was for seeing resemblances.

24 cf. Aphorism 84.

25 *all wits and understandings nearly on a level* this, of course, can never be fulfilled.

26 *words of the second intention* this refers to Aristotle's definition of the soul, *De Anima*, II.i. First intentions are primary conceptions of things formed by the direct application of the mind to things, e.g. a *tree*. Second intentions are secondary conceptions formed by the application of thought to first intentions in their relations to each other, e.g. the concepts of *genus, species, identity*.

27 *Anaxagoras* Accounts of the opinions of these philosophers are accessible in histories of philosophy, e.g. those by G. H. Lewes or Bertrand Russell. See notes 20-30 on pp. 246-7.

28 *realists* those who held that universals are alone true. *nominalists* those who held that universals are empty names, and individual things alone exist.

29 *seeking for the dead among the living* see Luke, 24:5. In Scripture, everything which concerns the passing interests of the body is called dead; the only living knowledge having regard to the eternal interest of the soul (Devey).

Essays: Of Studies (1597)

This is the text of 1597, without the alterations made in 1612 and 1625.

The essay is about book-learning, which Bacon defends in Book I of the *Advancement*. See also *Advancement* II.xix; xxii.7, 13. Rawley, his chaplain, said of Bacon, 'He was no plodder upon books; though he read much . . . for he would ever interlace a moderate relaxation of his mind with his studies, as walking or taking the air abroad in his coach, or riding, not fast but gentle, bowling, or some other befitting recreation; and yet he would lose no time, inasmuch as upon his first and immediate return he would fall to reading again.'

1 *abilities* to make men able.
2 *retiring* seclusion.
3 *expert men* men who have learned only from experience, not study.
4 *humour* peculiarity.
5 *craftie men* practical men.
6 *conference* discussion.
7 *writing* taking notes.
8 *wittie* ingenious, imaginative.

Of Truth, (1625)

1 *jesting Pilate* John, 18:38. Jesus said that he came into the world 'to bear witness unto the truth'. Pilate's comment 'What is truth?' is 'jesting' in the sense of jeering, derisive. See *Novum Organum* I.37, 67, 126 where Bacon refers to the New Academy, Plato's successors, who preached Acatalepsia, 'a denial of the capacity of the mind to comprehend truth', 'in jest and irony and in disdain of the older sophists'. This school and the Sceptics are referred to in the next sentence as 'the Sects'.
2 *Giddinesse* changeableness.

3 *discoursing Wits* reasoning intellects.

4 *imposeth* lays a yoke upon, restrains.

5 *Grecians* Lucian in *Philopseudes* (The Lover of Lies).

6 *Open day light* cf. Swift, *Tale of a Tub*, Sect. ix, 'How shrunk is everything, as it appears in the Glass of Nature! So that if it were not for the Assistance of Artificial Mediums, false Lights, refracted Angles, Varnish and Tinsel, there would be a mighty Level in the Felicity and Enjoyments of Mortal Men.'

7 *One of the Fathers* Augustine calls poetry 'the wine of error', Jerome 'the food of devils'. These are brought together in Cornelius Agrippa. See *Advancement* II.xxii.13.

8 *The Poet* Lucretius, who adorned the Epicurean philosophy in his poem *De Rerum Natura*. Bacon paraphrases the opening of Book II. See p. 61 above.

9 *not to be commanded* not to be overlooked, or inaccessible to others.

10 *with Pitty* cf. pp. 159, 173 below.

11 *Moue in Charitie* the image is from astronomy.
   rest in be sustained by.

12 *ciuill Businesse* conduct.
   cleare and Round plain and straightforward.

13 *Mountaigny* Montaigne in *Essais*, ii. 18, quoting Plutarch.

14 *He shall not finde Faith* in Luke, 18:8 it is a question, not a prophecy, and refers to religious belief, not honest dealing between men.

Of Reuenge (1625)

1 *Wilde* uncultivated.

2 *Salomon* in Proverbs, 19:11, though not in these words.

3 *the Arrow* Psalm, 91:5, 6.

4 *Cosmus* Cosimo de'Medici (1519–74). There is an Italian proverb, 'From them I trust, God preserve me; from them I do not trust I will preserve myself.'

5 *Job* Job, 2:10.

6 *in a proportion* to a proportionate extent. God, our Creator and Ruler, may treat us as He will; our friends have less power to help us and less right to give us pain.

7 *Fortunate* Augustus, Severus and Henry IV, the avengers, proved to be competent and good rulers. Avengers in private stations have no such success; as they are vindictive, so do they come to misfortune.

Of Aduersitie (1625)

1 *an high speech* a noble speech. Bacon translates, before quoting, the passage from Seneca, *Epistles*, 66. Notice that he preserves in his translation some of the brevity, balance and rhyme of the Latin.

2 *too high* above the natural standard of a person not a Christian.

3 *Security* i.e. freedom from care. Frailty implies that he suffers adversity. Again he translates, closely imitating the style of the original, though he misquotes, *fragilitatem* for *imbecilitatem*. See *Advancement*, II.xx.5.

4 *Transcendencies* extravagances of language and thought.

5 *Fiction* in Apollodorus *De Deorum Origine*, II.5.
 mystery a hidden meaning.

6 *Christian Resolution* the myth is interpreted in *Wisdom of the Ancients* sub Prometheus, where Hercules is a type of Christ. Here he represents Christian resolution.

7 *in a Meane* without exaggeration.

8 *Aduersity* probably referring to the Beatitude, 'Blessed are they that mourn', Matthew, 5:4.

Of Iudicature (1612, enlarged 1625)

The substance of this essay, 'Of the duty of a Judge', is to be found in Bacon's speech to Justice Hutton (*Life* &c, VI.201).

1 *Pronounce* proclaim solemnly.

2 *Shew of* under the guise of.

3 *Wittie* ingenious.

4 *Plausible* courting respect rather than applause.

5 *Aduised* deliberate.

6 *Cursed* ... Deuteronomy, 27:17.

7 *a Meere Stone* a boundary stone.

8 *Fons turbatus* ... Proverbs, 25:26, 'A righteous man falling down before the wicked is as a troubled fountain, and a corrupt spring.'

9 *Scripture* Amos, 5:7.

10 *as God vseth* ... Isaiah, 40:3, 4.

11 *Qui fortiter* ... Proverbs, 30:33, 'And the wringing of the nose, bringeth forth blood.'

12 *for Terrour* as a deterrent.

13 *Pluet super* ... Psalm 11:6, 'He shall rain snares upon them.'

14 *Iudicis* ... Ovid, *Tristia*, I.i.37, 'It is a judge's duty to consider not only the case but the circumstances of the case.'

15 *well tuned Cymball* Psalm 150:5. A garrulous Judge is a bad judge.

16 *represseth the Presumptuous . . .* James, 4:6; I Peter, 5:5.

17 *By-waies* secret proceedings.

18 *chop* bandy words.

19 *Foot-pace* the raised portion of the floor, on which the Judge's seat was placed. Precincts and Purprise both mean the area about the court.

20 *Thistles* Matthew, 7:16.

21 *Catching and Poling* rapacious and plundering.

22 *Amici curiae* 'Not friends, but parasites of the court.' Bacon is thinking of Coke who was suspended from his office of Chief Justice of the King's Bench in 1616 because he upheld the rights of his court over the Chancery. Bacon was instrumental in Coke's overthrow then.

23 *Poler* plunderer.

24 *Wether* stormy weather.

25 *Salus Populi . . .* not in the Twelve Tables, but in Cicero, *De Legibus*, III.3, 8. 'The safety of the people is the supreme law.'

26 *Consult* James often consulted with the judges before cases were tried. Coke opposed this practice, though Bacon approved.

27 *interuenient* involved.

28 *Trench to* encroach upon. The matter brought to trial may be simply one of property, though the principle behind it, and the consequence of it, may encroach upon some interest of the State.

29 *Salomons Throne* see 1 Kings, 10:19, 20. Bacon called himself a 'peremptory royalist' and was anxious to preserve the king's prerogative, which was in danger of being bargained away in exchange for supplies. To allow this to happen would vest all power in Parliament and, Bacon thought, thereby unbalance the machinery of government.

30 *Apostle* Paul, in 1 Timothy, 1:8, 'We know that the law is good, if a man use it lawfully.'

Of Marriage and Single Life (1612, enlarged 1625)

See Johnson's discussion of this topic in *Rasselas*, ch. 26.

1 *care of future times* an idea to which he refers in the opening of Book II of the *Advancement*.

2 *Impertinences* things which do not concern them.

3 *humorous* eccentric, following the predominant humour. It was thought that mental and physical qualities were determined by the

proportions of the humours—blood, choler, phlegm, melancholy—in a man.

4 *Vlysses* Cicero *De Oratione*, I.44, 'He preferred his old wife to immortality', because he left Calypso, who promised him immortality, for Penelope;' cf. *Advancement*, I viii.7

5 *Quarrell* a plea, a pretext.

6 *wise Men* Thales of Miletus.

7 *it rayseth* women who have married bad husbands are encouraged to be good in order to win over their husbands, whose affection will be all the more highly valued because of its rarity (Storr).

Of Loue (1612, enlarged 1625)

1 cf. Dr Johnson, 'Love is only one of many passions, and as it has no great influence upon the sum of life, it has little operation in the dramas of a poet [Shakespeare] who caught his ideas from the living world, and exhibited only what he saw before him' (*Preface to Shakespeare*).

2 *great Spirits* noble natures.

3 *Appius Claudius* the story of Appius and Virginia is told by Livy, Chaucer (*Physician's Tale*) and Macaulay (*Lays*). Bacon calls Appius 'wise' because, as one of the decemvirs, he codified the laws; 'austere' means rigorous, stern. Antony was, by contrast, intemperate and sensuous.

4 *Satis magnum . . .* 'We are a large enough theatre for one another', (Seneca, *Epistles*, I.7, where it is not a general proposition); cf. p. 33 above.

5 *Idoll* here both 'phantom, image', formed in the beholder's eye, and 'false god', the object of his adoration. Bacon classes love with envy, because both 'draw the spirits into the eyes' (*Sylva*, 944).

6 *braues* insults, by always exaggerating.

7 *in the Phrase* not only in the words but also in the thoughts.

8 *Arch-flatterer* by Plutarch, *De Adulatione et Amico*, II.
haue Intelligence have an understanding, are in league.

9 *. . . to be wise* a saying from the collection of *Sententiae* by Publius Syrus (fl. *c.* 44 B.C.); cf. *Troilus and Cressida*, III.ii.155: 'To be wise and love Exceeds man's might.'

10 *reciproque* mutual; in its second use it means 'reciprocity, the return of love'.

11 *the Poets Relation* referring to the story of Paris who chose beauty and love against wisdom and power.

12 *checke with* interfere with.

Of Death (1612, enlarged 1625)

1 *Children* Lucretius, in Books 1, 3, 6, of *De Rerum Natura*, repeats 'Even as children tremble and fear everything in blinding darkness, so we sometimes dread in the light things that are no whit more to be feared than what children shudder at in the dark, and imagine will come to pass.' It is used in Book 3 in the discussion on Death.

2 *Tales* children are frightened by stories of ghosts, etc.; men (according to Lucretius) by stories of punishment after death.

3 *Mortification* the friar's books have not been identified. To mortify is to put to death, and is applied to man's evil passions by St Paul. Hence the idea of inflicting pain on the body for the good of the soul.

4 *Naturall Man* guided by nothing but *nature*. The quotation may be misremembered from Seneca, 'The trappings of death are more terrifying than death itself.'

5 *Blackes* mourning garments, cf. Hamlet, ''Tis not alone my inky cloak, good mother, Nor customary suit of solemn black.'

6 *Mates* overpowers.

7 *pre-occupateth* anticipates, forestalls it by suicide.

8 *Otho* in Tacitus, *Histories*, II.49.

9 *Nicenesse* fastidiousness. The Latin is adapted from Seneca, *Epistles*, X.i.6, 'Consider how long you have been doing the same things! It is not only the brave man or the wretched man that may wish to die, but also the man who is consumed with ennui.' cf. also Montaigne, 'Of Judging of Others Death'.

10 *viue & vale* 'Goodbye, Livia! remember our married life while you live.'

11 *deserebant* 'Tiberius' strength and life were fast ebbing, but not his powers of dissimulation.'

12 *Vt puto . . .* 'I suppose I am becoming a god'.

13 *Feri . . .* 'Strike, if it be for the good of the Roman people.'

14 *Adeste . . .* 'Be quick, if anything remains for me to do.'

15 *Stoikes* cf. *Advancement*, II.xxi.5. Not a true picture of the Stoics, to whom life was a thing indifferent. Montaigne (*Essais*, III.12) quotes Seneca, 'The whole life of philosophers is a remembrance of death.'

16 *Qui Finem* Juvenal, *Satires*, X.358.
> A soul that can securely death defy,
> And count it Nature's privilege to die. (Dryden)

17 *Nunc dimittis* the song of Simeon (Luke, 2:29), beginning 'Lord, now lettest Thou Thy servant depart in peace.'

18 *Extinctus* Horace, *Epistles*, II.i.14, 'When his light is quenched his memory will be loved.'

Of Great Place (1612, enlarged 1625)

1 *Great Place* high office.
  Fame public opinion.
2 *Cum non* ... '(It is an old saying that) when you are no longer what you once were, there is no reason why you should wish to live' (Cicero).
3 *priuatenesse* private life.
4 *pusle* puzzle, entanglement.
5 *Illi Mors* ... 'Death falls heavily on him who, to others too well known, dies a stranger to himself', Seneca, *Thyestes*, ii.401.
6 *to Can* to be able.
7 *Conscience* consciousness.
8 *Gods Theater* if a man can contemplate, as God did, the spectacle of good works done by himself.
9 *Et conuersus* ... quoting Genesis, 1:31 from memory: 'And God turned to behold the works which His hands had made, and He saw that they were all very good.'
10 *a Globe of Precepts* a compressed mass of precepts, i.e. a model is worth a thousand directions.
11 *taxing* censuring.
12 *Brauerie, or Scandall* ostentation or defamation.
13 *set it down to* propose.
14 *best ... fittest* what was best originally may not be what is fittest now.
15 *expresse thy selfe well* explain your reasons clearly.
16 *Iurisdiction* see n. 22 on p. 238.
17 *interlace* mix up.
18 *For Corruption* it would seem that Bacon, as Chancellor, did not follow his own precepts.
19 *to steale it* to do it secretly.
20 *inward* intimate.
   close secret.
21 *Facilitie* readiness to yield to pressure.
   Bribery taking bribes.
22 *Salomon* Proverbs, 28:21.
   To respect Persons to show consideration for, to favour, individuals.
23 *Tacitus* Histories, I.49.50: of Galba, 'Had he never been emperor, no

man would have doubted his ability to reign.' Of Vespasian, 'He was
the only emperor who changed for the better.'

24 *Sufficiencie* ... administrative capacity.
Manners, and Affection morals and disposition.

25 *sensible* sensitive.

Of Simulation *And* Dissimulation (1625)

The 'politic' essays, which include this one and the next, 'Of Cunning', are
developments of the long essay on the Architecture of Fortune in *Advancement*
II.xxiii.

1 *Tacitus* in *Annals*, V.I. Livia was a match for the diplomacy of her
husband (Augustus) and the dissimulation of her son (Tiberius). The next
quotation is from the *Histories*, II. 76.

2 *Faculties seuerall* distinct and different abilities.

3 *Poorenesse* a drawback.

4 *generally* as a general rule of action.

5 *well mannaged* well trained.

6 *what he is* gives no one an opportunity to observe what he really is.

7 *industriously* purposely.

8 *Close Aire* *Sylva*, 866, 'close air is warmer than open air.' *Close*, in a
confined or sheltered place. The warm 'close' air would be less dense than
the cold 'open' air, hence the flow from 'open' to 'closed'. Bacon is
punning on 'open' and 'close' temperaments.

9 *in that kinde* in the same way.

10 *Mysteries* a reserved man has a right to hear secrets.

11 *Futile* *lit.* leaky, so, unable to hold his tongue.
Vaine empty-headed.

12 *Politicke and Morall* is a mark both of shrewdness and good character.

13 *a Mans Face* the face should not contradict what he has said, nor reveal
what he is about to say; cf. 'Of Cunning'. Essex gave all away by his
face.

14 *indifferent* impartial, neutral.

15 *Oraculous* ambiguous.

16 *ure* use, practice.

17 *(faire)* simply. They will not openly disagree, but will do so silently.

18 *Troth* truth; cf. *Hamlet*, I.v.63, 'Your bait of falsehood takes this carp
of truth.'

19 *spoile the Feathers* ... prevents the arrow from flying directly to the mark.

20 *Composition, and Temperature* combination and blending of qualities.

21 *Fame and Opinion* reputation.

Of Cunning (1612, enlarged 1625)

1 *We take Cunning* 'We understand by cunning ...' Because 'cunning' could also mean skill.

2 *Canuasses, and Factions* soliciting individuals or forming parties.

3 *the Reall Part of Businesse* the material part, namely, business.

4 *but in their own Alley* only in their own bowling alley.

5 *Mitte ambos* ... 'Send them both naked to those that know them not, and you shall perceive', attributed to Aristippus, fl. 400 B.C.

6 *wait vpon* observe closely.

7 *present dispatch* great urgency.

8 *crosse* thwart.
   doubts suspects.

9 *Nehemias* Nehemiah, 2:1, though this was not a piece of artifice.

10 *tender* delicate.

11 *Narcissus* Messalina was Claudius' wife and 'married' Silius during her husband's absence. Narcissus hired two prostitutes to tell Claudius. Tacitus, *Annals*, XI.29. 30.

12 *with a Letter* as Edmund in *King Lear*.

13 *Secretaries Place* Spedding suggests Sir Robert Cecil and Sir Thomas Bodley. Cecil became Secretary.

14 *the Cat in the Pan* if *Cat* is a form of *cate*, cake, then the proverb refers to tossing the pancake and so to changing sides, as it does in *The Vicar of Bray*, 'I turned a cat-in-a-pan once more, And so became a Whig, sir.' Bacon's meaning is clear.

15 *spectare* Tigellinus was one of Nero's favourites; Burrhus was prefect of the Praetorian Guard and, with Seneca, had been Nero's tutor. He opposed Nero's tyranny and was therefore poisoned, A.D. 63. After his death Tigellinus said, 'He [i.e. Tigellinus] was no trimmer like Burrhus, but had a single eye to the emperor's safety.' Tacitus, *Annals*, XIV.57.

16 *fetch* the image is of stalking game, going round about so as not to be scented, and beating a covert.

17 *Resorts and Falls* the general meaning is clear, but the particular meaning of the words is not. Some editors suggest that the image is of water,

others of mechanics (*resorts* as springs, machinery). I suggest *resorts*, expedients, the devices one has recourse to in business; *falls*, the issues, or the way things happen or turn out, (as in 'the fall of the cards').

sinke plunge into the depths *or* penetrate into the innermost parts (as ink sinks into blotting-paper).

18 *pretty Looses pretty*, tricky, astute, cunning; *looses*, the act of discharging an arrow, therefore 'shots'.

Conclusion final issue. Hence, they make astute guesses at the answers to problems.

19 *Wits of direction* intellects specially fitted to direct and decide matters (Reynolds).

20 *Salomon* 'The simple turns aside to the snare, but the prudent man looks well to his going', Proverbs, 14:15.

Of Masques and Triumphs (1625)

1 *Masques* were forms of dramatic entertainment combining dialogue, song and dance, and often elaborately staged. They were developed in Bacon's time by Jonson, Fletcher, Chapman, etc. They were a form of drama in which ladies and gentlemen could take part. In 1593 Bacon himself took part in masques given by the Inns of Court, and presented masques at the marriages of Princess Elizabeth and the Earl of Somerset.

Triumphs spectacles, pageants, tournaments.

2 *Daubed* lit, plastered over; referring to the expense of scenic decorations and devices.

3 *Dancing to Song* dancing while other people sing. 'Dancing in Song', i.e. while singing, is condemned as vulgar. Bacon approves ballet and opera.

4 *broken Musicke* music arranged for different instruments, a small orchestra.

in Quire in a gallery.

5 *Dainty* Bacon wants dignified words and music, not fastidiously dainty or elegant.

6 *some Motions* perhaps dumb show, before the actors come forward to speak their parts.

7 *Oes* stars, spangles.

Glory brightness.

8 *Vizars* masks.

9 *Antimasques* a performance, in contrast to the masque itself, usually extravagant, and performed by hired actors, as a prelude or an interlude.

10 *Antiques* buffoons.

11 *Turquets* puppets dressed as Turks.

12 *Iusts* a *joust* was a fight between single horsemen; a *tourney* between groups of knights; a *barrier*, between knights separated by a bar or railing.

De Augmentis Scientiarum

1 Sidney classifies poetry into religious, philosophical, and that which is an imaginary treatment of human life, which he subdivides into heroic, lyric, tragic, comic, satiric, etc. Bacon's classification is new.

2 *restrained* because in metre.

3 *imagination* for Bacon the Understanding is 'the seat of learning', and has three parts—memory, imagination, and reason.

4 *words or matter* most sixteenth-century critics regarded subject-matter as the characteristic quality of poetry. Bacon consigns metre to rhetoric.

5 *feigned history* all 'kinds' except Epic, Drama and Allegory (which is a mode rather than a 'kind') are relegated to 'rhetoric'. Only these three are aspects of Learning.

6 *feigned Relations* a Relation is an account of, say, an expedition and is opposed to a Biography and a Chronicle. A feigned Relation would cover most epics.

7 *typical History* symbolic or allegorical narrative.

8 *Heroical* because dealing with heroes. Used of Epic subject matter and of the accepted metre for epic.

9 *shadows of things* Epic poetry is a sort of wish-fulfilment.

10 *a more perfect order* poetry shows that men delight in more perfect order than fallen Nature affords. But for Bacon this is two-edged; while it points to man's need for the next world to satisfy the longings this can never fulfil except through art, it also is a hindrance to the pursuit of knowledge. See *Novum Organum*, I.62 above.

11 *nature of things* Bacon clearly delights in poetry and music, for refreshment and raising of the mind. But there is no doubt of his preference for 'reason and history'.

12 *as a toy* such writers as Erasmus, Elyot, Ascham and Sidney approved of drama; Gosson, Stubbes and others objected to all theatre. Bacon characteristically sees it as a means of educating people—especially since in a crowd men are more easily moved. In *De Augmentis*, VI.4, he recommends acting in schools.

13 *Parabolical Poesy*   parables, allegorical poetry. The fourfold interpretation of Scripture, against which Erasmus and Colet objected, saw four senses—literal, allegorical, moral and anagogical—in every Scripture text. See *Advancement*, II.xxv.17.

14 *Pythagoras*   according to Aristotle (*Metaphysics*, ch. 5) the Pythagoreans perceived in Numbers 'greater analogies with that which exists and that which is produced than in fire, earth or water'. They concluded 'that the elements of numbers are the elements of things'.
   Sphinx   a monster with the winged body of a lion and the breast and upper part of a woman. She posed a riddle to the Thebans and murdered all who could not guess it. Oedipus solved it, whereupon she slew herself.
   Aesop   the fables attributed to Aesop, who lived about 570 B.C., are now known to have been composed at a much later date.

15 *Apophthegms*   terse, pointed sayings, embodying important truths in a few words. Caesar is said to have made a collection. Here Bacon, whose own collection was published in 1625, is probably thinking of Stoboeus and Plutarch.
   a fable   see Shakespeare's *Coriolanus*, I.i.

16 *unskilful men*   nevertheless, Bacon was much indebted to Boccaccio, Natalis Comes, Fulgentius, Macrobius and others who preceded him in this field. See Lemmi, *Classical Deities in Bacon*.

17 *desiderata*   Book II of the *Advancement* surveys human learning and reports on the deficiency in any branch.

18 *Pan*   in his accounts of each myth Bacon amalgamates various stories. Consult a good Classical dictionary. Pan as the symbol of Nature dates from the early Stoics. In his interpretation Bacon selects from Macrobius' *Saturnalia*, Natalis Comes' *Mythologiae* (Venice, 1581) and Boccaccio, *De genealogiis deorum gentilium* (Venice, 1511).

19 *Pan*   Gr. πάν=all. According to the Homeric *Hymn to Pan* (transl. Chapman) 'And Pan they called him, since he brought to all, of mirth so rare and full a festival.' Bacon interprets the origins of Pan as accounts of Creation, deriving either from the One (Mercury) or the Many (Penelope's suitors).

20 *Anaxagoras*   see Lucretius, *De Rerum Natura*, I.830 f. Anaxagoras of Ionia, *c*. 440 B.C.
   Homoeomeria   likeness of parts, or the elementary seeds from which all things were made when Intelligence (*nous*) arranged the seeds of bone to form bones, of flesh to form flesh, etc. See J. Burnet, *Early Greek Philosophy* (1892, repr. 1945).

21 *Atoms* the atomic doctrine of Leucippus (*c.* 440 B.C.) and Democritus (*c.* 420 B.C.), which was particularly attractive to Bacon, is that matter is composed of atoms, different in shape and size, and combined in different ways to form different substances, but all atoms are composed of the same substance, are indestructible, always in motion, and physically, but not geometrically, indivisible.

22 *Thales etc.* the belief that Water, Air or Fire were the original substances from which all things were formed, was superseded by the establishment of the four 'elements', earth, air, fire and water, by Empedocles (*c.* 440 B.C.); cf. *Novum Organum,* I.63.

23 *Plato and Aristotle* referring to Plato's doctrine of 'Ideas' or Forms, in which particular objects are only imperfect manifestations of ideal Forms; and to Aristotle's distinction between matter and form, in which, at the simplest level, 'form' is the boundary imposed on 'matter'.

24 *Penelope and all her suitors* in the *Wisdom of the Ancients,* Bacon refers here to the Epicurean account of the Creation in Virgil's *Eclogues,* VI.31 f.

25 *entering in* Bacon amalgamates all three stories of the origin of Pan. The idea that God required the co-operation of Sin to create the Natural World is suggested by Augustine and Aquinas, and by Plato.

26 *Fates* Bacon is following Boccaccio's *De Genealogiis* here. There is an obvious connection between the concept of Fate, Necessity or Destiny, and the scientific belief in natural law; the 'thread' of an individual's fate is the same as the series of natural events that befall him. In the universe at large all events are linked in a causal chain.

27 *But if...* from Boccaccio, who is paraphrasing Cicero, *De Divinatione,* I.5.

28 *Fortune* the belief in Fortune or Luck denies that there is any rational ordering of human affairs, and by implication denies order and cause in Nature.

29 *vulgar* the common people.

30 *Epicurus* as reported by Seneca. 'Fate' now means, for Bacon, ordered causation in the universe; cf. opening of essay 'On Atheism'.

31 *Euthumia* i.e. tranquillity. Epicurus, according to Lucretius, regarded tranquillity as the greatest good. Therefore, he argued, the gods must be tranquil, and cannot disturb their state to take any interest in mankind.

32 *Horns* Bacon here follows Macrobius' *Saturnalia* in the interpretation of Pan's horns, beard and hoofs.

33 *chain* *Iliad,* VIII.19. Plato, *Theaetetus,* I.153c. see E. M. W. Tillyard, *The Elizabethan World Picture* (1943), ch. 4.

34 *top of pyramid* cf. *Advancement of Learning* II.vii.6: 'Knowledges are as pyramides, whereof history is the basis. So of natural philosophy,

the basis is natural history; the stage next .the basis is physic; the stage next the vertical point is metaphysic.'

35 *rays* cf. Boyle on *Electricity* (1675), p. 3, describing 'Electrical Attraction', 'the Amber ... being chaf'd or heated, is made to emit certain Rayes or Files of unctuous Steams.'

36 *interior of the earth* see n. 9, p. 218 above.

37 *meteors* a name then used for all atmospheric phenomena—winds, rain, snow, hail, dew, lightning, shooting stars, rainbows, etc.

38 *seven planets* i.e. Moon, Sun, Jupiter, Mars, Saturn, Mercury, Venus.

39 *superlunary comets* e.g. the comet of 1577, which Tycho Brahe showed was at least three times as far away as the moon.

40 *harmony* the spheres in their motion were believed to produce music, unheard by fallen man. See Tillyard, *The Elizabethan World Picture*. Bacon is concerned only with music as the symbol of the order in the Universe.

41 *gains its end* cf. *Hamlet*, II.i.61-3:

> And thus do we of wisdom and of reach,
> With windlasses, and with assays of bias,
> By indirections find directions out.

42 *heavens are spotted with stars* in ch. 6 of *The Intellectual Globe*, Bacon uses this idea to express a disbelief in the 'system' of the spherical universe.

43 *hunters* Bacon uses the term *Venatio Panis*, 'the Hunt of Pan' (*De Augmentis*, V.2), for proceeding from experiment to experiment in some orderly system. He opposes it to 'Novum Organum', which is proceeding from 'experiments to axioms, which may again point out new experiments'; cf. *Novum Organum*, I.82.

44 *capella* Virgil, *Eclogues*, II.63: 'The wild-eyed lioness pursues the wolf, the wolf pursues the kid, the kid herself goes gambolling in search of flowering clover.' Virgil continues: 'And I chase you. Each is drawn on by what delights him most.'

45 *dwellers in country* Virgil's panegyric on country life at the end of the second *Georgic* is relevant here.

46 *sui* Ovid, *Remedia Amoris*, I.343:

> The maid so tricked herself with art,
> That of herself she is least part.

47 *handiwork* Psalm 19:1; cf. *Advancement of Learning*, II.ii.1.

48 *spirits* suggested by Natalis Comes' account of the Muses as 'knowledge and those mental faculties which grasp it'.

49 *moderns* this is A. Donius in *De Naturâ Hominis* (1581), Book 2, ch. 21, which is titled 'Omnes operationis Spiritus esse Motum et Sensum'.

50 *tune of the thoughts* Bacon discusses the 'mind or soul' in *Advancement of Learning*, II.xi and *De Augmentis*, IV.iii.

51 *to the gods* In Laertius' 'Life of Epicurus'. Bacon often remarks (e.g. in the *Cogitata et Visa*) that religious superstition is the enemy of scientific investigation.

52 *windfalls* cf. p. 15 above.

53 *Syringa* a reed, therefore a pen.

54 *image and reflexion thereof* cf. p. 13 above.

55 *silvis* Aeneid VI.270:
>   Thus wander travellers in woods by night,
>   By the moon's doubtful and malignant light. (Dryden)

56 *Perseus* see, in general, the essay 'Of the true Greatness of Kingdoms and Estates'. Bacon draws on Machiavelli to add to the traditional interpretation of Perseus in Boccaccio, Natalis Comes, and Filgentius' *Mythologicon*. The account of Perseus is an amalgam of various sources.

57 *Pallas* Goddess of Wisdom.

58 *Chaeronea* Philip of Macedon won this hardly fought battle and so completed his conquest of Greece.

59 *Liguria* that part of Italy which lies round Genoa and Leghorn.

60 *Mount Taurus* the mountain-ridge of Asia Minor.

61 *Charles the Eighth* King of France 1483–98. His expedition to Naples was in 1494. See n. 12 on p. 233 above.

62 *Hercules divine honours* as a reward for ridding the earth of so many tyrants and monsters, Jupiter had Hercules carried to heaven from the pyre on which his body was being cremated.

63 *Caesar* the events are recounted in Shakespeare's *Julius Caesar*.

64 *Pertinax* Pertinax was Emperor for 87 days, after the murder of Commodus. The Empire was sold to Didius Julianus, by the Praetorian Guard, who later assassinated him when Severus marched on Rome to avenge Pertinax, A.D. 193.

65 *Lucretia* after the violation of Lucretia by Tarquin, Lucius Brutus led the revolt which drove the Tarquins from Rome and established the Republic in B.C. 509.

66 *raise envy* incite discontent; see essay 'Of Envy'.

67 *Dionysus* [or Bacchus] Bacon develops suggestions in the interpretations of Macrobius and Natalis Comes.

68 *Proserpine* Queen of the Underworld. Diodorus mentions three persons called Bacchus, one of whom was the son of Jupiter and Proserpine, one the son of Jupiter and Semele.

69 *Cobali, Acratus* Kobaloi, spirits of vulgar impudence in Aristophanes, *The Knights*, 635. Acratus, a demon attendant upon Apollo in Pausanias, *Description of Greece, Attica*, II.5.

70 *Ariadne, Theseus* Theseus deserted Ariadne at Naxos, after she had helped him escape from the labyrinth of the Minotaur.

71 *Pentheus, Orpheus* the stories are told in Ovid, *Metamorphoses*, III and XI.

72 *apparent good* Bacon develops this in the *Advancement*, II.xviii.4.

73 *every passion* Bacon describes the physical symptoms in *Sylva Sylvarum*, 713-22.

74 *disgust* this is violent, for Bacon; in particular the inclusion of knowledge in the list.

75 *antiperistasis* the resistance or reaction roused against any action (*OED*).

76 *ivy* cf. Spenser (*Faerie Queene*, II.xii.61) who says of the ivy 'Low his lascivious arms adown did creep'.

The Great Instauration: Part III—Natural History: Sylva Sylvarum (1627)

1 This experiment is repeated in *Novum Organum*, II.36, where it is the last experiment in the series of Instances of the Fingerpost. It is designed to illustrate 'the Transitory Nature of Flame and its momentaneous extinction'. See also ch. 7 of the *Description of the Intellectual Globe*.

2 *porringer* a small basin.

3 *pyramis* pyramid.

4 *wax* grow.

5 *Vulcan* like Vulcan (the god of fire) who was lame as a result of his fall (from heaven to the isle of Lemnos).

6 Also found in Bacon's *De Sono et Auditu* and his *Phaenomena Universis*.

7 *exile* thin.

8 *Sicilian Poet* the story of Hercules and his page Hylas is told in Theocritus, Idyll 13.

9 *quicksilver* mercury.

10 *vexing with separations . . . churlish* disturbed by distillations and extractions . . . and so made unworkable.

11 *spirits* see *Wisdom of the Ancients*, s.v. Proserpine. Bacon, with the alchemists, believed that all objects 'contained' spirits, fragments of the eternal creative power. In the *History of Life and Death*, § 11, he writes, 'this spirit is not a virtue, an energy, a soul, or a fiction: but a real, subtle,

and invisible body, circumscribed by place, and dimension'. See **Lemmi**, *Classical Deities*, pp. 74 f.

12 *colliquation* melting together.

13 *digestion or maturation* maturing by gentle heat.

14 *induration* hardening.

15 *consumption* decay.

16 This is repeated in *Novum Organum*, II.50, in *Thema Coeli* and the *History of Sulphur Mercury and Salt*.

17 *chemists'* alchemists'.

18 *sal* the alchemists believed that metals were formed from the union of two substances to which sulphur and mercury formed the closest available approximations. Paracelsus added salt, in order to explain the make-up of animal and vegetable matter as well as metallic.

19 *subterranies* substances formed underground, i.e. metals.

20 *fathers of their tribes* i.e. as constituents from which all other metals are made. Brimstone is sulphur.

21 *pneumaticals* gaseous substances.

22 *consents* agreements.

23 *maturation or concoction* ripening.

24 *air incensed* air set on fire.

25 *cession* yielding.

26 *magnalia naturae* 'great things of nature'.

27 *serring* pressing close together.

28 This and the next entry are repeated in *The History of Life and Death*. Bacon learned of coffee from Sandy's *Travels* (1615).

29 *not aromatical* not sweet-smelling.

30 *root and leaf beetle* betel is the leaf of a plant which is wrapped round parings of the areca nut and a little lime, and chewed in India (*OED*).

31 *aleger* cheerful (a word found only in Bacon).

32 *mandrake* any plant of the genus *Mandragora*; poisonous, having emetic and narcotic qualities.

33 *saffron* autumn crocus, which produces saffron, an orange-red colouring matter.

34 *folium indum* Indian leaf, the aromatic leaf of a species of *Cinnamomum*.

35 *ambergrease* a wax-like substance found floating in tropical seas, used in perfumery.

36 *Assyrian amomum* a species of aromatic plant.

37 *kermez* red dyestuff made from the dried bodies of an insect found on evergreen oaks in southern Europe and north Africa. 'Mineral

kermes', a preparation of antimony, was a popular medicine. There was also a confection called Alkermes.

38 *towards charge* the gross income per acre.

39 Repeated in the *Phaenomena Universis*. An experiment carried out by Philo in the second century B.C. (See A. C. Crombie, *Augustine to Galileo* (1961), ii. 38n., 260.)

40 *nexe* 'the cohesion existing between particles of matter' (*OED* with this the only quotation).

41 *ne detur vacuum* that there be not a vacuum.

42 *thinking for a vanity he spoke prettily* considering that it was all foolishness, he spoke very well.

43 *my father's servants* Bacon's father died in 1579. The event described here probably happened before Bacon was sixteen.

44 *nurse-children* foster children.

45 *two or three days before my father's death* i.e. 17 or 18 February 1579.

46 *have been entire, or have touched* i.e. sympathetic behaviour of parts that have once been connected together, or of parts that have once been in contact with each other.

47 *sixteen years old* i.e. in 1576.

48 *starting-hole* a loop-hole.

49 *blood-stone in powder* a powdered heliotrope (a precious stone streaked with red) supposed to stop bleeding.

50 *Crollius* Oswald Croll, *Basilica Chimica* (1609), pp. 278–82. There were many recipes for this salve. The moss from the skull of a man violently killed was called *usnea*. The seed from which it sprang was thought to have fallen from the sky. Robert Boyle cured nose-bleed by getting the patient to hold such moss in his hand.

New Atlantis

The world that was discovered to the west of Europe was *Novus Orbis*, the New World. Parts of that world were given similar names—Hispania Nova, Nova Francia, Nova Scotia, New England. Bacon adopts this form for his island—New Atlantis. Plato's Atlantis had been in the Atlantic and was now called America; Bacon's is in the Pacific, roughly in the area where the Insulae Salomonis (Solomon Islands) had been discovered in 1568.

1 *within a kenning* within sight, i.e. about 20 miles.

2 *boscage* woods.

3 *bastons* staves.

4 *writing tables* thin sheets of ivory or wood, for making notes on.

5 *pistolets* Spanish gold coins.

6 *water chamolet* a fabric made of goat's hair and wavy like water.

7 *subscription* the writing under the letter.

8 *whole* healthy.

9 *weal* welfare.

10 *kindly* naturally.

11 *tippet* cape.

12 Bacon portrays the inhabitants as having already mastered the secrets of Nature before the Revelation came to them. He sees them as in the situation in which he imagined the authors of the early myths, which he interpreted in *The Wisdom of the Ancients*, to have been. The prayer is what he imagined a study of God's works alone would lead one to make. As such it is an important part of his argument, that knowledge of God's works does not produce atheism. The father of the House of Solomon is both scientist and priest in this stage of their development, and he it is whom God allows to approach the pillar of light and find the ark.

13 *sindons* pieces of fine linen. Bacon perhaps suggests that the pieces were from the linen used to wrap the body of Christ.

14 *St Bartholomew* Bacon stresses the miraculous nature of the Revelation to the people of New Atlantis. It is the coming of God's Word, to add to their knowledge of God's Works, and includes the 'gift of tongues', a second Pentecost.

15 *with a countenance taking knowledge* with a look of intelligence.

16 *six-score years* this takes us back to 1500. The dates of the early voyages are Diaz, 1488; Columbus, 1492; Vasco da Gama, 1498; Vespucci, 1497–1504; Magellan, 1519–22.

17 *stirps* families.

18 *Pillars of Hercules* the Straits of Gibraltar.

19 *Paguin (Cambaline)* Pekin (Cambalu).
   Quinzy Hangchowfoo.

20 *a great man* Plato, in the *Critias* and *Timaeus*, describes Atlantis, the expedition into the Mediterranean, and its sudden disappearance. Bacon suggests there is historical fact behind Plato's evident fiction.

21 *Scala Caeli* a ladder to heaven (see Genesis, 28:12).

22 *entoiled* trapped.

23 Bacon enjoys accounting for the isolation of New Atlantis in terms of conjectures involving anthropology and history.

24 *lawgiver* His introduction is necessary to enable Bacon to complete his

fable by a description of ideal laws—a subject dear to him who had passed his life in the study and practice of law.

Solamona is oblique flattery of James, aimed at making him *want* Bacon's advice. Solomon, Solon and Lycurgus spring to mind as parallels to Bacon's lawgiver, Solamona. Bacon had described James as having a 'heart inscrutable for wisdom and goodness'.

25 *substantive* self-sufficing.

26 *doubting novelties* fearing innovations. As a lawyer and politician Bacon deprecated innovation. See his essay 'Of Innovations'.

27 *curious* The context suggests the modern meaning 'odd', 'singular', rather than 'inquisitive', 'prying'.

28 *Salomon's House* the foundation of such an institution was Bacon's hope. The Royal Society, founded in 1661, in part fulfilled his dream. Note that the Lawgiver and the founder of the House of Salomon are one.

29 *Natural History* see 1 Kings, 4:33.

30 *Six Days' Works* the arrangement of human knowledge according to the pattern set in the Biblical account of the six days of Creation was common in medieval and Renaissance encyclopaedists. Bacon divides Natural History into five parts—of ether, of air, of earth and sea, of the four elements, of species (stones, metals and living creatures), see *Works*, I.405–10, and V. K. Whitaker, *Francis Bacon's Intellectual Milieu* (Clark Memorial Library, 1962).

31 *God's first creature* light, for Bacon, symbolizes knowledge.

32 *took us off* relieved us.

33 *Spanish montero* a Spanish hunting cap. Note that the 'curious' gloves here are 'exquisite'. Bacon's detailed description shows his delight in clothing and dignified ceremony. He noticed everything around him.

34 *girt* belted.

35 *without any degrees to the state* without any steps leading to the canopy.

36 *deep caves* in the *Sylva* (68) Bacon says 'Heat and cold are Nature's two hands, whereby she chiefly worketh.' This is the opinion also of Telesius. Deep caves were thought useful for preserving vegetable matter, which decayed in air, for refrigeration, and for producing metals (because these were originally created underground). See *Novum Organum*, II.50. In what follows the whole of the *Sylva* is relevant.

37 *coagulations* thickening liquids.
   indurations hardening.

38 *insulation* exposure to the sun.
   meteors meteorological phenomena.

39 *salt* this is the first experiment in the *Sylva*.

40 *tincted upon* tinctured with.

41 *prolongation of life* The History of Life and Death (1623) is devoted to this topic.

42 *arefaction* drying up.

43 *inoculating* budding.

44 *trials* experiments.

45 *chirurgery* surgery.

46 *decocted* boiled down and concentrated.

47 *leavenings* fermenting agents.
    move stimulate.

48 *chilus* food ready to be absorbed into the blood.

49 *simples* they could so mix medical preparations that the body would absorb them as though they were uncompounded substances.

50 *diversity of heats* heat and the controlled variation of heat, was regarded as vital for all transmutations, and so of particular importance in alchemy. See John Read, *Prelude to Chemistry* (1936), pp. 143 f. *Dry* heat is ordinary fire, *moist* heat that found in horse-dung.

    pass divers inequalities Bacon gives a full account of the nature of fire in the firmament in his *Theory of the Firmament* or *Thema Coeli*. The quality of fire in the different heavenly bodies varied, he believed. Here he seems to mean that they could make heats corresponding to the various heats in the moon, comets, planets and sun, and reproduce the movements of such heats in circles, straight lines and bends, similar to the movements of the fiery bodies in the heavens. In *Novum Organum*, Book II, Bacon takes the Form of Heat as his example of how to investigate a Form.

51 *perspective houses* houses for optical experiments. Bacon wrote a short tract *Topica inquisitionis de luce et lumine*. For Bacon on microscopes and telescopes, see *Novum Organum*, II.39.

52 *fossils* any rock or mineral dug out of the earth.

53 *slides* fine shades. The material of Bacon's *Historia Sonī et Auditus*, written *c*. 1608, was taken over into the *Sylva*.

54 *basilisks* a kind of cannon. Bacon discusses Motion at greater length in *Novum Organum*, II. 36, 48, and in sections 8 and 9 of *Cogitationes de Natura Rerum*.

55 *motions of return* oscillations.

56 *equality* evenness, uniformity.

57 *mathematical-house* Bacon could not see the 'usefulness' of mathematics, and is significantly brief.

58 *swelling* puffed out, made to look more wonderful than it is.

59 *Mystery-men* men who enquire after 'mysteries', *i.e.* crafts.

60 *Compilers* Bacon collects experiments relating to Heat in *Novum Organum*, II.11–13.

61 *natural divinations* Bacon was interested, in the *Sylva*, in means of prognostication by natural means.

62 *Benefactors* Bacon is a 'Benefactor' when he takes the 'First Vintage' of the Form of Heat in *Novum Organum*, II.20.

63 *inventors* see note 13, p. 219 above.

64 *prayer* Bacon wrote such prayers, e.g. at the end of the *Plan of the Great Instauration* prefixed to *Novum Organum*. The Father of the House of Salomon is a priest of Nature and behaves rather like a Bishop.

The History of Henry VII (1622)

1 In 1597 Bacon piloted through the House of Commons a Bill relating to prevention of Enclosures and the maintenance of tillage. In a speech he made then he said, 'I should be sorry to see within this kingdom ... instead of a whole town full of people, none but green fields, but a shepherd and a dog' (*Life &c.*, II.82). The problem of the enclosure of arable and common land for sheep farming was one that all Tudor governments faced. Between 1489 and 1656 there were seven Royal Commissions and twelve Statutes relating to Enclosures. In Bacon's own time (1607) there was an insurrection in Northamptonshire directed against Enclosures. His interest in the first of the Tudor Statutes on Enclosures, that of Henry VII in 1489, is therefore part of his interest in contemporary problems, and his interpretation of the Statute—that it resulted in a fine national soldiery—reflects his concern (expressed in a paper on *The True Greatness of the Kingdom of Britain* (1608), in the essay 'On the True Greatness of Kingdoms and Estates', which he later inserted in the *De Augmentis*, VIII.3, and in *An Advertisement touching on Holy War* (1623)) that James, England's most pacific king, should pursue a war-like policy.

2 *demesnes* i.e. the land was no longer sub-let but held by the owner himself.

manured tilled.

rid dispatched.

3 *books of subsidies* the king's income depended partly on subsidies voted by Parliament. These were based on a percentage of the value of property assessed for each individual.

4   *lords of the fee*   the lords of whom the land was held and to whom, in return, homage and service were due.

5   *hinds*   farm employees.

6   *mannerhood*   A word found only here. *OED* suggests 'orderly condition, good order'; perhaps 'manliness'.

7   *amortise*   transfer (alienated them from their owners and transferred them to the holders).

8   *staddles*   young trees left standing when others are cut down.

9   *armed men*   there was, of course, no standing army.

10 *table*   either picture *or* abstract.

11 Bacon's account of the De Facto Act passed in 1495, to protect those who served Henry from being tried for their loyalty by some future occupant of the throne, is sufficiently clear. Throughout the Wars of the Roses, adherents of the unsuccessful party suffered for their support of the *de facto* king, on the grounds that he had not occupied the throne *de jure*. Henry's statute was made at the time when Perkin Warbeck was in Scotland and an invasion was threatened. It established the principle that the sovereign *de facto* must be considered to reign *de jure*, and his subjects not liable to penalties for obeying his orders or fighting to defend him. See Kenneth Pickthorn, *Early Tudor Government: Henry VII* (Cambridge, 1949), pp. 151–6.

12 *magnanimous than provident*   prompted more by nobility of purpose than by foresight.

13 *attainted*   charged with treason or felony.

14 *reason of estate*   the fundamental principle of the State.

15 *If . . . done*   2 Samuel, 24:17.

16 *conclude itself*   bind itself.

17 *He had parts . . .*   He had abilities . . . not so much suitable to be jotted down in a commonplace-book as general maxims, as to be carefully attended to.

18 *tender*   scrupulous in observing the rights of sanctuary.

19 *hospital of the Savoy*   in 1505 Henry built a Hospital on the site of the Savoy palace, burnt in 1381 by the rebels under Wat Tyler. He endowed it by his will.

20 *offers . . . wars*   threats and rumours of wars.

21 *war of his coming in*   ended by the defeat and death of Richard III at Bosworth, 22 August 1485.
    Earl of Lincoln   Lincoln and the Earl of Lovel supported the pretender Lambert Simnel, who claimed to be the Earl of Warwick (whom Henry kept safe in the Tower). They were defeated at Stoke in 1487.

Lord Audley Audley led the Cornish rebellion (occasioned by the levying of the subsidy to fight against Scotland) which was defeated at Blackheath on 22 June 1497.

22 *France* Henry made war on France in 1492, angered by the French annexation of Brittany. But he stood to gain nothing by the war and quickly concluded a peace in exchange for money.

Scotland Perkin Warbeck, encouraged by James IV of Scotland, raided the border country in 1496. Henry made a truce in 1497.

23 *Britain* i.e. Brittany. Henry was prepared to support Francis II, Duke of Brittany, against Charles VIII of France. The Duke died in 1488, and his daughter married Charles in 1491.

24 *Lovel* Lovel rebelled in Worcester in 1486 but was defeated and fled to Flanders. The following year he supported Simnel and was killed.

Perkin Perkin Warbeck pretended to be Richard, Duke of York, the younger of the two princes murdered in the Tower. He threatened Henry from Flanders, Ireland and Scotland, but when he landed in Cornwall in 1497 he ran away from his army, was captured, confined, and in 1499 executed.

Kent in 1495 some of Perkin's supporters landed at Deal. A hundred and fifty were captured and hanged.

25 *quanching* suppressing.

26 *forwardness* boldness.

27 *countenance* uphold.

28 *went to diminution* was curtailed.

29 *strain up his laws* stretch the laws by virtue of his royal prerogative.

30 *let down his prerogative* diminish his sovereign rights.

31 *mint* coinage.

32 *council-table* the equivalent of the Privy Council, which dates from the reign of Henry VIII.

33 *Warwick, Lord Chamberlain, Audley* executed respectively in 1499, 1495 and 1497. Sir William Stanley was Chamberlain of the Household, not 'Lord Chamberlain'.

34 *discharge their princes* exonerate them from blame.

35 *ancient authority* Thomas Morton, Bishop of Ely, later Chancellor and Cardinal, and Sir Reginald Bray had been with Henry before he became king.

36 *Empson and Dudley* the ministers who administered Henry's avaricious policy. They were executed by Henry VIII in 1510.

37 *high mind* haughty.

38 *confederates* allies.

39 *strangeness* unfriendliness.
40 *little envies* ambitious rivalries in little things.
41 *airs* as it were, 'information wafted on the breeze'.
42 *impropriate* appropriate, make his own.
43 *liegers* ambassadors.
44 *pensioner* one paid to serve him (by obtaining information, etc.).
45 *extreme curious, and articulate* very minute and specific.
46 *spials* spies.
47 *flies* spies.
48 *companiable and respective* sociable and considerate and attentive.
49 *till himself were declared* until he had declared his own opinion.
50 *a dark prince* a reticent and secretive prince.
51 *sad* firm, or orderly and regular, or grave.
52 *Queen of Naples* after the death of Elizabeth, Henry considered a second marriage. The Dowager Queen of Naples refused him.
53 *wit* usually wisdom, here implies intellectual and practical quickness and ingenuity.
54 *industries and watches* crafty expediencies and acts of vigilance.
55 *politic* shrewd and sagacious (with sense of 'cunning').
56 *entire and sincere* a man of more integrity and honesty.
57 *consort* agreement.
58 *he minded what he compassed* he applied himself diligently to what he planned to do.
59 *strange or dark* not cold or distant, nor frowning.
60 *exercised* i.e. in devotional observations.
61 *his tomb* Henry VII's chapel in Westminster Abbey.

The Trial of the Earl of Somerset (25 May 1616)

1 The Lord High Steward was the Chancellor, Ellesmere. The trial was in Westminster Hall on 25 May 1616. Somerset dressed in black satin and velvet; his hair was carefully curled, his face pale, his beard overlong, his eyes sunk in his head.
2 James was very anxious that no other matter should be pursued. Attempts had been made to suggest that Prince Henry's death could be laid to Somerset's charge.
3 *play prizes* to play for prizes.
4 *signet* Somerset had been Keeper of the Signet. The reference is either to Haggai, 2:23, 'I will make thee as a signet', or to Jeremiah, 22:24, 'As

I live, saith the Lord, though Coniah ... were the signet upon my right hand, yet would I pluck thee thence.'

5 *competent* which are required in such a case.

6 *Cain* Genesis, 4.

7 *Joab* 2 Samuel, 3:27.

8 *tables* the Ten Commandments.

9 *lieutenancy of God in princes* i.e. some divines have argued that disobedience to the King, God's lieutenant on earth, is a breaking of the commandments in the first part of the decalogue.

10 *nostri generis nec sanguinis* 'it is not of our lineage or blood'.

11 *that person* the Pope. Bacon refers to the death, probably by poison, of Alexander VI in 1503.

12 *a snare* Psalm 69:22; Romans, 11:9.

13 *cum sonitu* 'with a noise.'

14 *Quis modo tutus erit?* 'who shall be in any way safe?'

15 *concidit infelix alieno vulnere* 'the wretch collapses with a wound meant for another.'

16 *sagitta nocte volans* Psalm 91:5

17 *respondent* for whom the king and state must answer.

18 *Livia* probably Livilla, wife of Drusus, son of the Emperor Tiberius. She and Sejanus poisoned her husband, A.D. 23. Tacitus, *Annals*, IV.3, 8.

19 *Parisatis* I have failed to find this reference.

20 *triers* judges.

21 *affection* the determining of the mother of the child, in 1 Kings, 3:16–28.

22 *Weston* the underkeeper of the tower, who was appointed to supersede Cary at the instigation of Frances Howard, on 7 May 1613. He was hanged for the poisoning of Overbury in November 1615.

23 *toil* enclosed space into which the quarry is driven so that it cannot escape.

24 *Thrasonical* boastful.

25 *a better teacher* James first met Carr at a tournament at which Carr broke his leg. James visited him during his confinement and adopted the role of teacher to his new favourite.

26 *conversation* consorting together intimately—a wider meaning than the modern 'talking together'.

27 *Secretary* on the death of Lord Salisbury (May 1612) who had been Principal Secretary of State, James delayed the appointment of a successor and did business through the bed-chamber men of whom Carr, as Keeper of the Signet, was the most important. Throughout 1612 and 1613 there was much manœuvring of position to obtain the post of

Principal Secretary. Carr was technically committing treason in allowing Overbury to handle confidential matters of state.

28 *rounding in the ear* whispering.

29 *tables* lists of the contents.

30 *council-table* the Privy Council.

31 *inwardness* familiarity.

32 *ciphers and jargons* in the correspondence of Carr and Overbury, the King was *Julius*, the Queen *Agrippina*, Northampton *Dominic*, Suffolk *Lerma*, and Wolsey, the Archbishop of Canterbury, *Unctius*.

33 *Lord Privy Seal* Lord Henry Howard, Earl of Northampton, who might also have been tried had he not died on 14 June 1614.

34 *letters and industry* Overbury assisted Carr in his affair with Frances Howard but opposed the divorce and marriage.

35 *naught* wicked, immoral.

36 *ballads* there were many ballads on the death of Overbury.

37 *mineral* 'mineral' because brought up from the depths.

38 *Waade* Sir William Waade was superseded as Lieutenant of the Tower by Sir Jervis Elwes on 6 May 1613. Elwes was hanged in November 1615.

39 *Weston* see note 22.

40 *two days after* Overbury was arrested on 21 April 1613; fifteen days brings us to 7 May, the day Richard Weston took Cary's place, at the instigation of Lady Essex.

41 *trunks* i.e. through the means provided by them; lit. pipes, conduits.

42 *Franklin* the apothecary who supplied the poisons. He was hanged in November 1615.

43 *Mrs Turner* mistress of Sir Arthur Mainwaring, and a confidante of Lady Essex. Weston was her servant who carried messages between Carr and Lady Essex before the divorce. She was hanged at Tyburn, 14 November 1615. She introduced Franklin to Lady Essex and prepared the tarts, jellies, etc. that were sent to Overbury.
say-mistress on the analogy of *assay-master*, one who tests the virtue, fineness, quality, weight, of a substance.

44 *Mithridates* King of Pontus, the seventh of that name and surnamed the Great. He fortified his body against poison by drinking antidotes. On his defeat by Pompey in 63 B.C. he attempted to poison himself but failed.
treacle a medicinal compound used as an antidote against poisons.

45 *clip* Somerset tried to collect all correspondence relating to Overbury in the Tower and tampered with it.

46 *pardon for yourself* Somerset had tried to obtain the Seal to a general pardon for any irregularities that might have occurred during his tenure

of the Privy Seals in the interval between the death of Salisbury and the appointment of Winwood as Principal Secretary. The Lord Chancellor refused to seal it because it contained large clauses about felonies and misdemeanours. In a second attempt to obtain such a pardon, murder and treason were inserted! It was Somerset's attempt to obtain the first pardon that encouraged Winwood to follow up the rumours about Overbury's death. The draft of the second survived and was evidence against Somerset.

47 *convert* direct, address.
48 *elevation of the pole* an image from astronomy.
49 *toy* a piece of nonsense.
50 *periculum periculo vincitur* 'risk exceeded by risk.'
51 *flashes* something sudden, quick, transitory.
52 *progress* the Court was on its Summer Progress or journey to the western counties. News of events relating to Overbury was sent by Lady Essex to Somerset, who was with the King.
53 *dark words* ambiguous words.

Letters &c.

1 *honourable correspondence* the honour which your relationship with me.
2 *confirmed* firmly established. Bacon's mother thought her son's working late into the night was the cause of his bad digestion.
3 *more painful* cf. *Advancement*, I.ii.5, 6.
4 *contemplative planet* Mercury. For the belief that the heavenly bodies determine temperaments, see Burton, *Anatomy of Melancholy*, Part 1, Sect. 3, Mem. 1, Subsect. 3.
5 *second founder* because Bacon's father died before founding an adequate estate for him, the second son.
6 *my health is not to spend, nor my course to get* spending is not conducive to my well-being, nor does my way of life produce much in the way of income.
7 *province* the original reads 'providence' here, and below. With the rest of the sentence cf. p. 14 above.
   philanthropia a full gloss is the essay 'Of Goodness and Goodness of Nature'.
8 *countenance* repute in the world.
9 *encounter* opposition.

10 *Anaxagoras* his pupils included Euripides, Socrates and Pericles, who dissuaded him from starving himself to death. The day he found himself a beggar he exclaimed, 'To philosophy I owe my worldly ruin, and my soul's prosperity.'

11 *sorry* mean, poor, of little account.

12 *civil wars* Bacon is probably thinking of the religious civil wars in France in the late sixteenth century. He is prophetic of the Thirty Years War in Germany. In England in 1603 there was a conspiracy against the new king, which might have led to civil war—or at least looked threatening at the time.

13 *multum incola* . . . one of Bacon's favourite sayings, 'My soul hath long been a sojourner' (Psalm 120:6 in the Vulgate, where this is a complete sentence).

14 *congruity* agreement in character, appropriateness.

15 *ark* in 1598 Sir Thomas Bodley (1545–1613) offered to restore and refit Duke Humfrey's Library in Oxford. It was opened on 8 November 1602, and after 1610 was extended to accommodate the growing number of books.

16 *Gemitum Columbae* 'moaning of the dove'. A combined reference to Isaiah, 38:14 and Psalm 55:6.

17 *a higher flight* according to his letter to the Peers of 19 March, Bacon thought he was dying, 'it is no feigning or fainting'.

18 *suavibus modis* 'in the most agreeable manner'.

19 *inherited no hatred from my father* Bacon was naturally always conscious that his father had been Elizabeth's Lord Keeper. He is proud to assert that this dislike is not directed against him because of any act of his father.

20 *trick* to deck out, adorn.
   cavillations the use of legal quibbles.
   voidances evasive answers or arguments (a word used only by Bacon in this sense).

21 *neatness of conscience* Bacon seems to be saying that a display of greater scrupulosity than the case calls for would mask a hardness of heart (i.e. a lack of any sense of guilt).

22 *my matchless friend* the King's favourite, Buckingham, who delivered the letter for Bacon.

23 *usufructuary* a legal term meaning that Bacon had enjoyed only temporary rights in himself, the 'property' being the King's.

24 *oblation* an offering, a sacrifice.

25 *no new thing* Ecclesiastes, 1:9.

26 *Demosthenes* Demosthenes was banished from Athens after accepting

a bribe. He was welcomed back when Antipater made war against Greece, but shortly after poisoned himself to avoid being handed over to Antipater, 322 B.C.

Cicero as consul, Cicero defeated Catiline, but soon afterwards was banished when his enemy Clodius became tribune. He was welcomed back to Rome eighteen months later, but incurred the hatred of Mark Antony and was murdered at his instigation, 43 B.C.

Seneca Seneca was banished because of a love-affair. He returned after five years in Corsica and became tutor to Nero who ordered him to commit suicide on suspicion of being involved in the conspiracy of Piso, A.D. 65.

27 *banks, or mounts* 'mounts 'is the same as 'banks'. The image is one of investing money ('talent') in a bank that will not 'break' instead of in an 'exchange'.

28 *si nunquam fallit imago* Virgil, *Eclogues*, II.27, 'if the image does not deceive me'. He refers to the *Novum Organum* (1620).

29 *Natural Story and Inquisition* Natural history and inquiry—such as the *History of the Winds* and later the *Sylva*.

30 *particular laws* a work somewhere between the *Republic* and a legal handbook.

obnoxious to under the influence of the particular laws being discussed, and therefore not sufficiently general. He is repeating what he had said in the *Advancement*, II.xxiii.49. In *De Augmentis*, VIII.3, is a series of aphorisms on Universal Justice, such as he mentions here.

31 *digest* his *Offer of a Digest* was printed in 1629.

32 *embracement* perhaps 'cultivation'.

33 *exoriere aliquis Aeneid*, 4:625 'a something springing up'.

34 *platform* the existence of a plan may encourage the erection of the building. The work he is addressing to Andrewes is a dialogue on the rights and wrongs of a war against the Infidel. It is unfinished.

35 *experiment* Pliny lost his life observing an eruption of Vesuvius. Bacon alighted from his coach in order to stuff a chicken with snow, as an experiment in preserving by refrigeration.

36 *casting* vomiting.

stone a disease characterized by the formation of hard crystals in the body, especially the gall-bladder.

Suggestions for Further Reading

LIFE:

The *Letters and Life of Francis Bacon*, 7 vols., 1867–74, ed. J. Spedding, contains the Speeches and Letters. The best short life is that by R. W. Church (1889).

WORKS:

Works edited by J. Spedding, R. L. Ellis and D. D. Heath, 7 vols., 1857–9, and by J. M. Robertson (1905).

Essays: Editions with notes by E. A. Abbott (1881), Storr and Gibson (1891), A. S. West (1899).

Advancement of Learning: Editions by G. W. Kitchen (1861), W. A. Wright (Oxford, 1868, repr. 1957).

Novum Organum: Editions by T. Fowler (Oxford, 1889) and F. H. Anderson (New York, 1960).

COMMENTARIES:

Anderson, F. H., *The Philosophy of Francis Bacon* (Chicago, 1948).

Broad, C. D., *The Philosophy of Francis Bacon* (Cambridge, 1926).

Craig, H., *The Enchanted Glass* (Oxford, 1936).

Farington, B., *The Philosophy of Francis Bacon* (Liverpool, 1963).

Fisch, H., *Jerusalem and Albion* (1964).

Howell, W. S., *Logic and Rhetoric in England, 1500–1700* (Princeton, 1956).

James, D. G., *The Dream of Learning: An Essay on The Advancement of Learning, Hamlet, and King Lear* (Oxford, 1951).

Jones, R. F., *Ancients and Moderns* (St Louis, 1936).

Knights, L. C., 'Bacon and the Dissociation of Sensibility', in *Explorations* (1946).

Lemmi, C. W., *The Classical Deities in Bacon* (Baltimore, 1933).

Macaulay, T. B., 'Lord Bacon' (a review of Montagu's edition in the *Edinburgh Review*, July 1837).

Tillotson, G., 'Words for Princes', in *Essays in Criticism and Research* (Cambridge, 1942).

Wallace, K. R., *Francis Bacon on Communication and Rhetoric* (Chapel Hill, 1943).

Whitaker, V. K., *Francis Bacon's Intellectual Milieu* (William Andrews Clark Memorial Library, 1962).

Willey, B., *The Seventeenth Century Background* (1949).

Wilson, F. P., *Elizabethan and Jacobean* (Oxford, 1945).

INDEX